The Music of James MacMillan

The Music of James MacMillan

Phillip A. Cooke

THE BOYDELL PRESS

First published 2019
The Boydell Press, Woodbridge

ISBN 978 1 78327 370 6

The Boydell Press is an imprint of Boydell & Brewer Ltd
PO Box 9, Woodbridge, Suffolk IP12 3DF, UK
and of Boydell & Brewer Inc.
668 Mt Hope Avenue, Rochester, NY 14620–2731, USA
website: www.boydellandbrewer.com

A CIP catalogue record for this book is available
from the British Library

The publisher has no responsibility for the continued existence or accuracy of URLs
for external or third-party internet websites referred to in this book, and does not
guarantee that any content on such websites is, or will remain, accurate or appropriate

This publication is printed on acid-free paper

Printed and bound in Great Britain by
TJ International Ltd, Padstow, Cornwall

Contents

Plates

The author and publisher are grateful to all the institutions and individuals listed for permission to reproduce the materials in which they hold copyright. Every effort has been made to trace the copyright holders; apologies are offered for any omission, and the publisher will be pleased to add any necessary acknowledgement in subsequent editions.

Tables

Music Examples

Foreword

I clearly remember the night in 1990 when I witnessed something that would later change my perspective as a solo percussionist. I was watching the televised Henry Wood Proms in London. Playing at that precise moment was a musical work that would change not only my life but elevate the standing of solo percussion to a completely different level. The piece was the world premiere of *The Confession of Isobel Gowdie* by a young Scottish composer, James MacMillan.

I had never anticipated nor imagined such a powerful orchestral piece to be screened via the medium of television before. I was transfixed by the sheer power, changing of gears, waves of scintillating sound colours and the brilliance of each member of the orchestra who seemed to be pushed to their limits to provide such an immense sound meal. The music ended with an immediate elongated rapturous applause. I was breathless. The young composer with a small glistening ear-ring shyly took a bow and humbly accepted the shower of adoration. I knew I had witnessed something incredibly special and important. I also knew I had to contact this composer immediately to ask if he would consider writing a percussion concerto for me. The rest is history. 1992 saw the arrival of one of our great percussion concertos *Veni, Veni, Emmanuel*. It was the first ever percussion concerto to be performed in the history of the Proms.

From that night in 1990 James MacMillan's music has been an essential part of my life. Pieces can come and go but with James's music each new work is a landmark, a statement whereby we are sucked into a web of musical power and passion that questions our very being. There is no medium that James MacMillan shies away from; he often embraces the instruments which are sometimes less common in a solo medium, such as the Cor Anglais in *The World's Ransoming* and his Viola Concerto, not to mention two percussion concerti; he transcends them into an emotional rollercoaster for performers and our audiences.

I fondly remember performing *Veni, Veni, Emmanuel* in Washington DC with the National Symphony Orchestra and the great Slava Rostropovich conducting. Mr Rostropovich adored this concerto, so much so that we performed it again at the Evian Festival in France. It was after the final performance in Washington DC that Rostropovich invited James and me to his fascinating apartment opposite the Kennedy Centre. In the tiny kitchen enjoying a totally informal delightful traditional Russian meal Rostropovich exuberantly popped the question to James, 'Please would you write a cello concerto for me?'

Of course Rostropovich had always been such an inspiration to me not only as a formidable musician but as one who devoted so much of his energy in broadening the repertoire for solo cello. To be present during that moment and thankfully witnessing the positive reply from James caused the hairs on my arms to stand to attention! I knew I was witnessing a remarkable era for music with the birth of a piece of history which would hail yet another momentous piece from this young composer. I followed James throughout that journey and so many more.

James writes music with musicians and audiences in mind. In doing so he receives widespread recognition, popularity and respect from all sectors. As a musician one wants to 'serve' the music rather than 'using' the music as a means to show off one's skills. There is always a delicate wire between the music and the audience, which is created by the musicians as a bridge. This is even more profound through James's activities as a prolific conductor and unselfish supporter of other living composers. He celebrates the power of music, the power of the musician and the power of listening. He is not afraid to allow his music to scream and rumble or suspend in mid-air from emulating a delicate piece of silk – leaving time at the door. He trusts his instincts and he trusts those who participate in his music.

I think of James's music as stars shining above us, always there for us to indulge in amid the turmoil of the world. Although much of his music embraces the realities of world events, present and historic with the tight thread of religious connotations, there is always the feeling of hope. He is also deeply proud and respectful of his geographic upbringing in Scotland and frequently embraces the wonders and impact that his Scottish heritage has on his music.

I am especially excited to be contributing to the first ever official book about Sir James MacMillan. The dedication from the author Phillip Cooke to produce this major publication is much appreciated and will valuably serve so many generations to come, allowing the life and music of this great composer to continue impacting our lives in the most profound ways.

Dame Evelyn Glennie, CH
Cambridgeshire, England

Prologue

Writing a book on a living composer is a double-edged sword: for all the freedom granted by being the first person critically to assess much of the music comes the constant feeling of worry and guilt that you might get some valuable information wrong. Having no vast bibliography of secondary literature is both a blessing and a curse; there is certainly much less to read and absorb, to verify or contradict, but there are far fewer places to turn to for corroborating views or analyses. With the composer in question very much still alive and producing, there is always the possibility of contacting him for another interview, or for that key bit of information that has alluded you – whether he wants to respond or not. In short, writing this book is something of a voyage into the unknown, or the little known, with the ultimate hope being to end up somewhere of value and experience, for both the author and the wider musical world.

I first encountered James MacMillan's name before I had heard any of his music; it was during my undergraduate degree at Durham University in a workshop given by MacMillan's former tutor (and my soon-to-be tutor) John Casken. Casken informed the composition class that there was 'little money in contemporary composition' (a typically matter-of-fact statement from the then Head of Composition at Manchester University) and that the 'only composer who made money from serious composition is James MacMillan'. Who was this James MacMillan who made all this money? How did he do it? I did not take the time to find out, but I remembered his name. I met him for the first time a few years later in Manchester, whilst I was studying with Casken; MacMillan was at the university on one of his visits to work with the BBC Philharmonic as part of his role as composer–conductor. During our brief meeting, I had a nosebleed and spent much of the time hiding behind a piano – an auspicious introduction.

I first encountered his music in any real fashion whilst working in a music shop in Oxford; here we were encouraged to listen to some of the CDs we were trying to sell, and I slowly made my way through all the contemporary music the shop stocked. It was the Westminster Cathedral Choir recording of MacMillan's *Mass* that really drew my attention and opened my ears to many things; the music seemed so vibrant, colourful, modern and memorable, and I was instantly hooked. I listened to all the CDs that were available at the time (c.2002–03) and built up a large collection of bootleg recordings of his pieces, though it was the *Mass* that still captivated me most. By the time I had completed my doctoral studies in 2007, I had become familiar with much of MacMillan's work; I had attended the 'Darkness into Light' festival of his music in London in 2005; and I had delivered a paper on his music at various universities a year later. It was only after securing my first permanent academic position at the University of Aberdeen, and having had experience as co-editor of a book on the music of Herbert Howells, that I thought about attempting this project.

One thing I should clarify is that I work predominantly as a composer (a much less successful composer than MacMillan). I teach composition in university and in the rare event that someone recognised my name it would probably be for my exploits in writing music. I mention this not as some sort of poor disclaimer, but because I feel that this has had a direct bearing on this book: the way I have approached it, the pieces I have elected to discuss and the narrative that I have chosen to pursue. My musical training has been predominantly as a composer, so it is understandable that this would shape any musicological work I would undertake; and it has undeniably shaped the scope and design of this book. I could have subtitled the book a 'composer portrait' (which I did consider), as this would describe not only the act of portraying MacMillan in words, but my own thoughts, feelings and concerns in this matter.

This book is not an analytical study of MacMillan's work (perhaps that will come in the future) but rather a look at the composer's most important pieces, viewed through the lens of his life, beliefs and aesthetics. I imagine the book as paving the way for future study on the composer, where forthcoming musicologists and critics can disagree with my opinions and belittle my efforts to better their own books and papers. In any case, it should provide the biographical information that many scholars may need for their studies until someone provides something more comprehensive. The pieces I have chosen are a reflection of both my own perception of MacMillan's most important works and my own efforts as a composer of largely vocal and choral music. That is not to say that I have endorsed his choral works over his other output, but rather to suggest that someone from a different background may have chosen a completely diverse selection of pieces in which his choir works did not feature (though in doing this they would be failing to recognise the most expanding part of the composer's oeuvre).

There are works that scholars and critics would omit at their peril: *The Confession of Isobel Gowdie*, *Veni, Veni, Emmanuel* and the *Seven Last Words from the Cross* are three that spring to mind. There are large-scale works such as the operas, the symphonies, the concerti and the oratorios that are amongst his most high-profile compositions, and would probably make most surveys and studies. For a composer of over 250 works, it is not possible to include every piece, whether in detail or in passing, and I am aware that the majority of MacMillan's work (particularly the shorter choral pieces) never gets mentioned. I feel that I have covered most of the significant pieces from his early tone-poem *The Keening*, through his breakthrough works in the early 1990s to the various large-scale offerings that have characterised his output from the mid-1990s onwards. The works chosen cover most of MacMillan's operatic and theatrical pieces (only *Parthenogenesis* is not looked at in any great detail), his two great Passion settings, two of his four symphonies, several of his concerti and other prominent tone-poems and oratorios. There are many substantial pieces that do not get covered in the book, much to my chagrin: the Fourth Symphony, the *Stabat Mater* and his two later piano concerti to think of a few. Some works are chosen to highlight a narrative or theme in the book rather than for their size and profile; this is certainly the case with the clarinet quintet *Tuireadh*, which I chose to study over the larger and more dramatic clarinet concerto *Ninian*. It may also seem perverse to spend time looking at a congregational mass setting from the composer's early career rather than exploring the modernist chamber works he was also writing at the time, but that would do a disservice to the *St Anne's Mass* and the continuing significance of *The Tryst* that is housed within it.

The book is largely chronological, though sometimes bunching similar pieces together to enhance a point or topic; the places where I deviate from this scheme are in chapters six and seven, where I side-step from the linear to take a more specific look at the composer's politics and his choral outpouring. There are key themes that appear throughout the book, and I have tried to bind them together (as they are in MacMillan's music at large), with the composer's Catholicism being one of the strongest and most enduring. It may seem churlish, writing about a composer whose musical output is so bound up with his faith, not to deal with this influence head-on and with more gusto. However, I have tried not to make MacMillan's Catholicism the main theme of this book: I am not a theologian, nor a religious man; I can only respond to the music with the tools available to me, those of a composer and academic. For all MacMillan's statements on faith, religion and Catholicism, he remains a composer, someone who combines notes and rhythms to create a meaningful whole. For all I know, James MacMillan may be a great composer and a bad theologian; it is not for me necessarily to comment on the latter.

The lack of secondary literature is an issue when attempting a book such as this; this is the first book of its type on MacMillan (as far as I am aware) and represents the most extensive appraisal of his music to date. There are some wonderful academic articles to draw on from journals such as *Tempo* and *The Musical Times*, particularly from trailblazer Richard McGregor, as well as significant offerings from the likes of James Telford, Patrick Russill and Keith Potter (to name but a few). There are two fabulous PhD theses that have been immensely useful to the preparation of this book, from Dominic Wells (Durham University, 2012) and George Parsons (Sheffield University, 2016), with an honourable mention of Helen Burrows's chapter on MacMillan in her University of East Anglia submission from 1999. I wish I could be as positive about the doctoral scholarship that is currently coming from the United States: alas, I have read too many ill-informed, factually incorrect and sub-standard DMA theses that have been written in the past decade, with authors often quoting inaccuracies from previous DMA submissions and thus creating a never-ending cycle of poor scholarship. Many of these theses are the written requirement for choral conducting degrees and have neither the detail nor the breadth of their PhD counterparts. I hope at the very least that this book will eliminate some of the biographical errors from future academic work.

After journal articles and doctoral theses, much of the 'research' involves newspaper and magazine articles, CD liners, the two TV documentaries, radio programmes and interviews with the composer from various platforms with differing amounts of reliability. It is perhaps too easy to rely on 'reception theory' in the absence of scholarship: there are reviews of most of MacMillan's major works and they tell a story of their own. I have tried to keep my use of newspaper reviews to a minimum, using them mainly for MacMillan's operatic works, where the reviewers have had the most to say (often in quite unpleasant terms). Some of the contributions from long-term MacMillan stalwarts such as Stephen Johnson and Ken Walton have been particularly illuminating, with their nuanced writing style often a surprising inspiration. There are many interviews from MacMillan available to read, watch or listen to, and if you look hard enough you can find the quote you want. I have been fortunate to interview MacMillan four times, as well as to spend time with him at other events and to be in email correspondence at others; one of the pitfalls of corresponding with a living composer is that they do not always remember some of the facts correctly, particularly regarding dates and venues. MacMillan's own scores and the Boosey & Hawkes website have often come to my rescue.

To return to my opening, writing a book on a living composer is a double-edged sword, and to carry on this martial metaphor, I will live or die by that sword. Writing this book has given me a true insight into James MacMillan as both a man and an artist, and I have learned much about both him and the art of composition in the twenty-first century. It is my hope that this book will be the first of many on the composer and his wonderful music.

Acknowledgements

I would like to thank all who helped in the encouragement and creation of this book which first began as a nascent idea in 2006, whilst I was a PhD student at Cardiff University. I had recently given a short paper on James MacMillan at both Cardiff and Bristol Universities and was filled with grand plans to write a book. It took nearly eleven years before I began the project in earnest.

I would like to thank the publishers Boydell & Brewer and particularly their music editor Michael Middeke for his encouragement and belief in the project and for showing faith in a relatively inexperienced author. Many thanks also to MacMillan's publisher Boosey & Hawkes, especially Ethan Kelly, who has regularly provided me with scores, reviews and other materials related to the composer.

I could not have completed the project without the support of the University of Aberdeen, which not only granted me research leave in 2017 but also gave me a Principal's Excellence Award in 2018, which helped to cover some of the associated costs of this project. Thanks to my colleagues Dr Edward Campbell and Professor Peter Stollery for their support and encouragement and to my PhD students Sarah Rimkus, Edward Rhys Harry and Eoghan Desmond for their understanding. A big thank you to another student of mine, Joseph Stollery, for his diligent work in researching and preparing the list of MacMillan's works and recordings that sits handsomely at the end of this book. Many fellow writers on MacMillan have been equally supportive and giving of their time and expertise, particularly Richard McGregor, Timothy Rolls, George Parsons and Dominic Wells. It has been hugely edifying to have experienced much good will and kindness from the academic community towards this project and a genuine feeling of support from many quarters.

A big thank you must also go to Sir James MacMillan himself, who has been incredibly generous with his time over the past two years, both in person and by email. We have met in Aberdeen, Glasgow, Stroud, Cumnock and Windsor, and I feel that I have got to know him as both a man and a composer during this period; he has been kind, interested in and sympathetic to the project throughout. It is to be hoped that he enjoys reading this book as much as I have enjoyed researching and writing it.

A final thank you to my family: my wife, Carolyn, and my children, Amelia and Alexander, who have not only put up with me being away for long periods of time but have endured all the introspection and neuroses that accompany such an undertaking. I could not have done it without them.

P. A. C.
Oldmeldrum, Aberdeenshire, 2018

Permissions

The Confession of Isobel Gowdie

© Copyright 1992 by Boosey & Hawkes Music Publishers Ltd. Reproduced by permission of Boosey & Hawkes Music Publishers Ltd.

Tuireadh

© Copyright 1992 by Boosey & Hawkes Music Publishers Ltd. Reproduced by permission of Boosey & Hawkes Music Publishers Ltd.

Seven Last Words from the Cross

© Copyright 2003 by Boosey & Hawkes Music Publishers Ltd. Reproduced by permission of Boosey & Hawkes Music Publishers Ltd.

Veni, Veni, Emmanuel

© Copyright 1994 by Boosey & Hawkes Music Publishers Ltd. Reproduced by permission of Boosey & Hawkes Music Publishers Ltd.

Visitatio Sepulchri

© Copyright 1992 by Boosey & Hawkes Music Publishers Ltd. Reproduced by permission of Boosey & Hawkes Music Publishers Ltd.

Think of how God loves you

© Copyright 2010 by Boosey & Hawkes Music Publishers Ltd. Reproduced by permission of Boosey & Hawkes Music Publishers Ltd.

Missa Dunelmi

© Copyright 2010 by Boosey & Hawkes Music Publishers Ltd. Reproduced by permission of Boosey & Hawkes Music Publishers Ltd.

Divo Aloysio Sacrum

© Copyright 1992 by Boosey & Hawkes Music Publishers Ltd. Reproduced by permission of Boosey & Hawkes Music Publishers Ltd.

Kiss on Wood

© Copyright 1995 by Boosey & Hawkes Music Publishers Ltd. Reproduced by permission of Boosey & Hawkes Music Publishers Ltd.

The Children

© Copyright 1996 by Boosey & Hawkes Music Publishers Ltd. Reproduced by permission of Boosey & Hawkes Music Publishers Ltd.

Inés de Castro
© Copyright 1996, 2014 by Boosey & Hawkes Music Publishers Ltd. Reproduced by permission of Boosey & Hawkes Music Publishers Ltd.

The World's Ransoming
© Copyright 1996 by Boosey & Hawkes Music Publishers Ltd. Reproduced by permission of Boosey & Hawkes Music Publishers Ltd.

Dunblane Cathedral hymn-tune
© A. F. Barnes. Published in *Hymns from the Church Hymnary*, rev. edn (Edinburgh: Oxford University Press, 1927)

Cello Concerto
© Copyright 1996 by Boosey & Hawkes Music Publishers Ltd. Piano reduction: © Copyright 1997 by Boosey & Hawkes Music Publishers Ltd. Reproduced by permission of Boosey & Hawkes Music Publishers Ltd.

Symphony: 'Vigil'
© Copyright 1998 by Boosey & Hawkes Music Publishers Ltd. Reproduced by permission of Boosey & Hawkes Music Publishers Ltd.

Quickening
© Copyright 1999 by Boosey & Hawkes Music Publishers Ltd. Reproduced by permission of Boosey & Hawkes Music Publishers Ltd.

A New Song
© Copyright 1998 by Boosey & Hawkes Music Publishers Ltd. Reproduced by permission of Boosey & Hawkes Music Publishers Ltd.

A Scotch Bestiary
© Copyright 2004 by Boosey & Hawkes Music Publishers Ltd. Reproduced by permission of Boosey & Hawkes Music Publishers Ltd.

Beatus Vir
© Copyright 1992 by Boosey & Hawkes Music Publishers Ltd. Reproduced by permission of Boosey & Hawkes Music Publishers Ltd.

Christus Vincit
© Copyright 1995 by Boosey & Hawkes Music Publishers Ltd. Reproduced by permission of Boosey & Hawkes Music Publishers Ltd.

A Child's Prayer

Mass

Magnificat

O Radiant Dawn

Os mutorum

Symphony No. 3: 'Silence'

The Sacrifice

St John Passion

Violin Concerto

Clemency

St Luke Passion

1 | *The Keening* – Cumnock, Edinburgh and Durham

In a candid and somewhat brutal article in *The Guardian* in 2004 James MacMillan talks very openly and honestly about his childhood, growing up in working-class west Scotland in the 1960s. The article, entitled 'Silence of the lambs', vividly describes the religious divisions that were present at the time and the difficulties the young MacMillan found in a society 'dominated by machismo, hard-drinking and sporadic violence'.[1] The article, written in response to a new edition of Dennis Sewell's *Catholics: Britain's Largest Minority*, finds MacMillan reminiscing on what one can only imagine are difficult memories of animal cruelty and anti-Catholic bullying in his formative years.[2] Though the article seems to revel in the portrayal of this cruelty (MacMillan certainly does not hold back in his description of the loose sheep that had wandered into a local estate to find its untimely end at the hands of the boys and their 'sexually aroused Alsatians') it does give a very personal insight into the composer's early years: his fears, his family, his education, his love of football and most importantly, his religion. In many ways, the article can be read as a metaphor for MacMillan's music: it is emotionally direct, heart-on-sleeve and has the beguiling mix of dramatic violence and tender consolation that are the hallmarks of the composer's mature works. Although ostensibly an article on religious divisions, it still finds space for warmth, humour and humanity and these are the characteristics that have helped to make James MacMillan one of the most successful British composers of recent years.

James Loy MacMillan was born in Kilwinning, Ayrshire, in south-west Scotland, on 16 July 1959, the first child of James MacMillan Senior (1931–2019) and Ellen Loy (1935–2008). Both MacMillan's parents were from Ochiltree, a small village west of the larger settlement of Cumnock, and both attended the same school, St John's Roman Catholic Primary School, which MacMillan Junior would attend in the 1960s. James MacMillan Senior was a

---

1   James MacMillan, 'Silence of the lambs', *The Guardian* (28 February 2004).
2   Dennis Sewell, *Catholics: Britain's Largest Minority* (London: Penguin, 2002).

joiner and carpenter and it was whilst he was employed to carry out repair work at Drongan Primary School (another small village near Cumnock) in the mid-1950s that he met Ellen, who was a trainee teacher at the time. They married at St John's Church, Cumnock in 1958 and James MacMillan Junior was born a year later. Two further children were born in 1961 and 1964. The MacMillan family moved from Ochiltree to Cumnock (then a town of c.12,000 inhabitants, though now closer to 25,000) in 1963 and it was here that MacMillan attended both primary and secondary school.

Like many Roman Catholic families in the west of Scotland there was a link with Ireland, in this case through MacMillan's maternal family: his mother's grandfather came to Scotland from Ireland in the late nineteenth century. The family hailed from Crossmaglen in County Armagh (in what is now Northern Ireland) which became one of the epicentres of strife during the 'troubles' of the twentieth century.[3] It was MacMillan's maternal grandfather (George Loy, 1900–96) who was the young composer's first musical influence, taking MacMillan to brass band rehearsals and buying him his first musical instrument, a cornet, in 1968. Like many in the area at the time, George Loy was a miner, though MacMillan recalls: 'he spent most of his working life under the ground but when he was above ground he loved taking part in bands, choirs and listened all the time'.[4] George Loy was ever-present at MacMillan's concerts until his death in 1996, so experienced the fruition of his musical influence with his grandson's success in the early 1990s and beyond.

In the 'Silence of the lambs', MacMillan talks warmly of his mother and father and their place in his upbringing and emotional development. He refers to his father as 'quiet, thoughtful and sensitive', 'strangely out of place' with the vicious sectarianism and violence that MacMillan portrays in Cumnock during this period.[5] He recollects 'one of my earliest memories ... is observing him on his knees before a statue of [the Virgin] Mary, lost in a distant humble introspection ... the first time I saw him weep was at the death of Sister Clarissa,

---

[3]   MacMillan recalls a dramatic event when his grandfather's cousin (an early IRA volunteer) came to stay with the family in Ayrshire in the early 1920s, hiding from the 'Black and Tans' (a Royal Irish Constabulary Special Reserve that was set up to fight insurgents during the Irish War of Independence). The fact that two branches of the MacMillan/Loy family could have faced each other 'across the barricades' of this conflict only goes to highlight the internecine nature of Irish independence. See Phillip Cooke, Interview with James MacMillan, Royal Conservatoire of Scotland, 30 November 2015.

[4]   Ibid.

[5]   MacMillan, 'Silence of the lambs'.

a feisty, eccentric nun who had taught him in Primary One [first year of Scottish Primary School] and me a generation later.'[6] MacMillan's portrayal of a working-class man who 'preferred the company of his family to that of hard-drinking men' is both tender and enlightening, it is no surprise that MacMillan refers to his father's sensitivity as 'showing me more about being a man than any of the other masculine madness surrounding me at the time'.[7]

MacMillan describes his mother as 'strong and intelligent', Catholic but with a 'palpable anti-authoritarian and anti-clerical streak'.[8] He recalls that she 'talked politics to me all the time – not just our "backyard stuff" – but of a much bigger picture'. It was his mother who suggested the young MacMillan buy a 'proper grown up paper like the ones published in London' when copies of the *Morning Star* started arriving at the house in the early 1970s.[9] It was arguably through his mother that MacMillan gained the religious sensitivity that he has carried all his life, as he explains: 'My mother was aware that there were still a lot of important people in Scotland who were unnaturally obsessed in an unsavoury way with the existence of third- or fourth-generation Irish Catholics in "their" country: strangers in a strange land.'[10] This sensitivity found early fruit in *The Confession of Isobel Gowdie* in 1990 and a more strident voice in MacMillan's infamous 'Scotland's Shame' address at the Edinburgh Festival in 1999.

Having moved to Cumnock in 1963, MacMillan began attending St John's Roman Catholic Primary School in the centre of the town (the school closed in the 1980s). Here he was taught by the nuns of the Sacred Heart, a Catholic sisterhood, established in London in the early part of the twentieth century, which quickly spread its mission throughout the UK and further afield. It was at primary school that MacMillan received his first experience of the interaction between music and worship, reminiscing that 'there was always a new hymn, chant or antiphon to prepare ... liturgies coming hard and fast, week after week, shaping the community's year'.[11] This experience was pivotal for the young MacMillan, as he reminisced: 'I felt especially nourished by the

---

[6]   Ibid.

[7]   Ibid.

[8]   Ibid.

[9]   Ibid. The *Morning Star* is a British Socialist daily tabloid newspaper. The paper was founded as the *Daily Worker* in 1930, a mouthpiece for the Communist Party of Great Britain, moving to its current political position and title in 1966.

[10]   Ibid.

[11]   Ibid.

Plate 1   James MacMillan (aged 7) with Sister Suzanne and Brother John
at St John's Roman Catholic Primary School, c.1966
(unknown photographer)

nuns and seemed able to contribute a lot for them.' The reciprocal relationship between music and liturgy and between musician and congregation filtered down throughout MacMillan's music in the coming years, reaching its apogee in the work he carried out for St Columba's Church in inner-city Glasgow.[12]

It was during these years that MacMillan began to become aware of music from outside his familial and religious environment. By the age of ten he showed a great interest in Beethoven's *Fidelio*, claiming that 'the social message grabbed [him] as much as the music did' and a lifelong love of Wagner's music resulted in visits to Glasgow to attend Scottish Opera's productions of *Tristan und Isolde* and *Götterdämmerung*.[13] There was a wide variety of music-making taking place in Cumnock which MacMillan was directly or indirectly involved with, ranging from the 'Berlin Octet giving a concert at the local music club' to the great 'community pride in local

12   Ibid.
13   Mary Miller, 'Music for a new Scotland', *The Scotsman Weekend* (21 March 1992).

amateur operatic and oratorio societies' which gave performances of Handel and Gilbert and Sullivan.[14] The rich mixture of music being performed at all levels at the time greatly appealed to the young MacMillan, as he recalled: 'The reason I'm a musician is because of the interaction I've had with friends, relatives and teachers who were all doing music.'[15] This understanding of community, both social and musical, has continued to be of importance for MacMillan throughout his compositional career, as he commented in 2015: 'There is something about the British composer ... that is open to composing in the community and writing music for their own community ... and I loved doing that, writing for little groups of amateurs who might have wanted me to write them a piece or working with children.'[16]

Secondary school followed, initially at St Conval's Secondary School in Cumnock, though this was a difficult time for MacMillan when he felt 'bullied and threatened.'[17] As he recalled to Mary Miller in 1992: 'There was ... a then not unusual working-class resistance to classical music, and he, the son of a carpenter in the mines and a teacher soon to turn to social worker, was regarded as a sissy, despite his passion for football.'[18] This sobering experience, combined with the feeling of disenchantment with his peers and religious intolerance as described in 'Silence of the lambs', made for a difficult transition to early adulthood for MacMillan; fortunately the transfer to the larger Cumnock Academy which occurred in 1973 provided the receptive and encouraging environment for his nascent musical abilities to flourish. Much of this encouragement came in the form of Herbert (Bert) Richardson, the head of music at the academy who arrived at the same time as MacMillan and inspired the young composer's musical activities from the outset.[19] Richardson was a musician 'deeply interested in Renaissance church music' who had been a pupil of George McPhee at Paisley Abbey and quickly started a choir at the school which MacMillan joined.[20] There was a great mutual respect

---

[14]   MacMillan, 'Silence of the lambs'.

[15]   Cooke, Interview with James MacMillan, 30 November 2015.

[16]   Ibid.

[17]   Miller, 'Music for a new Scotland'.

[18]   Ibid.

[19]   MacMillan dedicated his 1993 work for brass ensemble, *They saw the stone had been rolled away*, to Richardson.

[20]   Miller, 'Music for a new Scotland'. Paisley Abbey is a Church of Scotland parish kirk, 12 miles west of Glasgow and roughly 35 miles north of Cumnock. George McPhee is a choir director of some longevity, having taken up his position at the abbey in 1963.

between pupil and teacher, with Richardson recalling MacMillan as not only a 'gifted performer, but as a remarkable catalyst' able to cajole other students and teachers into various musical projects and performances.[21] MacMillan has reciprocated his praise, stating Richardson was an 'inspirational music teacher' full of 'infectious enthusiasm' who had a 'love of music that took over his life'.[22] Certainly much of MacMillan's positivity towards Richardson stems from the older man introducing the choir to the music of Palestrina, Victoria and Lassus and more standard Baroque fayre from the likes of Bach and Handel, an early choral grounding that set MacMillan in good stead for the outpouring of works for choir that appeared from the 1990s onwards. MacMillan reminisces that Richardson thought of him as 'a bit of a collaborator ... on his wavelength' and the warmth between the two men suggests an intense collaborative bond that inspired MacMillan to creativity and originality outside the usual school confines.[23]

It was whilst under Richardson's tutelage at Cumnock Academy that MacMillan composed one of his earliest pieces, the *Missa Brevis*, that he began in 1977. The work is unusual in that it predates much of the juvenilia that MacMillan composed during his university days and has more stylistic congruence with the choral works he composed in the 2000s. Although the Sanctus was first performed in 1977 by MacMillan's school choir (conducted by the composer) and later given its first public performance by McPhee and the Paisley Abbey choir, it was not be performed as a whole until 2006 and was published a year later. The work is undeniably influenced by Richardson's espousal of Renaissance music but also by the music of the leading Anglican composer of the time, Kenneth Leighton (1929–88). Leighton and Richardson were friends and it is no surprise that he brought this music to MacMillan's attention. MacMillan was instantly attracted to Leighton's music and this was a major contributing factor in his decision to go to Edinburgh University and study with him (Leighton was the Reid Professor of Music) after finishing secondary school. As MacMillan recalls, *Missa Brevis* 'was written before I even met Kenneth Leighton, it was a time where I was excited I was going to study with him, so I was looking at a lot of his work'.[24]

---

[21]   Ibid.

[22]   Elizabeth Buie, 'James MacMillan: My Best Teacher', *Times Educational Supplement Scotland* (9 September 2011).

[23]   Ibid.

[24]   Cooke, Interview with James MacMillan, 30 November 2015.

The *Missa Brevis* wears its influences on its sleeve: there is a cleanness of line and thinness of texture that is reminiscent of Palestrina, with a sense of austerity and chromatic inflection that is entirely Leighton; as MacMillan commented, 'it's not Renaissance pastiche, it's a form of archaic counterpoint given a modern flavour'.[25] The piece is undeniably a 'youthful' work and one can imagine the young MacMillan working his way through a head full of diverse musical sources and techniques: it has none of the thumbprints of the composer's later choral work save perhaps the mix of the dramatic and reflective that is a constant theme of MacMillan's oeuvre. It is interesting that MacMillan felt that the work was ripe for publication in 2007 and it highlights a growing awareness of his earlier work that has gradually taken place, with more and more early pieces, that had either been unpublished or discarded, reaching publication as the composer's style evolves. MacMillan made 'little tweaks here and there' in readying the work for performance and publication, as he explains: 'I tidied up the Kyrie and some of the word-setting in the Sanctus, but the Gloria, Agnus Dei and the Ite, missa est (cf. 'At the conclusion') are as they were.'[26] How much 'tidying up' MacMillan actually did to the *Missa Brevis* is not stated, though his reference to it being 'like the adult composer helping the boy composer' gives some indication.[27] It is nevertheless an interesting document of MacMillan's early compositional developments and the undoubted influence of Richardson.

It was whilst at Cumnock Academy that MacMillan met his future wife, Lynne Frew, who also sang in Richardson's school choir, and they became a couple in 1976 at the age of seventeen. Lynne MacMillan (they married in 1983) also went to Edinburgh University, though to study law, becoming a practising lawyer in 1983. She has been a tireless supporter of MacMillan's music from his early days in 'a little band which I played keyboard in' through to her pivotal role in the creation and continuation of The Cumnock Tryst music festival which the couple set up in 2014.[28] She shares MacMillan's Catholic

---

[25]   MacMillan, as quoted in Rebecca Tavener, liner notes to *Tenebrae: New Choral Music by James MacMillan*, Linn CD, CKD 301 (2007), 5.

[26]   Ibid.

[27]   Ibid.

[28]   Cooke, Interview with James MacMillan, 30 November 2015. MacMillan refers to his 'little band' as doing 'covers of heavy stuff like the Rolling Stones, we never actually played anywhere, and we used to record things in the basement. It was all pre-Punk, the sort of things you are ashamed to say you liked, like *Tales of the Topographic Oceans* [Yes, 1973] and *The Lamb Lies Down on Broadway* [Genesis, 1974]. Whether these works will benefit from a 'little tweak here and there' and come to light remains to be seen.

faith and in recent years, like her husband, has become a Dominican of the Third Order (also known as Lay Dominicans, individuals or couples following the same spiritual path as the Dominican Order). She has always had a love of music and studied for an Open University degree in music in the early 2010s.

MacMillan began studying at the University of Edinburgh in 1977 and his four years at university were a happy and productive period which resulted in many works for diverse instrumental combinations and ensembles. His decision to move to Edinburgh was motivated by more than geography or national prestige, as he commented: 'I do not know what drew me there ... I had got it into my head that, in those days, the place to study composition was university'.[29] Certainly, MacMillan's interest in a 'broad-based musical experience' which gave him access to the whole gamut of musical history pointed him in the direction of university rather than a conservatory education (such as at the Royal Scottish Academy of Music and Drama [RSAMD] where MacMillan had taken lessons as a teenager) and the lure of studying with Leighton only reinforced this decision.[30]

MacMillan's relationship with Leighton was warm if a little distant – he recalls the older composer as 'quite shy, quite quiet ... he smoked a pipe during lessons and there was a big dog sat at his feet' – a remnant of a more relaxed time in academia.[31] However, MacMillan has been quick to point out how much he learned from Leighton and how effective he was as a teacher: 'he was very good, very generous, but also very pointed in his teaching ... I learnt a lot from him'.[32] Perhaps some of the most unexpected music that Leighton exposed MacMillan to was that of the Italian avant garde, particularly the music of Luigi Dallapiccola (1904–75). Leighton had studied in Italy in 1951 (with Goffredo Petrassi) on a Mendelssohn Scholarship, so was well-versed in contemporary Italian music. MacMillan recalls that Leighton was 'particularly good at showing how Dallapiccola transcribed his piano music into orchestral music ... it was an amazing insight' and that the orchestration of *Quaderno musicale di Annalibera* (1952, orchestrated in 1954 and given the

29   Ibid.

30   MacMillan, James, 'MacMillan on University', YouTube (https://www.youtube.com/watch?v=L8Nm5c-yZvE&t=19s), accessed 24 January 2019. MacMillan had trumpet and some harmony and counterpoint lessons at the academy, but no formal composition lessons.

31   Cooke, Interview with James MacMillan, 30 November 2015.

32   Ibid.

title *Variazioni*) was the 'single most important orchestration' that MacMillan had witnessed.[33]

Perhaps the most salient examples of Leighton's influence on MacMillan's early music come in the form of two short choral works written during MacMillan's university studies: *The Edinburgh Te Deum* (1978) and *The Lamb has come for us from the House of David* (1979). Both works stem from MacMillan's early association with the Dominican Order: at university he lived upstairs from the Dominicans and was involved in the music provision for the order, and both pieces are dedicated to Dominican Fathers.[34] Like the *Missa Brevis*, MacMillan 'rediscovered' and edited the works in the 2000s with both being published, performed and recorded shortly afterwards (in fact, despite being written in 1978, *The Edinburgh Te Deum* had to wait until 2011 to have its first performance).[35] *The Edinburgh Te Deum* is the more substantial of the two and has a level of chromaticism and complexity that is missing from the *Missa Brevis*, the opening appoggiatura theme in the organ (redolent of Leighton) quickly giving way to dramatic choral outbursts that seem to suggest similar gestures in *Seven Last Words from the Cross* and later pieces. The work has an angularity and austerity that makes it difficult to find much of the mature MacMillan present, though the youthful confidence in textural and harmonic changes point toward future works, both choral and instrumental. *The Lamb has come for us from the House of David* is perhaps closer to the choral music of mature MacMillan, certainly in terms of tone and delivery: it has a warmth and serenity that pervades the whole piece. Although the parallel second-inversion triads and stacked fourths that finish the work may come directly from Leighton's church music, there is a sense of immediacy in this piece that is often missing from the older composer's work. Dominic Wells refers to the work as being 'very much in the style of Herbert Howells', and although the link between the ageing doyen of English church music and a young, socialist, nationalist Scot might be tangential, there is a certain similarity between the opening figure of *The Lamb* (which MacMillan uses

---

[33] Ibid. Richard McGregor, 'James MacMillan: a conversation and commentary', *The Musical Times*, vol. 151, no. 1912 (Autumn 2010), 96.

[34] *The Edinburgh Te Deum* is dedicated to Father Aidan Nicholls OP, who later became a leading Catholic writer, and *The Lamb has come for us from the House of David* is dedicated to Father Allan White OP.

[35] The work only acquired the 'Edinburgh' of its title in 2011, MacMillan having written another *Te Deum* in 2001.

throughout the work) and Howells' 'Master Tallis's Testament' from the *Six Pieces for Organ* (1945).[36]

MacMillan wrote an impressive amount of music during his university days, much of which has been discarded by the composer (other than the two aforementioned choral works, and two others from this period that were repackaged in the 2010s: *A child is born in Bethlehem*, 1978, and *Hymn to the Blessed Sacrament*, 1980).[37] MacMillan appears to have taken every opportunity available to him to have his music performed in the university, beginning with the Baudelaire setting *Poème* in 1978 (for flute, violin, piano and counter-tenor) through to such works as *Canons and Interludes* (flute, oboe and piano) and *Ostinato* (piano) in 1980. As Miller states: 'his work bore the smudges of continual dabbling ... there was the Boulez month, the Webern fortnight and six weeks of would-be Messiaen', and the titles of the works alone suggest abrupt switches from programmatic to absolute music as the whim took him.[38] MacMillan also wrote the incidental music for an Edinburgh University Theatre Company production of Shakespeare's *A Midsummer Night's Dream* in 1979, for which he also acted as musical director, and conducted a performance of Gluck's *Alceste* in 1981. All of this suggests an incredibly fruitful musical period for MacMillan, which also included winning prizes and his first professional commission, *A Study on Two Planes* (1981).

One of the most substantial pieces from the Edinburgh period to have received public performance and publication is the *Symphonic Study*, written in 1981 but not performed and published until 2014.[39] Like the *Missa Brevis* and

---

[36]   Dominic Peter Wells, 'James MacMillan: Retrospective Modernist' (PhD, University of Durham, 2012), 83.

[37]   I am greatly indebted to James Telford's excellent article 'Reconciling Opposing Forces: The Young James MacMillan – A Performance History', *Tempo*, vol. 65, no. 257 (July 2011), 40–51, which goes to extraordinary lengths to document the works and performances of MacMillan during his Edinburgh days.

[38]   Miller, 'Music for a new Scotland'. Perhaps the most intriguing piece suggested by Telford's article is *Ainulindalë*, a Tolkien-inspired work for flute, clarinet, piano and double bass from 1980.

[39]   MacMillan is coy as to the original title of the work, stating that 'it had some other title at the time, a typically useless student one' (Ken Walton, 'Preview: James MacMillan conducting the BBC SSO', *The Scotsman*, 11 January 2014). In an interview with the author he was a little more candid, reminiscing that 'it was *Symphony in One Movement* or something' (Cooke, Interview with James MacMillan,

the other choral works from this period, the work required invasive 'surgery' prior to performance, with MacMillan simplifying some of the orchestral textures ('some things had to be made more practical') and making numerous corrections and edits.[40] Despite the older MacMillan's corrective hand, the *Symphonic Study* is a fascinating document of the composer at an important juncture in his compositional career. The work finds MacMillan writing for orchestra for the first time with a subtleness and naturalness that belies his age and inexperience. The work wears its influences earnestly: the pulsing, staccato string chords with woodwind interjections at measure M could be taken straight from *The Rite of Spring* and the slow, elegiac middle section has a Shostakovichian intensity that is unusual in MacMillan's mature orchestral work. There are certainly moments in the *Symphonic Study* that point towards the works on which MacMillan's reputation rests: the long opening pedal in the double basses (some 28 bars) suggests similar passages in *The Confession of Isobel Gowdie* and the powerful brass outbursts punctuating the texture are reminiscent of such works as *Veni, Veni, Emmanuel*. The work is unusual in that it does not feature the highly ornamented melodic lines and heterophonic passages that are the hallmarks of later works, though the piece contains many of the same gestures that are found throughout the composer's oeuvre. MacMillan referred to the work as 'a little bit indulgent', but there was 'a lot in it I found still quite useful for me to go back to and revisit'; whether the work will reach the same audience as his more recent work remains to be seen, but it nevertheless shows the composer striving for a musical voice that he achieved in earnest five years later.[41]

It was during his university days that MacMillan attended that mecca for modernist composers that was the Darmstadt New Music Summer School, grown to prominence in the former industrial town in western Germany. MacMillan attended the summer school in 1980, the same year that he first visited the St Magnus Festival in the Orkney Isles. The experience of attending Darmstadt appeared to have had a galvanising effect on the 21-year-old MacMillan, but rather than launching him into the vanguard of European modernism it produced the opposite effect: 'I had been to Darmstadt and found

---

30 November 2015). Whether this coyness is because the work is not actually a symphony, or because it had an embarrassing programmatic title, is unclear. The *Symphonic Study* was premiered on 11 January 2014 in a concert that also featured the world premiere of *The Keening*.

[40]   Walton, 'Preview: James MacMillan conducting the BBC SSO'.

[41]   Cooke, Interview with James MacMillan, 30 November 2015.

it problematic ... there was an ideological restrictiveness that worried me.'[42] If anything, the experience 'left [him] gasping' at the incongruity in opportunities available through state support to British (or more specifically Scottish) composers and their German counterparts.[43] In 1981, with the experience of Darmstadt still fresh in his mind, MacMillan turned his attention to life after Edinburgh and his postgraduate studies with John Casken.

MacMillan studied for a PhD in musical composition at the University of Durham from 1981 to 1987, passing the degree in January 1987. His decision to study with Casken (1949–), then only thirty-two and ten years MacMillan's senior, was both practical and pedagogical: he had become engaged to Lynne in 1981 and did not want to be too far from his fiancée who was studying in Edinburgh (Durham is less than two hours from Edinburgh by train).[44] There were other possibilities for study at the time, particularly the University of Sussex (based in Brighton, much further from Edinburgh) with Jonathan Harvey (1939–2012), a prospect that would have rendered a very different outcome for MacMillan's compositional direction. MacMillan has referred to Casken's music as a form of 'soft, English modernism', with Casken belonging to a group of composers that could be described as 'modernism, with a "soft belly"'.[45] Though these terms may seem pejorative, MacMillan has always been quick to express his gratitude for Casken's teaching and the high esteem in which he holds his mentor's music. As he stated: 'I was fascinated by ... John, who had studied in Poland with people roundabout Lutosławski, and his [Casken's] wonderful orchestral pieces such as *Orion over Farne* that he was writing while I was studying with him.'[46] Certainly MacMillan appreciated Casken's 'open-mindedness and openness to the past and a non-

---

[42]   MacMillan, as quoted in Rebecca Tavener, liner notes to *Alpha and Omega*, Linn CD, CKD 439 (2013), 4.

[43]   James MacMillan, 'Neglect of Scots Composers', *The Herald* (23 April 1986). The year that MacMillan attended Darmstadt featured a teaching staff of Brian Ferneyhough, Gérard Grisey and Wolfgang Rihm.

[44]   For more information on Casken, see Arnold Whittall, 'Elegies and Affirmations: John Casken at 60', *The Musical Times*, vol. 150, no. 1909 (Winter 2009), 39–51 and Andrew Clements, 'John Casken', *The Musical Times*, vol. 123, no. 1667 (Spring 1982), 21–23.

[45]   Cooke, Interview with James MacMillan, 30 November 2015.

[46]   Ibid. Casken studied with the composer Andrzej Dolbrowolski (1921–90) on a Polish government scholarship in 1971, whilst in Poland he had 'consultations' with Lutosławski.

ideological stance regarding what the past can/should mean' and that he was 'a great teacher: very friendly, very humane ... just what I needed'.[47] Casken's attachment to his adopted homeland of rural Northumberland and the history and culture of that region is found in works such as the aforementioned *Orion over Farne* (1984, rev. 1986), the choral work *To fields we do not know* (1984) and the orchestral song cycle *Still mine* (1991–92): it is no surprise that MacMillan found his music nourished and encouraged by Casken and his personal aesthetic. The close relationship has continued since MacMillan's studies ended, with MacMillan conducting the BBC Symphony Orchestra in Casken's Violin Concerto at the Barbican in London in 2005, dedicating the dramatic scena *Parthenogenesis* from 2000 to his former tutor and writing the short piano quartet *Chant for John* in 2007 for Casken's retirement from academic life.[48]

MacMillan spent two years studying full-time at Durham but moved to part-time study in 1983, coinciding with his marriage and Lynne beginning a law apprenticeship in Ayr.[49] He took a job at a small preparatory school called Drumley House School in the town of Mossblown in Ayrshire (some 13 miles west of Cumnock) where the young couple were given a small cottage in the grounds. They spent two years there with MacMillan 'doing part time teaching and writing' with frequent trips to Durham to have sessions with Casken.[50] In 1986 the couple's circumstances changed again with MacMillan taking a lectureship at Manchester University, covering the absences of composers Geoff Poole and Robin Walker, Lynne now working for the Scottish Consumer Council in Glasgow. He spent nearly two and a half years in the position, regularly commuting between Manchester and Scotland, 'north on Friday, south on Sunday night'. It was whilst in Manchester that MacMillan finished his PhD.[51]

MacMillan's PhD consisted of eight works written between 1982 and 1987, five of which (*Three Dawn Rituals*, *The Road to Ardtalla*, Sonata for Piano, *Two Visions of Hoy* and *Festival Fanfares*) form the backbone of his early corpus

---

[47]   MacMillan, as quoted in Tavener, liner notes to *Tenebrae: New Choral Music by James MacMillan*, 4. Cooke, Interview with James MacMillan, 30 November 2015.

[48]   MacMillan chose Casken's 1985 large ensemble work *Vaganza* as one of his 'Private Passions' in the BBC Radio 3 programme on 2 March 1996.

[49]   MacMillan refers to his wedding as 'like a pauper's wedding ... it was like the middle ages'. Cooke, Interview with James MacMillan, 30 November 2015.

[50]   Ibid.

[51]   Miller, 'Music for a new Scotland'.

of performed work and remain in his published catalogue today. Two of the works (*Study on Two Planes* and *Songs of a Just War*) have been withdrawn by the composer and one work (*The Keening*) was initially withdrawn but edited, performed and published in 2014 for the same concert that featured the *Symphonic Study*. Many of the works are for solo or chamber ensembles of varying instrumental combinations (as was the vogue for young British composers of the time writing for the likes of Lontano, Fires of London and the London Sinfonietta), excepting *The Keening* and *Festival Fanfares*, and the portfolio is arguably the beginning of MacMillan's mature compositional voice. MacMillan's comments in the introduction to the portfolio are telling and form a blueprint for much of his subsequent work, particularly the works of the next fifteen years: 'The works in this portfolio are not so much concerned with stylistic unity and consistency as with balancing a strongly subjective expression with the need to shape the music into an effective dramatic (or even melodramatic) entity.'[52] The choice of words such as 'subjective expression' and 'dramatic' are succinct and will occur again and again in reviews of the composer's works; however, the use of the word 'melodramatic' is even more nuanced, for here MacMillan uses it without negative connotation (though the use of brackets suggests a nod towards a different semantic interpretation), but future critics would often use the term as a pejorative to criticise over-dramatic elements in MacMillan's work.[53]

MacMillan also makes another statement of real importance for his compositional aesthetic in this introduction: 'There emerges one other major trait: a desire to give expression to received cultural characteristics from my own background, which is Scottish and Celtic ... the ultimate purpose in this was not to write "national" music, but paradoxically to attain an individual voice.'[54] Again, this quote from the 28-year-old MacMillan reads like a 'mission statement' for his future work and will be discussed at length in later chapters.

The works in the portfolio are heavily influenced by Casken as well as the leading British composer of the period, Peter Maxwell Davies (1934–2016), with whom MacMillan formed a close association in the late 1980s. Casken and Maxwell Davies's ability to harness aspects of extra-musical subject matter into a mainstream British modernism were of paramount importance and an influence on MacMillan, and works such as *The Road to Ardtalla* (or *An rathad*

---

52   James MacMillan, 'Music Composition' (PhD, University of Durham, 1987), i.

53   For example, Whittall refers to the 'blood-boltered melodrama of the opera *Inés de Castro*' (Whittall, 'Elegies and Affirmations: John Casken at 60', 46).

54   MacMillan, 'Music Composition', ii.

do dh'Ardtalla as MacMillan refers to the piece in his commentary, using the Gaelic translation) and *Two Visions of Hoy* are in a direct lineage from *Orion over Farne* and works such as Maxwell Davies's *Runes from a Holy Island* (1977) and *A Mirror of Whitening Light* (1977). *The Road to Ardtalla* is perhaps the most emblematic of the 'soft modernism' espoused by Casken, as much of the inspiration for the work could be argued as coming from a Romantic (both lower- and upper-case) wellspring. MacMillan had his honeymoon on the Isle of Islay (off the west coast of Scotland) in July 1983 and as he recalls, 'my most evocative memory of the place was walking along the south coast of the island from Port Ellen towards Ardtalla on a blazing hot Sunday morning'.[55] The work is a paean to the memories of 'heat, sun, sea, tenderness, peace, green land, the beloved, distant mountains, quietness, soft Gaelic speech, whisky', though the final work is no bucolic rhapsody with some of the most spikey, modernist music to be found in the portfolio.[56] In a 1990 article in *The Musical Times*, Keith Potter refers to the work as a 'good example of the kind of well-made pieces turned out, perhaps in their hundreds, by British composition students in the wake of the explosion of interest in the post-war European avant-garde in this country in the 1960s'. 'Well-made' the work may be, but it is not an identikit pastiche of Maxwell Davies, rather one of the first flourishes of MacMillan trying to reconcile the prevailing modernism with his own desire for 'subjective expression' and 'an individual voice'.[57]

The Keening (1985–86)

By far the most substantial work in MacMillan's PhD portfolio is the large orchestral work, *The Keening*, which was written between 1985 and 1986 and which represents the culmination of his academic studies. Not only is the piece the most extensive MacMillan had written to date; it is also the one that points most towards his mature compositional works and the success of *The Confession of Isobel Gowdie*. *The Keening* takes its title from the sensation when 'mourners break into an impromptu chant, expressing their grief and describing the character and virtues of the deceased and the circumstances of

---

[55]   Ibid., 21.

[56]   Ibid., 21.

[57]   Keith Potter, 'James MacMillan: A New Celtic Dawn?', *The Musical Times*, vol. 131, no. 1763 (Winter 1990), 13.

his death' found in ancient folk traditions of Ireland and Highland Scotland.[58] The lament (or keening) that MacMillan portrays in the piece would become a hallmark of his work and reach full voice in numerous pieces throughout his career (such as *The Confession of Isobel Gowdie* and *Tryst*). The work takes as its basis the Scottish lament tune of *Great is the Cause of My Sorrow* (also referred to as *Murt Ghlinne Comhann*, 'The Lament for Glencoe'), a melancholy folk tune referencing the Massacre of Glencoe which took place in 1692 (see Example 1.1).[59] MacMillan never states the tune in any discernible fashion in *The Keening*, rather taking the melodic contour of the original tune and using it as a loose framework for the opening A section (bars 1–71), though transposed from the C minor that is often used in traditional music (including The Whistlebinkies version on their 2015 album *The Whistlebinkies 2*[60]) to

Example 1.1   Opening sixteen bars of *Great is the Cause of My Sorrow* which forms the basis for *The Keening*

Example 1.2   Opening seven bars of *Great is the Cause of My Sorrow* showing melodic contour and appropriation in *The Keening*

---

58   MacMillan, 'Music Composition', 72.

59   A literal translation of *Murt Ghlinne Comhann* is 'Murder (or massacre) of Glencoe'.

60   There is more information on The Whistlebinkies in chapter two.

Table 1.1   Formal structure of *The Keening*

Section	Bar numbers
A	1–71
B1	71–94
A1	95–151
C	152–95
D	196–375
C1	376–400
A2	401–34
A	435–93

B minor and doubled in note value. MacMillan's own interpretation of this development can be seen in Example 1.2.[61]

Choosing the lament as a basis for the orchestral work was a significant decision made by MacMillan, as he explains: 'the choice of melody and its title take on an added significance and inject the work with an external emotional force'.[62] The added 'emotional force' is the key to the importance of *The Keening* in MacMillan's development and earmarks the work as more significant than works such as *The Road to Ardtalla* and *Two Visions of Hoy* that may have sprung from a similar aesthetic wellspring. The melodic contour of the lament is most apparent in the opening solo viola section, where the muted solo violas (accompanied by horns, harps and alto flute) have a loose canonic interpretation of the material from Example 1.1. The modal material of this opening returns three further times (see Table 1.1): as a variation for strings (beginning at bar 95), a spiky brass variant (beginning at bar 401) and as a full string reprise at bar 435.

The relationship between the modal and chromatic material in *The Keening* is very similar to *The Confession of Isobel Gowdie* and MacMillan treats the material in a similar fashion in both pieces: both begin with a slow unfolding of a modal collection of notes which is gradually embellished (both texturally and rhythmically) until new material takes precedence. Both works feature a reprise of the modal music before dramatic climaxes finish the pieces

---

[61]   MacMillan, 'Music Composition', 74.

[62]   Ibid., 72.

and in both there is the sense that the softer material is an undercurrent throughout, obscured and often dominated by the more strident music. It is easy to assume that *The Keening* is a prototype for *Isobel Gowdie*, MacMillan refining his compositional practices in the later work, and in many ways, this is the case. However, there are subtle differences in *The Keening* that make the work a vital part of MacMillan's oeuvre.

Perhaps one of the most striking of these is the inclusion of a Wagner-inspired section (section C in Table 1.1; Example 1.3) which MacMillan states 'was initially provoked by the music from the beginning of Act II Scene 4 of *Die Walküre*'.[63] The link between Wagner's tale of gods and Valkyries and MacMillan's Celtic threnody might seem a little incongruous, but, as he says, 'since a Valkyrie is the Norse equivalent of a Banshee ... the analogy is not out of place. Celtic mythology has it that when a banshee is heard wailing, death is imminent.'[64] The appropriation of extant music (whether traditional, liturgical or concert works) to fit a pre-existing, extra-musical concept is something MacMillan features throughout his works and Wagner (particularly quotations from *Tristan und Isolde*) returns in works as diverse as the Symphony No. 2 (1999), the *St John Passion* (2007) and the *Miserere* (2009).

The Wagner allusion occurs in bars 152–95, starting with the first trumpet and trombone in octaves pitted against a held string sonority with microtonal *glissandi*. MacMillan refers to the Wagner influence on this section: 'The musical "image" from this moment in the opera which has percolated through

Example 1.3   Moment in Wagner's *Die Walküre*, when Brünnhilde appears to Siegmund to announce his fate, that inspired material in *The Keening*

63   Ibid., 78.

64   Ibid., 78.

to my work is the use of slow, solemn leitmotivs announced in the brass.'[65] It would be a keen-eared listener who would detect any Wagnerian influence on this section, but the inclusion of this material (and MacMillan's willingness to openly admit the inspiration) shows the framework of allusions, influences and inspirations that provide the stimuli for many of the composer's works.

It is quite hard to believe that *The Keening* had to wait twenty-seven years for its first performance and even more unusual that for a long period the piece was not listed in MacMillan's published works. As he recalled: 'Nobody asked for it at the time, and almost immediately things got busy for me ... in the melee of all that, *The Keening* simply got forgotten.'[66] Certainly the outpouring of new works that coincided with MacMillan's return to Scotland in 1988 meant there was little time to promote the work, and the string of new commissions made for financial security in an uncertain time for the composer. The work is listed in the 1990 article by Keith Potter in which he surveys MacMillan's output to date, but Potter's assertion that '*The Keening* owes something to the "texture music" of the Poles and Ligeti' is odd, as it is hard to discern any aspects of the work that are reminiscent of Penderecki and his contemporaries.[67] Certainly by the mid-1990s the piece had disappeared from MacMillan's list of works and it had to wait a generation to be heard in the concert hall.[68]

Not long after the completion of *The Keening*, MacMillan's studies were completed and his PhD viva voce took place at the Department of Music, University of Durham, in January 1987. His external examiners were Robert Saxton and Adrian Thomas, he passed with no corrections and, as his contract at Manchester University finished, he returned to Scotland and to the next stage of his life.

---

[65]   Ibid., 78.

[66]   Walton, 'Preview: James MacMillan conducting the BBC SSO', 45.

[67]   Potter, 'James MacMillan: A New Celtic Dawn?', 15. Whether Potter saw the score is debatable. He certainly would have had no access to a recording or any 'realisation' of the work. In the same article it states that *The Keening* would have its premiere at the Musica Nova festival in Glasgow in November 1990, but, for whatever reason, this performance did not take place.

[68]   MacMillan is surprisingly proud of *The Keening* and twice referred to wanting to perform the work again (Phillip Cooke, Interviews with James MacMillan, 30 November 2015, and Candleriggs, Glasgow, 29 March 2017).

2 | *The Tryst* – Glasgow and the Road to *Isobel Gowdie*

1988 would turn out to be a pivotal year for James MacMillan, one that saw the emergence of the composer he is today. With his teaching post at Manchester University finishing in July 1988 and all academic commitments completed at Durham it made sense, both personally and professionally, to return to Scotland and to Glasgow where Lynne was already based, working for the Scottish Consumer Council. Although a logical move in many ways, the homecoming was not the return of the prodigal son that it may have appeared. MacMillan returned to a Scottish music scene he had largely been absent from for the past six years and creative contacts were not initially forthcoming. His first action was pragmatic: 'I came back and signed on the dole'; though this action was short-lived as with Lynne's earnings and MacMillan's first forays into freelance composing his position became increasingly secure.[1] What MacMillan may not have been aware of at the time was how integral to his professional development these first, tentative months in Glasgow were, for the return to his homeland brought forth a sudden surge of new works that culminated in *The Confession of Isobel Gowdie* in 1990 and his position as Scotland's pre-eminent compositional voice.

The move to Glasgow followed on from a period of creative silence that coincided with the completion of *The Keening* and the PhD portfolio, and very little music was written in the latter part of 1986 and 1987. This was undeniably a period of creative introspection and aesthetic soul-searching (as many composers do when leaving the safe confines of academia and study) in which MacMillan was looking for 'a switch in style or a reorientation of technique or stressing of different priorities'.[2] The move away from pieces that had 'a lot of concurrencies with music that has been seen to be important in

---

[1] Cooke, Interview with James MacMillan, 29 March 2017. The 'dole' is an informal British term for benefit paid by the state to the unemployed.

[2] Potter, 'James MacMillan: A New Celtic Dawn?', 14.

Britain' to something more recognisable with MacMillan's oeuvre of today, 'a more exciting music ... music which is visceral ... physical, rhythmic' was taking place.[3] As was noted in 1992: 'It was a time for taking stock ... for leaving behind his earlier concern with the avant-garde, and discarding the pastoral strains in some of his own earlier music.'[4] A 'switch in style' did occur during this fallow period and MacMillan points to the now withdrawn work *Litanies of Iron and Stone* (1987) as 'the work that really started it off'.[5]

Litanies of Iron and Stone is written for clarinet, soprano saxophone, trombone and tape (one of the few works in MacMillan's output to feature a pre-recorded element) and was completed in September 1987. MacMillan reminisces about the time: 'there was a whole group of us ... we spent the whole summer in the electronic music studio of Glasgow University working on an electro-acoustic component to the piece, but all that equipment is now obsolete and it sounds it'.[6] The limitations of the technology and the cumbersome nature of the electro-acoustic process ('days and weeks to get one little thing right') were immensely frustrating to MacMillan and he withdrew the piece in the early 1990s.[7] But the withdrawal of the work should not detract from its importance in the forging of a new style by the composer: in fact MacMillan regularly states his desire to return to the piece in some fashion or other, and in the light of publication and performance of works such as the *Symphonic Study* and *The Keening* it may well happen.[8] Whether *Litanies* is the piece that earmarks the 'switch in style' is debatable as many of the hallmarks of MacMillan's new 'visceral' style can be traced to *The Keening*, which is in many

---

3   Ibid., 14.

4   Miller, 'Music for a new Scotland'.

5   Potter, 'James MacMillan: A New Celtic Dawn?', 14.

6   Cooke, Interview with James MacMillan, 30 November 2015. MacMillan wrote an article for *The Guardian* in 1988 entitled 'Electro-Acoustic Music' in which he was less than charitable about contemporary electro-acoustic composers: 'a lot of recent British electronic music is frankly second-rate, relying on a crude and artless exploitation of flashy sound effects' (6 May 1988).

7   Cooke, Interview with James MacMillan, 30 November 2015.

8   'I'd like to go back to that piece, *Litanies of Iron and Stone*, because there is material I can still use, perhaps in a different context' (Cooke, Interview with James MacMillan, 30 November 2015). 'There is a piece called *Litanies of Iron and Stone* which I "ditched" because the electronic material wasn't good enough, I'd like to go back to that as there is some material I could reuse' (Cooke, Interview with James MacMillan, 29 March 2017).

ways a prototype for works such as *Tryst* that MacMillan shortly embarked on, following his return to Scotland.

The new style that emerged from MacMillan's creative silence, his electro-acoustic experiments and his return to his homeland can largely be characterised by a greater interaction with his national culture, his Celtic heritage and his religious beliefs; much of the political and modernist rhetoric that dominated his earlier work was abandoned (though not wholly) in favour of a new striving for an identity, one forged from his own experience and relation to that tradition. Most works that immediately followed his move to Glasgow and immersion into Scottish society feature direct inspiration from Scottish or Celtic influences and the relationship between composer and national traditions becomes much more intertwined and integral than the 'Romantic and gestural' associations espoused in earlier works such as *Two Visions of Hoy* and *The Road to Ardtalla*.[9] 'Tradition' has never been a dirty word for MacMillan and this sets him apart from his modernist forebears; as early as 1990 he referred to tradition (whether it be Scottish, Celtic or Western Art Music) as 'a river irrigating history' and he has repeated the sentiment throughout his career.[10]

Whether the success of MacMillan's return to Scotland was serendipitous or calculated is hard to discern and it well may be a bit of both, but certainly he chose an important time to return to his homeland, with the nationalist debate beginning in earnest again and a new-found confidence in the Scottish contemporary music scene emerging. It is hard to imagine that works such as *Into the Ferment* and *Tryst* would have been composed if MacMillan had not moved to Glasgow – the inspiration and the opportunities would not have been forthcoming south of the border.

---

9   Potter, 'James MacMillan: A New Celtic Dawn?', 15. The 'Romantic and gestural' *Two Visions of Hoy* (1986) may be the 'pastoral strains' that MacMillan refers to in Miller, 'Music for a new Scotland'.

10   Potter, 'James MacMillan: A New Celtic Dawn?', 15. He carried on the watery metaphor in a 1992 article in *The Scotsman* in which he refers to tradition as 'a deep reservoir of cultural experience ... from which the vapours rise to inform the work which I'm doing now. So in that way, I'm a traditionalist' (Miller, 'Music for a new Scotland'). In 1997, he stated: 'I have an attitude to the past which regards tradition like a river running through history, irrigating human experience at any given time.' Julian Johnson and Catherine Sutton, 'Raising Sparks: On the Music of James MacMillan', *Tempo*, no. 202 (October 1997), 32.

The Tryst (1984) / *St Anne's Mass* (1985)

One of the stimuli behind his change of style was the incorporation of a short piece that MacMillan wrote in 1984, *The Tryst* (not to be confused with *Tryst*, the orchestral work, or *After the Tryst*, the violin and piano piece), into many of his large-scale pieces during the late 1980s and beyond. This brief song is in a pastiche Scottish folk ballad style, largely traditional in design, and a setting of a poem of the same title by William Soutar (1898–1943) in a broad Scots dialect (see below). The poem is an intimate description of two lovers (a 'tryst' meaning a private romantic rendezvous between lovers) and the night-time assignations that take place, and MacMillan wrote the piece for his wife shortly after they were married. The piece was first composed as it was intended, as a folk ballad, initially for his own folk group Broadstone (with whom MacMillan toured bars and folk clubs in west Scotland) then by the group The Whistlebinkies. The Whistlebinkies is a Glasgow-based folk group which performs both folk and art-music pieces in its eclectic repertoire and features amongst its members the flautist and composer Eddie McGuire (1948–) who MacMillan got to know very well.[11] The group recorded *The Tryst* in 1999 on an album entitled *Timber Timbre* on which MacMillan himself sang.

> The Tryst, by William Soutar
> O luely, luely, cam she in
> and luely she lay doun:
> I kent her by her caller lips
> and her briests sae smaa and roun.
>
> Aa throu the nicht we spak nae word
> nor sindered bane frae bane:
> aa throu the nicht I heard her hert
> gang soundin wi ma ain.
>
> It was about the waukruif hour
> when cocks began to craw:
> then she smooled saftly throu the mirk
> afore the day would daw.

---

[11]   For more information on The Whistlebinkies see www.whistlebinkies.co.uk (accessed 10 May 2017).

O luely, luely, cam she in
and luely was she gane:
and wi her aa ma simmer days
like they had never been.[12]

The melody of *The Tryst* is attractive if unremarkable; emotive, yet melancholic and detached (see Example 2.1), much of this springing from Soutar's text which MacMillan states as having 'commitment, sanctity, intimacy, faith ... love, but it is also saturated with a sadness as if all these things are about to expire'.[13]

MacMillan published the piece in 1991 as *Scots Song* (and later in 1996 as *Three Scots Songs* with other Soutar settings 'The Children' and 'Ballad') in an arrangement for voice and piano, though the opaque piano accompaniment with bell allusions and pregnant pauses gives the work an over-serious and over-composed veneer that belies its original simplicity. It was the appropriation of *The Tryst* into a trio of works from 1985 to 1989 that give the piece real significance in both MacMillan's musical development and his change of aesthetic direction: those three works were the *St Anne's Mass* (1985), *Búsqueda* (1988) and *Tryst* (1989).

The composition of the short congregational mass setting, the *St Anne's Mass*, in 1985 would not ordinarily appear to be of great consequence in a corpus of works that includes operas, symphonies and concertos; however, the impact of this work (both congregationally and artistically) is continuing to be felt in MacMillan's work and imbues the piece with lasting significance. It was the decision to use *The Tryst* as the Sanctus of the *St Anne's Mass* that began the process of bringing elements of Celtic or Scottish music into the composer's idiom, and although pre-dating some of the PhD works, it was an important way-marker in MacMillan's change of style. MacMillan uses the material from *The Tryst* almost verbatim, simplifying the melody for congregational use by omitting the grace notes and smaller note values (see Example 2.1).

---

[12]   Glossary: *luely* (softly); *kent* (knew); *caller* (fresh); *breists* (breasts); *sinder'd* (parted); *bane* (bone); *gang* (go); *waukrife* (wakeful); *smool'd* (slipped away); *mirk* (dark); *afore* (before); *wud* (would); *daw* (dawn); *gaen* (gone); *simmer* (summer). www.williamsoutar.com/poems/tryst (accessed 10 May 2017).

[13]   James MacMillan, liner notes to *James MacMillan: Veni, Veni, Emmanuel; Tryst*, Naxos CD, 8.554167 (1998), 3.

Example 2.1   Comparison of melody from *The Tryst* and the Sanctus from the
St Anne's Mass

The use of a pre-existing melody with Scottish heritage (in this case self-composed, but in a pastiche style) as the basis for a larger work is a technique MacMillan used often, and to great effect shortly after the *St Anne's Mass* with *The Keening* and its use of *Great is the Cause of My Sorrow* (as shown in chapter one). But the folksong melody is obscured and 'stretched' in *The Keening* to be almost unrecognisable to even the most observant listener, but in the *St Anne's Mass* the impulse is very different – *The Tryst* is instantly recognisable and a point is surely made. The appropriation of a melody which initially accompanied a secular text to one that is sacred is nothing new (composers in the Renaissance often used a secular melody as the basis for a mass composition, such as in the *L'homme armé* tradition) but there is something quite striking about such a depiction of erotic love being used for a sacred purpose. In using *The Tryst* material, MacMillan has transformed the music from being a love song for his wife to being a 'love song for the Church', to which the characteristics of 'commitment, sanctity, intimacy, faith ... [and] love' ring true. This transformation of tradition, religion and heritage are key to the incorporation of *The Tryst* in many future works and to its longevity as a musical inspiration for the composer.[14]

The *St Anne's Mass* is probably MacMillan's most performed work, as it became a standard congregational setting, initially in the west of Scotland though soon after throughout the rest of the UK, culminating in it becoming the congregational mass of the archdiocese in Westminster. Much of the work's popularity stems from its inclusion in the popular hymnbook *Laudate*, which is widely used across the Catholic Church and in other denominations in the UK. With its wistful tone and 'folksy' quality, the work has had continued popularity with parishioners and will no doubt continue to do so. The *St Anne's Mass* was written for a small Catholic primary school of the same name in Mossblown, Ayrshire (the school closed in 2011) whilst MacMillan was working at Drumley House School in the mid-1980s. As he recalls: 'It was written for children ... they asked me to go down and work with them and there was an important mass coming up, so I said I would write them a couple of things ... so it was the children of St Anne's primary who sang the *St Anne's Mass* for the first time.'[15] MacMillan revised the work in 1996 in preparation for publication, then again in 2011 using the new translation and including a new Gloria.[16]

It is interesting to note that the *St Anne's Mass* and the Piano Sonata were the only works MacMillan completed in 1985; it is hard to imagine two quite so different pieces coming from the same composer in the same period. The Piano Sonata is modernist and brutal with its depiction of a harsh Ayrshire winter and pre-dates MacMillan's shift in style, whilst the mass is warm and traditional (in both the ethnic and tonal sense) and points towards the great outpouring of choral music that occurred in later years. If they were opposites in 1985, it was the gradual coalescence of these two distinct aesthetics that characterised MacMillan's music from 1988 onwards – 'sometimes they are close, sometimes they are distant ... there are elements of both I'm trying to pursue'.[17]

---

[14]   James MacMillan, as quoted in Wells, 'James MacMillan: Retrospective Modernist', 195.

[15]   Cooke, Interview with James MacMillan, 30 November 2015.

[16]   The 1996 revision of the work was largely due to 'photocopies [of the work] going around the archdiocese ... I had no control over it' (Cooke, Interview with James MacMillan, 29 March 2017). The new English translation of the Roman Missal came into usage in 2011 and MacMillan revised the *St Anne's Mass* and the later *Mass* (2000) to incorporate this new text.

[17]   Cooke, Interview with James MacMillan, 30 November 2015.

Búsqueda (1988)

If there is one work that acts as a symbol of MacMillan's new aesthetic after the period of creative silence, it is *Búsqueda* from 1988, for in this work, more than others, for the first time the composer brought art and folk music, politics and religion together in an individual and integral way. It should be considered one of his most important creations. In fact, MacMillan has emphasised this by stating it was a 'piece that allowed me, for the first time to be myself ... in music without trying to qualify ... or having to write to the criteria that is laid down by a modernist dictat'.[18] *Búsqueda* (Search) is a music theatre piece in the tradition of the expressive works for singers, actors and ensemble that were written by the likes of Peter Maxwell Davies and Harrison Birtwistle in the 1960s and 70s, and is scored for large chamber ensemble, three sopranos, eight actors and speaker. The work was commissioned by the Edinburgh Contemporary Arts Trust (ECAT) and the first performance was given by the ECAT ensemble, conducted by the composer, at the Queen's Hall, Edinburgh in June 1988.

The work was commissioned as a companion piece to Luciano Berio's work of the same instrumental forces, *Laborintus II* of 1965, and both works were performed at the première of *Búsqueda*. The piece is a highly original amalgamation of texts taken from the Mothers of the Plaza de Mayo of Argentina (also known as the Mothers of the Disappeared) with sections of the Latin Ordinary of the Mass, and represented MacMillan's most daring text setting to date.[19] It was the beginning of MacMillan's interest in Liberation Theology, a heavily politicised form of religious theory in which religion is redefined in a secular context. This practice, which began in Latin America in the late 1960s, suggests a certain level of humanism, as it aims to transform society by overcoming the conditions of poverty, oppression and violence: with MacMillan's interest in Marxism (he had been a member of a junior Marxist organisation) and Christianity, it would seem a natural place of compositional inspiration. The poems of the Mothers of the Disappeared were translated by

---

[18]   Interview with James MacMillan, during the Second Annual Vancouver New Music Festival, 1998. web.archive.org/web/20030418031812/http://www.sfu.ca/twentieth-century-ltd/macmillan1.html (accessed 14 April 2015).

[19]   The Mothers of the Plaza de Mayo (Asociación Madres de Plaza de Mayo) is an association of Argentine mothers whose children were 'disappeared' during the military dictatorship between 1976 and 1983. They took their name from the Plaza de Mayo, in front of the presidential palace in Buenos Aires, where they first demonstrated against state terror.

Gilbert Markus OP (a Dominican friar and close collaborator of MacMillan's who worked in Central America in the 1980s and campaigned for human rights in that region) and other members of the Búsqueda organisation in Oxford, from where the piece took its title.

The Ordinary sections of the Mass (Kyrie, Gloria, Credo, Sanctus, Agnus Dei) are used as a musical and textural background, which MacMillan refers to as a 'structural scaffolding for the development of the piece', over which the vernacular texts give *Búsqueda* its narrative drive and momentum.[20] Not all the Latin text is used, with MacMillan choosing important and significant phrases, often to enhance and comment on the mothers' poems. The Kyrie and Agnus Dei are used in whole but only the beginning of the Gloria and crucial sections of the Credo are present, leading to powerful interjections such as 'Come back my darling and take away my thorn ... *Crucifixus etiam pro nobis*' and 'Sad is your young life – broken now – *et homo factus est*'. The use of the Latin text not only provides the framework for the piece, but also emphasises the plight of the Mothers of the Disappeared, with the shared theme of a mother's grief at the loss of a son.

Richard McGregor notes that many of MacMillan's works from this period are 'focused on aspects of loss, grief, and hurt refracted through some form of musical and/or religious commentary which addressed human suffering', and *Búsqueda* is a clear example of this.[21] There is a humanitarian element to MacMillan's engagement with the texts and the use of the Ordinary sections, with the suggestion that the liturgy is 'the mediator, the means of "making good" or ameliorating the suffering'.[22] In 1997 he stated: 'There's something in being in artist which needs to make sense out of chaos ... taking the chaos and making it right ... perhaps it's futile, but it comes from a humanitarian urge.'[23]

On a musical level, *Búsqueda* has many of the hallmarks of MacMillan's later works: the unison Ds in the brass (bars 158–61) denoting a change of section, the softly unfolding modal collections with dramatic brass interjections (bars 96–141) and the keening strings elaborating important pitches (bars 162–95) can all be found in works from *Búsqueda* onwards. In fact, *Búsqueda* and *Tryst* (1989) share much similar material and long sections (bars 267–303 in the

---

[20]   James MacMillan, programme note to *Búsqueda*, www.boosey.com/cr/music/James-MacMillan-B-squeda/3524 (accessed 11 May 2017).

[21]   McGregor, 'James MacMillan: a conversation and commentary', 84.

[22]   Ibid., 84.

[23]   Johnson and Sutton, 'Raising Sparks: On the Music of James MacMillan', 14.

former, bars 277–99 in the latter) based on the same falling three-note motifs, as shown in Example 2.2.

The use of *The Tryst* material in *Búsqueda* is the same as the folksong appropriation in *The Keening*: it is elongated to the point of being no longer recognisable as the original melody, but what remains is the mood and 'feeling' of the initial piece. MacMillan reserves *The Tryst* for the Agnus Dei section of *Búsqueda* (beginning at rehearsal mark S), the most reflective and poignant section of the work. He introduces the 'melody' in the cellos and double bass, gradually presenting the pitches of the original until the whole modal collection has been stated and the melancholy vein of *The Tryst* permeates the whole work. The soft harp arpeggios and improvised soprano lines highlight the same notes and emphasise this most reflective part of the piece. Coincidently, the three-note motifs of Example 2.2 are the same pitches transposed as the first three notes of *The Tryst*, further strengthening the presence of this material. Whether the inclusion of *The Tryst* in this section of *Búsqueda* makes an association with the mother's love for her lost child, or whether MacMillan is reiterating the 'love song for the church' is not apparent, but his decision to use this material at the most emotive section of the work is clear.

Búsqueda was warmly received by audience and critics alike after its first performance, with *The Guardian* stating that 'much of this music was violent and shocking; much of it had a wounded, exhausted serenity that was profoundly moving' and *The Independent* praising 'music of shattering directness, clearly defined emotion and angry idealism.'[24] MacMillan is today ambivalent about the piece, referring to it as a 'young man's piece', as 'being of its time ... [it] sounds like a 1980s-composer thinking it was the 1960s!'[25] Certainly, the work has not aged quite as well as some of his other pieces from this period, but this is mainly due to the waning of music theatre as an important vehicle of musical expression for composers; it will always be redolent of its 1960s and 70s heyday together with such pieces as Maxwell Davies's *Eight Songs for a Mad King* (1969) and *Miss Donnithorne's Maggot* (1974). But that should not detract from its importance in MacMillan's compositional development and the way it pointed towards new sounds and new discoveries, as the composer noted in 1997: 'it was a rite of passage piece'.[26]

---

[24]   Quotations taken from www.boosey.com/cr/music/James-MacMillan-B-squeda/ 3524 (accessed 11 May 2017).

[25]   Cooke, Interview with James MacMillan, 30 November 2015.

[26]   Johnson and Sutton, 'Raising Sparks: On the Music of James MacMillan', 14.

Example 2.2   Use of the same falling three-note motifs in *Búsqueda* and *Tryst*

A work that covers similar religio-political ground to *Búsqueda* is *Cantos Sagrados* (Sacred Songs) from 1989, written for choir and organ and commissioned and first performed by the Scottish Chamber Choir in 1990.[27] The work juxtaposes sacred and secular texts in a comparable way to *Búsqueda* and features the same themes of Liberation Theology as the earlier piece. In the first and third movements, MacMillan sets poems by Ariel Dorfman, an Argentine-Chilean-American novelist, playwright and human rights activist; the first poem 'Identity' continues the 'search' of *Búsqueda*, with a fragmented phone call giving the text for a frantic and desperate search for the identity of a found body. The delivery is highly staccato, urgent and agitated, with the choral texture punctuated by dissonant, declamatory organ chords. As in *Búsqueda*, MacMillan introduces sections of the traditional Latin liturgy, here using the 'Libera animas' (Deliver the souls of all the faithful departed from the pains of hell) from the Latin Requiem as a soft, homophonic coda to the movement, easing some of the desperation of earlier. Patrick Russill refers to this moment as MacMillan 'channelling righteous anger into heartfelt prayer, all the more forceful for being so expressively contained'.[28]

The third movement, 'Sun Stone', covers similar ground to the first with MacMillan setting the final words of an executioner to his victim. Again, MacMillan blends Latin and English, with a section of the Creed, 'Et incarnatus est' (He became incarnate by the Holy Spirit ... For our sake he was crucified), providing a backdrop for the disturbing events described. The final line of the

---

[27]   MacMillan orchestrated the work in 1997, with the first performance given by the Royal Scottish National Orchestra and Chorus in March 1998.

[28]   Patrick Russill, 'Cantos Sagrados', *The Musical Times*, vol. 137, no. 1837 (Spring 1996), 36.

executioner, 'Forgive me compañero', is delivered increasingly quietly, and more earnestly until the last whispered utterance leaves a powerful and resonant mark on the drama that has unfolded.

It is perhaps the second movement of *Cantos sagrados* that is the most striking, full of 'memorable beauty and haunting bewilderment'.[29] It is a setting of a prayer to the Virgin of Guadalupe by Ana Maria Mendoza (translated again by Gilbert Markus) with its central theme of bitterness and irony at an American Indian praying to the same Virgin as the Conquistadors who are ravaging her country. The final lines are extremely poignant: 'Why is it, Sweet Virgin, sweet mother, why is there another Virgin of Guadalupe, 'Patroness of the Conquerors?'. The movement is deceptively simple with the same melody present throughout (see Example 2.3), a melody in 4/2 repeated over slowly unfolding chords in 3/2 in the lower voices.[30]

Stephen Johnson notes that 'the tension between the developing thoughts [of the narrator/poet] and un-developing musical patterns heightens the poignancy of the poem' and there is something arresting about this static nature of this expressive movement.[31] Perhaps it is this expressivity that has led to the work's continued success and relevance, for regular performances have continued long since the piece's premiere. It has aged better than its companion work, *Búsqueda*, though the irregular staccato interjections of the opening movement have a curiously anachronistic feel, what Johnson calls 'almost like a brutalized Sondheim'.[32] It is probably the second movement which has led to the work's longevity, with the simple melodic lines and static harmonies suggesting much of the composer's later choral works. The instrumentation and form of the piece have made it much more accessible than the unusual scoring of *Búsqueda*, and the 'sacred songs' of *Cantos Sagrados* seem much more contemporary than the music theatre of the earlier work. MacMillan has reiterated this: 'opera happens, chamber opera happens and choral music does, maybe *Cantos Sagrados* suits the living culture more than music theatre, which has fallen by the way.'[33]

---

29   Ibid., 36.

30   The pitches of this melody in the first soprano part form the same D major tonality/ modality as *The Tryst*, further cementing the link between the text of Mendoza's 'prayer' and the 'love song to the church' of MacMillan's folksong.

31   Stephen Johnson, 'James MacMillan', *Tempo*, no. 185 (June 1993), 4.

32   Ibid., 4.

33   Cooke, Interview with James MacMillan, 30 November 2015.

Example 2.3   Bars 5–7 of 'Virgin of Guadalupe' from *Cantos Sagrados*

Cantos Sagrados was the highpoint of MacMillan's interest in Liberation Theology and other than a small fragment of *Catherine's Lullabies* (1990) no other work after this was so openly influenced by the ideology. His opinion on the movement and its relationship to his work has changed over the years (as has his political persuasion: see chapter six). In 2000, he described the two works as 'naively ... being inspired by the basic principles of Liberation Theology', whereas in 2007 he stated that 'Liberation Theology has had its day and become a historical thing', preferring to call it the 'preferential option for the oppressed'.[34] By 2015 he was unequivocal: 'I look back at it as quite a dangerous time for theology and also for the church when opportunists, both inside and outside the church were making a move in trying to influence that church, and to an extent I fell for it because I was a believer and also someone who believed in social justice. You can have both without taking the whole quasi-Marxist package.'[35]

---

[34]   James MacMillan, 'God, Theology and Music', *New Blackfriars*, vol. 81, no. 948 (2000), 19; MacMillan, as quoted in Tavener, liner notes to *Tenebrae: New Choral Music by James MacMillan*, 16.

[35]   Cooke, Interview with James MacMillan, 30 November 2015.

Into the Ferment (1988)

One of the first substantial contacts that MacMillan made on his return
to Scotland was Kathryn McDowell, the then development officer of the
Scottish Chamber Orchestra (SCO), and it was McDowell who suggested that
MacMillan should be the composer-in-residence for the second of Peter Maxwell
Davies's Strathclyde Concertos projects.[36] The project was a collaboration
between Strathclyde Regional Council (the local authority for Glasgow and the
west of Scotland from 1973 until 1996) and the SCO. The orchestra's associate
composer/conductor, Maxwell Davies, was to write a series of ten concertos
over a ten-year period for the principal members of the orchestra. Each concerto
was accompanied by an educational project that related to the work and was
designed and delivered by a young Scottish composer-in-residence.[37] MacMillan
was the chosen composer for the project associated with Davies's *Strathclyde
Concerto No. 2* (1987, for cello and orchestra) and from this association resulted
Into the Ferment.

The links with both Maxwell Davies and the SCO proved to be invaluable
in MacMillan's professional development and were key to him becoming
established in his homeland and beyond. The link with the SCO was
particularly fruitful in the late 1980s and 90s as MacMillan was appointed
affiliate composer in 1990 and composed a series of works including *Into the
Ferment*, *The Exorcism of Rio Sumpúl* (orchestral version) and *Tryst*. There is
no doubt that MacMillan benefitted from the endorsement of McDowell and
Ian Ritchie (the then managing director of the SCO), but the relationship was
reciprocal with the orchestra gaining significant kudos from its 'discovery' of
Scotland's 'outstanding talent' and MacMillan's success after *The Confession of
Isobel Gowdie*.[38] It was a good time for the composer to return to Scotland: with
Maxwell Davies's patronage and publicity, new music was coming to the fore
in Edinburgh, Glasgow and the home of Maxwell Davies's St Magnus Festival,

---

[36]   MacMillan dedicated the 1989 chamber orchestra work *The Exorcism of Rio Sumpúl*
to McDowell.

[37]   For more information on the Strathclyde Concertos project see: www.maxopus.
com/resources_detail.aspx?key=58 (accessed 16 May 2017). The young composers
involved in the project reads like a who's who of contemporary music in Scotland, with
Bill Sweeney, Eddie McGuire, Sally Beamish and Alasdair Nicolson all having the role at
some point.

[38]   John Purser, *Scotland's Music: A History of the Traditional and Classical Music of
Scotland from Earliest Times to the Present Day* (Edinburgh: Mainstream, 1992), 274.

Kirkwall in the Orkney Isles. MacMillan was to become the 'poster boy' for a new generation of Scottish composers and a new-found confidence in Scottish contemporary music.[39]

The link with Maxwell Davies was equally important to MacMillan in the same period, as it cemented further MacMillan's place at the top table of Scottish music. As mentioned in chapter one, MacMillan first attended the St Magnus Festival in 1980 where he was present at the 'world premiere of that piece, *The Yellow Cake Revue*, with that beautiful little piano piece' (*Farewell to Stromness*) and returned in 1988 to review the festival for *The Guardian*.[40] Following on from MacMillan's involvement with the Strathclyde Concertos he returned to Orkney to assist Maxwell Davies on the older composer's annual composition course in 1989 and MacMillan's work has featured regularly in the festival, including the premiere of *Tryst* by the SCO in 1989. MacMillan wrote a short piano quintet, *For Max*, for Maxwell Davies's seventieth birthday in 2004 and was full of praise in the programme note: 'I have always had a great admiration for him and regarded him as a kind of mentor.'[41]

Into the Ferment was first performed by the SCO and the Ayrshire Schools Orchestra, conducted by the composer at the Magnum Leisure Centre, Irvine (a small town on the Ayrshire coast, some 30 miles west of Glasgow) in December 1988. The work is scored for orchestra with a second chamber orchestra of fourteen players, the larger group being written for the schools' orchestra and the smaller for players from the SCO. The piece is based on Robert Burns's poem 'Willie brew'd a peck o'maut' (1789, see below), a depiction of three friends and their whisky-tasting exploits, and each of the nine sections of the work is headed by a quotation from the poem or from a different Burns offering.

Willie brew'd a peck o'maut, by Robert Burns
Willie brew'd a peck o' maut
O Willie brew'd a peck o' maut
And Rob and Allan cam to see;
Three blyther hearts, that lee-lang night,
Ye wad na found in Christendie.

---

[39] If you are in doubt about MacMillan's status as a poster boy, see Gerald Larner, 'New men for the New music', *The Guardian* (14 August 1990).

[40] Interview on BBC Radio 3, *In Tune* (15 March 2016). MacMillan's review of the 1988 St Magnus Festival: 'Orcadian Delights', *The Guardian* (23 June 1988).

[41] James MacMillan, programme note to *For Max*, www.boosey.com/cr/music/James-MacMillan-For-Max/46369 (accessed 17 May 2017).

Chorus:
We are na' fou! We're nae that fou',
But just a drappie in our e'e!
The cock may craw, the day may daw,
And aye we'll taste the barley-bree!

Here are we met, three merry boys,
Three merry boys I trow are we;
And mony a night we've merry been,
And mony mae we hope to be!

It is the moon, I ken her horn,
That's blinkin' in the lift sae hie;
She shines sae bright to wyle us hame,
But, by my sooth, she'll wait a wee!

Wha' first shall rise to gang awa',
A cuckold, coward loun is he!
Wha' first beside his chair shall fa'
He is the King amang us three! [42]

MacMillan took the project 'very seriously, both the educational work and the commission itself' and wanted to write a piece that 'could survive beyond its first performance'.[43] He knew the Ayrshire Schools Orchestra quite well having played trumpet with them in his youth and the addition of the SCO principal players made for an exciting commission. He recalls the educational project as involving 'going down to Ayrshire every day for eight weeks', working and improvising with the school-children on the work, and that the experience taught him a lot.[44] Certainly the opportunity to write a successful piece for amateurs was of paramount importance to MacMillan (he mentions Maxwell Davies's work with children in his PhD commentary[45]) and with funding and

---

[42] Glossary: *maut* (malt whisky); *fou* (drunk); *drappie* (droplet); *daw* (dawn); *ay* (always); *barley-bree* (whisky); *lee-lang* (live long); *ken* (know); *blinkin* (glinting); *lift* (sky); *wyle* (lure); *by my sooth* (upon my word); *loun* (fool). www.robertburns.org/works/281 (accessed 16 May 2017).

[43] Cooke, Interview with James MacMillan, 29 March 2017.

[44] Ibid.

[45] MacMillan, 'Music Composition', 85.

goodwill at the time in ready supply, it was an important commission in which to invest all his energies.

Into the Ferment is a curious mix of styles, genres and influences and represents the first in a line of colourful, somewhat satirical orchestral works that includes *Britannia* (1994) and *A Scotch Bestiary* (2004). The opening movement, 'The Storm', immediately recalls Benjamin Britten's 'Storm' from the *Four Sea Interludes* from *Peter Grimes* (1945) with its cascading woodwind and string figures, pounding percussion and harp *glissandi*. The second movement, 'Here are we met three merry boys', has a feeling of Malcolm Arnold with the three orchestral trombones representing the three drunken protagonists of Burns's poem (see Example 2.4).

The third movement, 'In dispraise of whisky', finds MacMillan in full Maxwell Davies mode with a boisterous reel gradually exposed alongside *fortissimo* brass interjections, giving the impression of festivities and revelry. The fourth movement, 'We are na' fou!', is perhaps closest in tone to *Tryst* and the works that follow, with a unison melodic line filtered through the upper orchestral voices but interrupted by rhythmic hockets throughout. The 'Nocturne' that follows leads to a reprise of the second movement in 'Three merry boys again (sometime later)' before a seventh movement, 'Wha' first shall rise to gang awa', which again sees MacMillan straying into Maxwell Davies territory with the inebriated brass trio slurring their way through material that does not sound too dissimilar to *Farewell to Stromness* (complete with comedy mutes and *glissandi*). The eighth movement, 'Man to man ... shall brithers be', is more reflective and serious, depicting what MacMillan refers to

Example 2.4   Bars 48–51 of 'Here are we met three merry boys' from *Into the Ferment*

as 'a different light ... friendship and brotherhood are being strengthened by this occasion'.[46]

MacMillan makes an unusual musical decision in this movement by using the very same material as he later used for the final movement of *Cantos Sagrados*: the two are identical, leading to questions about this process. As will become evident, MacMillan was very happy to reuse, recycle and re-appropriate material from his pieces throughout his career and had already done so with *The Tryst* and the *St Anne's Mass*. However, the large-scale appropriation of this material from *Into the Ferment* into *Cantos Sagrados* is unusual, particularly as it is without any apparent extra-musical significance. One can only surmise that the feelings of 'friendship and brotherhood' that MacMillan espoused in this movement are similar in some way to the act of forgiveness that the executioner asks for in 'Sun Stone', a humanitarian impulse that connects works from across times and cultures. *Into the Ferment* ends with a short, rousing finale, closing this characterful but important work in the composer's output.

Richard McGregor notes that the works from the time of MacMillan's return to Scotland feature an 'increasing engagement with Celtic elements', and *Into the Ferment*, with its references to Burns, reels and whisky, certainly fits this description.[47] There is an earnestness to MacMillan's 'Scottishness' in the work that seems at odds with his relationship with his homeland in later pieces, almost as if MacMillan is hiding behind other composers – a sense of Maxwell Davies parody perhaps? Nevertheless, the homage to all things Scots was a success with the schools and the SCO and provided MacMillan with an important contact in the musical world of his homeland.

A work that shares a similar 'engagement with Celtic elements' is the piano concerto *The Berserking* of 1990, which was first performed by the Scottish National Orchestra with the pianist Peter Donohoe in September 1990. The work takes its title from the 'Berserkers', the Viking warriors who prepared for battle by taking copious amounts of alcohol and other substances to lose their fear and inhibitions, thus becoming feared warriors. However, in doing so, they became more vulnerable to organised attack and often their pre-battle exertions were fruitless and largely suicidal. MacMillan states in his programme note to the work: 'As a Scot living in the modern

---

[46]   James MacMillan, programme note to *Into the Ferment*, www.boosey.com/cr/music/James-MacMillan-Into-the-Ferment/3961 (accessed 16 May 2017).

[47]   Richard McGregor, 'A Metaphor for the Deeper Wintriness: Exploring James MacMillan's Musical Identity', *Tempo*, vol. 65, no. 257 (July 2011), 28.

world this behaviour seems very familiar! I see its pointlessness as resembling the Scots' seeming facility for shooting themselves in the foot in political and, for that matter, in sporting endeavours ... in fact the initial inspiration for *The Berserking* came from watching a soccer game in which Glasgow Celtic turned in a characteristically passionate, frenzied but ultimately futile performance against Partizan Belgrade.'[48]

The sense of this 'Berserking' can be felt most in the opening movement which is loud, chaotic and exhilarating, starting with percussive effects from the woodwind, brass and string players before growing to brutal climaxes and crescendos. MacMillan mentions 'a sense of swaggering futility in the way the energy is "misdirected" into climaxes without resolutions and maintained in a continual state of hyper-activity and excess'.[49] Indeed the movement has the feeling of unrelated 'blocks' of material colliding and crashing into each other, rather than a continuous musical development. The 'hyper-activity' that MacMillan describes may be referring to his use of quasi-minimalist material in this movement (see Example 2.5), an unusual departure for the composer and one that may show his admiration for the Dutch composer Louis Andriessen (1939–).

Andriessen's anti-avant-garde stance appealed to MacMillan in the late 1980s (the wind-band piece *Sowetan Spring* of 1990 is directly inspired by him)

Example 2.5   Bars 135–38 of the first movement of *The Berserking* (piano part only)

---

[48]   James MacMillan, programme note to *The Berserking*, www.boosey.com/cr/music/James-MacMillan-The-Berserking/6452 (accessed 18 May 2017). The game MacMillan is referring to was on 27 September 1989 in the European Cup Winners Cup competition, in which Celtic beat Partizan Belgrade 5-4, but the tie ended up level at 6–6 over two matches. Celtic exited the competition on the 'away goals' rule. He may also be reminiscing about Scotland's 'gallant failures' at the 1974 and 1978 football World Cups which would have left a tangible mark on the teenage MacMillan.

[49]   Ibid.

and he contemplated studying with him after his doctoral studies, but received a negative response from the Dutch composer.[50] The 'hard-edged' minimalism espoused by Andriessen can also be found in his pupil Steve Martland (1954–2013), to whom *The Berserking* is dedicated: whether Martland's form of 'muscular' minimalism influenced the work is hard to say, but there is a sense of over-repetition and lack of goal-orientation that is synonymous with much minimalist music.

The Celtic elements of the work are most prominent in the second and third movements, where any notion of the piece being programmatic seems to dissipate. The second movement is 'slow, reflective and delicate and has a simple verse and refrain structure like a folksong, creating an aura of traditional Scottish music'.[51] This reference to Scottish music is most prominent in bars 439–51, one of the first references to Hebridean psalm-singing in MacMillan's music, with its weaving, heterophonic lines, circling and embellishing a unison pitch.

Perhaps the most obvious interaction with Scottish music occurs at the very end of the piece where a trio of harp, celeste and piano emerges from an orchestral climax, repeating interlocking fragments of modal music with a decidedly folk-like hue. MacMillan refers to this ending as a 'meaningful resolution' to the 'deliberately aimless climaxes' of the first movement and reveals that 'the themes have been there throughout the piece, but acquire special significance because of both the scoring and the sense of suspended time that is conveyed'.[52]

The idea that folk music, or vernacular music, was used as a 'meaningful resolution' to a piece became a key tenet of MacMillan's mature music and can be found in many later pieces, perhaps most prominently in the *Seven Last Words from the Cross* in 1993. It relates directly to the consistent inclusion and reference to *The Tryst* in MacMillan's music. Drawing on McGregor's suggestion that liturgy 'ameliorates the suffering': the use of folk music ameliorates more dissonant music and gives the true conclusion to a work which other music cannot: reference to traditional music is pervasive in MacMillan's later music, but always carries the same significance and meaning.

---

[50]   MacMillan recalls Andriessen returning his scores with a note saying words to the effect of 'your music is nothing like mine, therefore I can't teach you' (Cooke, Interview with James MacMillan, 30 November 2015).

[51]   MacMillan, programme note to *The Berserking*.

[52]   Johnson and Sutton, 'Raising Sparks: On the Music of James MacMillan', 28.

Tryst (1989)

One of MacMillan's most accomplished pieces before *The Confession of Isobel Gowdie* is *Tryst* from 1989, first performed by the SCO, conducted by Paul Daniel, at the St Magnus Festival, Orkney in June 1989. As well as being a succinct example of MacMillan's compositional aesthetic in the late 1980s, it also proved to be an important 'calling card' for his professional reputation in his homeland. The success of *Tryst* at the St Magnus Festival (where MacMillan was composer-in-residence for the 1989 festival) led to his appointment as the affiliate composer of the SCO and ultimately to the commission of *Isobel Gowdie* and the success that work had at the 1990 Proms.

The title of *Tryst* unsurprisingly comes from the inclusion of *The Tryst* material in the work, as MacMillan states: 'Not only has it cropped up in this piece, but it has provided both the title and the emotional core of the music.'[53] *The Tryst* theme occurs in an elongated fashion, like its use in *Búsqueda*, in the third section of the work (C), the slow, burgeoning heart of the piece. MacMillan initially introduces the first three pitches of the theme (A-D-E) in the upper second violin part in an expressive, characteristic fashion (see Example 2.6).

The following pitches of the theme (F♯–A–B) are added in bars 318, 320 and 324 (all in the second violin) with the canonic texture of the work beginning to fragment and become more animated (see Example 2.7).

As in *Búsqueda*, *The Tryst* melody is not easily recognisable in *Tryst*, in fact, as Dominic Wells suggests, it is clear only to 'those familiar with the melody or who are actively searching for it'.[54] However, the same essence of feeling or mood is captured in this movement, as with the Credo section of the earlier

Example 2.6   Bars 310–15 of *Tryst* showing first appearance of *The Tryst* theme

---

[53]   James MacMillan, programme note to *Tryst*, www.boosey.com/cr/music/James-MacMillan-Tryst/5742 (accessed 18 May 2017).

[54]   Wells, 'James MacMillan: Retrospective Modernist', 187.

Example 2.7   Bars 318–24 of *Tryst* showing further revealing of *The Tryst* theme

piece: 'commitment, sanctity, intimacy, faith ... love'. What is different with the inclusion of *The Tryst* in this work compared to *Búsqueda* is that MacMillan is here alluding to the original tune with its connotations of romantic love, rather than the 'love song for the church' of the tune's appearance in the *St Anne's Mass*.

Tryst is one of MacMillan's most uncompromising orchestral works, full of rhythmic energy and declamatory outbursts, but with very little of the juxtaposition of styles and material that characterises other works of this period. The central slow section, C (in which *The Tryst* appears) does feature more reflective music, but it is often obscured and fragmented and does not carry the same emotional gravitas as the ending of *The Berserking* or the eighth movement of *Into the Ferment*. The work also alludes to modernist composers of the twentieth century, with Stravinsky's *Rite of Spring* (1913) an obvious influence in the faster sections (A and E) and Messiaen's *Et exspecto resurrectionem mortuorum* (1964) recalled in the homophonic wind chords that begin the second section (B).[55] The form of the work is unusual with sections B and C sharing material and section D restating material from A (see Table 2.1). MacMillan further emphasised that 'the final section [E] combines fast music with chordal ideas from the middle section [C]'.[56]

The success of *Tryst* in June 1989 showed how successful MacMillan's return to Scotland had been and how much he had achieved in just under a

---

[55]   MacMillan stated in 1997: 'I can think of pieces I wrote ten years ago, like the orchestral piece *Tryst*, which make certain allusions to Stravinsky. There was a deliberate attempt to exorcise his influence by grappling with it head on.' Johnson and Sutton, 'Raising Sparks: On the Music of James MacMillan', 7.

[56]   MacMillan, programme note to *Tryst*.

Table 2.1   Formal structure of *Tryst*

Section	Bar numbers
A	1–199
B	200–76
C	277–411
D	412–582
E	583–685

year – from uncertainty in both his aesthetic and his employment to being lauded as the future of Scottish music was an incredible achievement. The 1980s had been a decade of searching and experimenting, but one that had ultimately proved hugely successful; however, the real successes lay in the next couple of years and in a series of works that brought the composer to even greater exposure and acclaim.

Scots Songs – The Confession of Isobel Gowdie, Tuireadh and Veni, Veni, Emmanuel

'Imagine Vaughan Williams's *Tallis Fantasia* updated and then invaded by Stravinsky's *Rite of Spring*, and you get a rough idea of the new Prom work by the positive young Scottish composer, James MacMillan', said *The Guardian* after the first performance of *The Confession of Isobel Gowdie* in 1990.[1] The same review would go on to call the premiere an 'instant success'. The work 'grabbed the Prom audience in a way rare with new music'. *The Telegraph* wrote that 'MacMillan's command of even the most complex musical material is as impressive as his emotional conviction', and *The Independent* savoured the work's 'many brilliant and beautiful moments'.[2] These comments are typical of the chorus of approval that greeted the premiere of *Isobel Gowdie* on 22 August 1990 in a Prom given by the BBC Scottish Symphony Orchestra (BBC SSO) conducted by Jerzy Maksymiuk. *Isobel Gowdie* was the work that transformed MacMillan's compositional career and thrust him into the artistic spotlight in his native Scotland, the rest of the United Kingdom and further afield. If one work represents a composer, his style, techniques and aesthetic, then that work for James MacMillan is *The Confession of Isobel Gowdie*. He is inextricably linked with the piece, its sounds, its effects, its gestures, its meanings and its legacy – *Isobel Gowdie* is a vivid representation of everything the composer believes in (or perhaps *believed* in), put forth in a powerful and emotional fashion that has resonated with audiences ever since that first London performance. It is both the culmination of his early work (in a trajectory from *The Keening*, *Búsqueda* and *Tryst*) and the beginning of his most successful and fecund period that

---

1   Edward Greenfield, 'James MacMillan', *The Guardian* (25 August 1990).

2   Ibid., 39. Robert Henderson, 'Witch-hunts and Renaissance bawdy', *The Telegraph* (24 August 1990). Stephen Johnson, 'The current way of things', *The Independent* (24 August 1990).

included *Veni, Veni, Emmanuel*, *Seven Last Words from the Cross* and the *Triduum*. It is both his musical and aesthetic 'calling card' but also his most analysed, discussed and criticised work, dividing opinion again and again after each performance and recording.

Plate 2   James MacMillan and Jerzy Maksymiuk (Photo: William Long, 1990)

The Confession of Isobel Gowdie (1990)

The success of *Tryst* at the 1989 St Magnus Festival and MacMillan's appointment as affiliate composer of the Scottish Chamber Orchestra had resulted in his profile being raised substantially, and it was no surprise that commissions from Scotland's other musical bodies soon appeared. The Scottish National Orchestra commissioned *The Berserking* in 1989 and a commission from the BBC SSO for the 1990 Proms arrived shortly after. The work was given a prime Saturday night televised concert position sandwiched between the Proms staples of Beethoven's Symphony No. 4 and Sibelius's Violin Concerto (played by the impressive young Korean violinist Dong Suk-Kang) and despite the majority of the audience, one imagines, being there for the more established works, it was *The Confession of Isobel Gowdie* that caused the greatest commotion – and that is no mean feat for a work that deals primarily with a post-Reformation witch trial, satanic intercourse and a hysterical execution. There was something in *Isobel Gowdie* that appealed to the audience, something 'accessible, meaningful and highly personal' that chimed with those present and led to MacMillan repeatedly being called to the stage to take the applause – a new compositional voice had arrived.[3]

The Confession of Isobel Gowdie takes as its inspiration the witch trials that occurred with alarming regularity in Scotland (as in other parts of Great Britain) in the 150 years or so after the Reformation, when 'as many as 4500 Scots perished because their contemporaries thought they were witches'.[4] Isobel Gowdie was a woman from Nairn (in the north of Scotland) who confessed in 1662, under severe torture, to being a witch. As MacMillan explains, she:

> confessed to having been baptised by the devil and joining a coven of 13 who met at night; she had journeyed to the centre of the earth to feast with the King and Queen of the fairies; she could fly, or become a hare, a cat or a crow; she used waxen images and bags of boiled toads to cause inflictions.[5]

---

[3] Johnson, 'James MacMillan', 2.

[4] James MacMillan, programme note to *The Confession of Isobel Gowdie*, www.boosey. com/cr/music/James-MacMillan-The-Confession-of-Isobel-Gowdie/3115 (accessed 29 May 2017).

[5] Ibid.

Gowdie was subsequently tried and then 'strangled at the stake and burned in pitch amid scenes of hysterical fright and sadism'.[6] MacMillan makes a very bold claim in the programme note to the work: 'On behalf of the Scottish people the work craves absolution and offers Isobel Gowdie the mercy and humanity that was denied her in the last days of her life.' He goes further by hoping the work 'captures the soul of Scotland in music'.[7] These collective ambitions clearly show *Isobel Gowdie*'s 'increasing engagement with Celtic elements' that characterises the works of this period (such as *The Berserking* and *Into the Ferment*), though there is an intensity of vision and design in the later work, allied with an increased religiosity, that suggests a departure from the earlier pieces. MacMillan goes to some lengths to point out that the persecution of witches at this time was a 'phenomenon known to Catholic and Protestant Europe', suggesting that his inspiration from the events was not purely religiously motivated, even if the piece does highlight sectarian tensions (something he stressed in other works from this period, most persuasively in the *Sinfonietta* of 1991).[8] The work does, however, have multiple religiously inspired themes acting as undercurrents to the piece (more of which shortly), and MacMillan's assertion that the work is 'the Requiem that Isobel Gowdie never had' places the piece firmly in the Catholic firmament, as does the 'miserere nobis' (have mercy on us) inscription that finishes the score.[9]

MacMillan stated in 1990 that *The Confession of Isobel Gowdie* was a 'warning against the pogrom, against fascism, against the witch hunt'; it was one of the first times that he mentioned the perceived racism in Scotland that became the main topic of 'Scotland's Shame' in 1999.[10] He continues: 'witch-hunting tendencies can blossom and erupt in our own society just as much as it did in the sixteenth and seventeenth centuries … we saw this in the Nazi Holocaust of fifty years ago'.[11] Here MacMillan shows that on one hand *Isobel Gowdie* is a historically informed tone poem with clear religious symbolism, but on the other that the story of oppression and intimidation has parallels with contemporary society as much as the Central American inspired works, *Búsqueda* and *Cantos Sagrados*.

---

[6]   Ibid.

[7]   Ibid.

[8]   Ibid.

[9]   Ibid.

[10]   Proms featurette, *The Confession of Isobel Gowdie*, www.youtube.com/watch?v=fNPolWpX9no (accessed 17 February 2017).

[11]   Ibid.

One of the ways that MacMillan attempts to 'capture the soul of Scotland' is by using pre-existing material as a musical and textual framework for the piece, what he calls a 'multitude of chants, songs and litanies (real and imagined) coming together in a reflective outpouring'.[12] These are half-heard, half-stated and often buried deep in texture, fragmented and not easily decipherable. The sources (that MacMillan has acknowledged) include the folksong *The Cruel Mother* and the *Lux aeterna* (let perpetual light shine) plainsong from the Requiem Mass. Dominic Wells makes a very persuasive argument for *The Tryst* theme also being present; certainly the opening modal section with the emphasis on the pitches of C-D-F♯-G-A suggests the same sound-world as the original tune and its use in works such as *Tryst*.[13] With *Isobel Gowdie* being composed very soon after *Búsqueda*, *After the Tryst* and *Tryst*, it is no surprise to find the melody alluded to in some fashion.

The Confession of Isobel Gowdie begins with a distinctive MacMillan device of a drone, being characteristically Scottish as well: here the notes C and D are played by the bassoons, clarinets and horns, all in the same register. The musical lines gradually become more animated as the pitch collection expands: G (bar 7), F♯ (bar 9) and A (bar 16). It is a dense, expressive modality and MacMillan continues this gradual development of material against the fixed pentatonic collection until the introduction of a B♭ in the first violas in bar 47. Despite some chromatic inflections, the modality is preserved until a distinct change of mood, mode and material occurs at rehearsal mark D (bar 65). This opening modal threnody is MacMillan at his most Celtic, his most reflective and his most subdued, and it is in this section that both *The Cruel Mother* and the *Lux aeterna* themes are first presented (see Examples 3.1 and 3.2).

The inclusion of the *Lux aeterna* quotation is not without meaning as MacMillan's desire for his orchestral work to be the 'Requiem that Isobel Gowdie never had' naturally would include some reference to religious practice, and a section of the Requiem Mass is the obvious choice. It is interesting that MacMillan chooses one of the most transcendent and optimistic sections of the rite as a quotation, rather than something more mournful and dramatic such as the Dies irae or the Libera Me. Although the opening may seem an odd place to put the *Lux aeterna* material (coming as it does in the Communion towards the end of the Requiem Mass) the growing significance of the plainsong throughout *The Confession of Isobel Gowdie* and its reappearance at

---

12   MacMillan, programme note to *The Confession of Isobel Gowdie*.
13   Wells, 'James MacMillan: Retrospective Modernist', 190–95.

Example 3.1a   *The Cruel Mother* folksong

Example 3.1b   Bars 23–25 of *The Confession of Isobel Gowdie* showing allusion to *The Cruel Mother*

Example 3.2a   The *Lux aeterna* plainsong

Example 3.2b   Bars 26–34 of *The Confession of Isobel Gowdie* showing the appropriation of the *Lux aeterna* plainsong

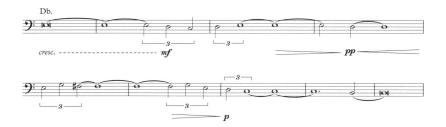

the climax of the work show that MacMillan is clearly aligning the chant with the events that inspired the piece.

Following the opening threnody comes much more fragmented music (bars 65–127), where the modal material jostles with static woodwind chords, brass interjections and animated percussion. It is interesting to see how MacMillan transforms the keening string *glissandi* of the opening section from a soft lament to a terrifying wail: the strings that were marked 'like a sigh' now carry directions 'like a scream' and 'shrieking' – the mode of delivery might be similar, but the effect and the gesture is very different. Amongst all this, the trombones deliver a harmonised version of the *Lux aeterna* theme, hymn-like in its simplicity and directness (see Example 3.3).

The music continues to fragment and crescendo until it reaches one of the most dramatic and gestural moments of the whole work (bars 127–29): the thirteen, full-orchestral chords that are hammered out as loudly as possible across the full range and register of the orchestra. The thirteen chords obviously relate to Isobel Gowdie confessing to joining a coven of thirteen, but the number also has had satanic connotations throughout history (a brief Internet search will bring up a wide variety of information on this topic). MacMillan stated that the number was significant 'for good and ill – sometimes it's an unlucky thirteen, but it also has sacramental qualities as well that one finds in Christian traditions throughout Europe from that time'.[14] The influence of the *The Rite of Spring* that *The Guardian* mentioned in its review can be felt in

Example 3.3   Bars 80–83 of *The Confession of Isobel Gowdie* showing harmonisation of the *Lux aeterna* plainsong

---

[14]   Stephen Johnson, *Discovering Music: James MacMillan's 'The Confession of Isobel Gowdie'*, BBC Radio 3 (28 February 2010). MacMillan does not go into any further

this section, and there are further parallels between the works, not least in the sacrificial nature of both pieces. MacMillan referred to the thirteen chords as 'probably the most simplistic gesture in the whole piece ... sometimes the most simple gestures are the best', and the directness of this brutal moment bears witness to that.[15]

The material that follows this dramatic moment (bars 130–345) becomes progressively more dissonant, angular and virtuosic as the musical fragments and gestures from earlier in the work are juxtaposed in an increasingly frenetic fashion, what Stephen Johnson refers to as a 'demonic ceilidh'.[16] MacMillan utilises one of his favourite techniques for extending faster sections, the rhythmic hocket (as seen in *Into the Ferment* and *Tryst*) and the piece whirls to a desperate crescendo at bars 329–36 with a repeated B note played *fortissimo* in the upper strings and woodwind. Out of this comes strident brass chords marked 'frantic, like an eruption' and these alternate with equally loud and dissonant woodwind trills as the music reaches fever pitch. Just when it appears the work will reach a horrifying finale, the music stops dead (bars 345–47) and the lower strings are exposed playing the same harmonisation of the *Lux aeterna* theme as was played by the trombones in Example 3.3. MacMillan refers to this moment as 'serenity ... resignation ... undisturbed by the chaos that has preceded it', and the sudden reappearance of this material, played quietly and slowly, is as striking as the earlier thirteen chords.[17] The work continues with the juxtaposition of the woodwind and brass material with the *Lux aeterna* in the strings, though each time the former gets shorter and latter longer, picking up more string instruments with each iteration. After the final appearance of the woodwind and brass material (bar 367; now commuted to half a bar) the full string orchestra enters with a concluding variation of the *Lux aeterna* theme, though MacMillan keeps a reference to the previous interjections with clusters of tubular bells and militaristic side-drum. From this string music, MacMillan reveals an impassioned recapitulation of the threnody that began the work, replete with the same keening figures and folksong references. From its emotional (and registral) high point at bars 407–8 the music begins to contract and quieten, reaching a *pianissimo* unison C at bars 415–16. And there the piece could feasibly have ended, achieving the unison that the opening

---

detail regarding the 'sacramental qualities', but he may be referring to the cult associated with St Anthony and the number thirteen.

[15]   Proms featurette, *The Confession of Isobel Gowdie*.

[16]   Johnson, *Discovering Music: James MacMillan's 'The Confession of Isobel Gowdie'*.

[17]   Ibid.

drone subverted, but MacMillan has one final musical device, as gestural as the thirteen chords – a long crescendo on the unison C for the whole orchestra (though strangely not including the flutes), starting at *pianissimo* before climaxing at *fffff* in a thrilling finale.

Much has been written about this final crescendo, not least the similarities between the unison in MacMillan's *The Confession of Isobel Gowdie* and in Alban Berg's *Wozzeck*. Stephen Johnson, slightly tongue-in-cheek, writes 'if that wasn't a direct rip-off from *Wozzeck* then surely the word "plagiarism" has lost all meaning', and fellow critic David Wright was less effusive when calling it 'plagiarised Berg'.[18] MacMillan seems to be aware of the similarities to *Wozzeck*, stating in an interview with Richard McGregor in 2010 that 'I was aware of the Berg' and that the unison crescendo was 'an extension of the drone'.[19] Whether or not the crescendo is a conscious or unconscious 'rip-off' of Berg, it is clear that, along with the similarities to *The Rite of Spring*, hocketing from Andriessen and a string threnody redolent of John Tavener or Henryk Górecki, you are left with a complex web of influences and interactions – 'echoes of safe 20th-century styles'.[20] Certainly the familiarity of MacMillan's musical building-blocks is one of the reasons for the work's instant appeal. As well as looking back to historical events in *Isobel Gowdie*, MacMillan is equally retrospective with the music he chooses to acknowledge – a shared cultural history is forged between composer and audience.

The form and narrative of the work are also key to the success of *The Confession of Isobel Gowdie*. The work's form, a simple arch or ternary form, with the modal threnody bookending the central scherzo material, is easy to comprehend. The narrative element is a little more complex, with MacMillan not attempting to portray the grim events in music: 'I've never really wanted to write programme music and I especially took fright at this story ... to actually tell the story in music or even attempt it would be a little voyeuristic I think.'[21] Despite this, it is difficult to divorce the musical events from the actual events, particularly the more gestural moments that seem to be more than 'a complicated act of contrition' and err towards a literal depiction of the horrifying event.[22] MacMillan states that he does not mind 'at all how people

---

18   Johnson, 'James MacMillan', 2. David Wright, 'From the Heartbeat', *The Musical Times*, vol. 133, no. 1796 (October 1992), 535.

19   McGregor, 'James MacMillan: a conversation and commentary', 89.

20   Johnson, 'James MacMillan', 2.

21   Johnson, *Discovering Music: James MacMillan's 'The Confession of Isobel Gowdie'*.

22   MacMillan, programme note to *The Confession of Isobel Gowdie*.

describe, or make their own pictures in their own minds' regarding his music but even he baulked when asked if the aforementioned crescendo 'represented the flames rising up the stake, and Isobel herself going up in smoke.'[23] The pseudo-programmatic element to *Isobel Gowdie* (backed by MacMillan's evocative programme note and interviews) has undoubtedly aided audiences in understanding the work, or at the very least approaching the work on their own terms – something the composer continued in his works in the 1990s.

Not every quarter has been complimentary of *The Confession of Isobel Gowdie*, whether that be the popular press or music journals: for many the work is too direct, too emotive and too popular. The *Daily Telegraph* music critic, Ivan Hewett, dismissed the work as 'full of pathos' with 'no real substance'; the piece had 'no discourse', just 'pure gesture'.[24] Venerated musicologist Arnold Whittall referred to the piece as 'blatantly rabble-rousing', and even long-term MacMillan stalwart Stephen Johnson found the work 'shameless'.[25] Certainly there are moments in *Isobel Gowdie* that stray into some people's perceptions of 'bad taste', but the music's ability to provoke reactions both pro and contra is part of its strength and part of MacMillan's appeal as a composer; whatever charged images *Isobel Gowdie* creates for the listener, later works would do more and go further – such as the unabashed ending to *The World's Ransoming* of 1996.

MacMillan regularly cites *Búsqueda* as being the 'piece that allowed me, for the first time, to be myself'. The work paved the way for many of the musical developments that were to follow; however, one could view *Isobel Gowdie* as being equally important and opening as many new musical avenues as the earlier work. Perhaps the most important of these is the giving of a prominent voice to MacMillan's Catholicism in an overt and non-liturgical fashion, and bringing this key part of his aesthetic to the fore. Though religious themes are present in much of his work prior to *The Confession of Isobel Gowdie*, they are often part of a wider representation of political or national concerns (such as in *Búsqueda* or *Cantos Sagrados*); many works after *Isobel Gowdie* see MacMillan's Catholicism promoted to the driving force. This can be demonstrated by viewing two specific years before and after *Isobel Gowdie* (1989 and 1993) and the religious inspirations stated (see Table 3.1).

---

23   Ibid. Johnson, 'James MacMillan', 3.

24   Ivan Hewett, *Music: Healing the Rift* (London: Continuum, 2003), 196–97.

25   Whittall, 'Elegies and Affirmations: John Casken at 60', 46. Johnson, 'James MacMillan', 3.

Table 3.1 Increasing use of religious themes in MacMillan's music after
The Confession of Isobel Gowdie

1989	*Tryst*	The *Tryst* theme; no stated religious inspiration
	The Cumnock Orcadian	No stated religious inspiration
	Ruin	No stated religious inspiration
	Cantos Sagrados	Secular texts; sections of the *Requiem* and *Credo*
	The Exorcism of Rio Sumpúl	Depiction of community 'exorcism' during El Salvadorian civil war
1993	*Visitatio Sepulchri*	Setting of a fourteenth century liturgical drama; section of the *Te Deum*
	Kiss on Wood	Based on Good Friday versicle, *Ecce lignum crucis*
	Angel	Representation of angelic beings
	... here in hiding ...	Setting of *Adoro te devote* by Thomas Aquinas
	They saw the stone had been rolled away	Relating to Easter story
	Memoire imperiale	A variation on *Garb of Gaul*; no stated religious inspiration
	Seven Last Words from the Cross	Various biblical texts

It is hard to divorce *Isobel Gowdie* from MacMillan's religion. Particularly when viewed through the prism of his later work, the similarities between Gowdie's fate and the Passion story are stark. MacMillan has never denied this, and his comments that the final pages of the score feature a 'sense of resignation and release, maybe even joy' echo Christian sentiments and the suggestion of final redemption.[26] He emphasised this in an article he wrote in 2000 entitled 'God, Theology and Music' in which he stated:

---

[26] Johnson, *Discovering Music: James MacMillan's 'The Confession of Isobel Gowdie'*.

My choice of this particular archetype [Isobel Gowdie] was similar to my choice of the Disappeared [in *Búsqueda*] as archetypes because, in their lives and in their experiences of hatred and death and rejection, they resonate with the original archetype of Christ in the Passion narrative.[27]

The Passion narrative soon became a regular feature in MacMillan's work, a recurring idée fixe that unifies the composer's oeuvre, as he said in the same article: 'I seem to be drawn again and again to the Passion ... I do seem to be going round and round the same three days of history.'[28]

The Confession of Isobel Gowdie continued to open doors for MacMillan after its successful Proms premiere; the composer himself conducted a London performance with the Philharmonia Orchestra in October 1991 that led to his appointment as visiting composer with the orchestra. As was recalled by John Wallace (a trumpeter from the orchestra): 'the impetuous maestro [Giuseppe] Sinopoli rushed from the stalls after the Philharmonia's first rehearsal, and proposed an immediate appointment', even if the orchestra currently had a composer-in-residence![29] MacMillan's relationship with the Philharmonia continues to be strong, with MacMillan being the founder and director of the orchestra's *Music of Today* series from 1992 to 2000, in which he conducted and introduced much new repertoire, often from Eastern Europe and the former Soviet Union.[30]

The MacMillans had their first child, Catherine, on 22 September 1990, during a busy end to the year that saw a further performance of *Búsqueda* at the Edinburgh Festival (with leading actress Diana Rigg in the speaker role) and MacMillan as the featured composer at Musica Nova in Glasgow with the premiere of *The Berserking*. Catherine MacMillan was the inspiration for two pieces, the more substantial being *Catherine's Lullabies* (1990) for choir, brass

---

[27]   MacMillan, 'God, Theology and Music', 19.

[28]   Ibid., 19.

[29]   Miller, 'Music for a new Scotland'.

[30]   *Music of Today* is a regular series of early evening concerts in which the director or a visiting composer introduces contemporary music, often largely unknown to the regular Philharmonia audience. Other directors of *Music of Today* have included Julian Anderson (1968–) and Unsuk Chin (1961–). MacMillan refers to having performed 'Ustvolskaya and some of the younger Russians' (Interview with James MacMillan, during the Second Annual Vancouver New Music Festival, 1998).

and percussion, which was premiered in Glasgow on 10 February 1991.[31] This is one of MacMillan's most obscure published pieces (and certainly one of his least well-known choral works); it is rarely performed and is currently without a commercial recording. Although written for his newborn daughter, the lullabies are not intended in the traditional fashion of coaxing a child to sleep but rather to 'use the subjective experience of parenthood as a focus for more universal ... human truths'.[32] In fact MacMillan stated in 1992 that *Catherine's Lullabies* included 'the loudest music he has yet written', further emphasising the perceived contradiction between the title and the subject matter.[33] The work continues the trend in MacMillan's work of the late 1980s of combining sacred and secular texts, this time including excerpts from the Credo, the Magnificat, Isaiah, Ecclesiasticus and the Litany of Saints with a section of a poem from a mother of the Plazo de Mayo (see chapter two). As MacMillan explains, the texts 'are the finest lullabies for our children – effective endearments, seeds of hope and freedom to blossom in the future'.[34] *Catherine's Lullabies* was the final time MacMillan set a Liberation Theology text and began a gradual move away from overtly politicised narratives in his work, though not a complete abandonment of political engagement, as future pieces would show.

Tuireadh (1991)

If *The Confession of Isobel Gowdie* represented a work 'on behalf of the Scottish people' that offered 'absolution' and 'mercy' for an event, deep in Scottish history, then *Tuireadh* found MacMillan covering similar ground in a much more contemporary event that shocked modern-day Scotland. On 6 July 1988, the North Sea oil and gas production platform, Piper Alpha (some 110 miles north-east of Aberdeen), exploded, the resulting fires killing 167 men. A further 62 were rescued from the sea. The disaster was a grievous wound to not just the families of those affected, but also to the confidence and prestige of a nation that had achieved much economic success from the off-shore industry. Of the

---

[31]   The other is the short piano piece *Angel* from 1993.

[32]   James MacMillan, programme note to *Catherine's Lullabies*, www.boosey.com/cr/music/James-MacMillan-Catherine-s-Lullabies/5648 (accessed 1 June 2017).

[33]   Edward Greenfield, 'An echo of the pure sound of prayer', *The Guardian* (6 August 1992).

[34]   MacMillan, programme note to *Catherine's Lullabies*.

167 dead, 30 bodies were never recovered.[35] A memorial was commissioned from the Scottish artist Sue Jane Taylor (who had spent time on Piper Alpha the year before the disaster) which was erected in the Rose Garden of Hazelhead Park, Aberdeen in 1991.[36]

MacMillan was contacted by a mother of one of the deceased men to see if he would 'write a musical equivalent' of Taylor's work that would act as 'some kind of [musical] memorial for the dead'.[37] MacMillan describes how the mother 'wrote movingly of her visit to the scene [of the disaster] for a memorial service' and how the 'ceremony became a rite of passage for those whose loved ones had not been found'.[38] *Tuireadh* is the Gaelic word for lament (or requiem) for the dead and the piece is dedicated to the victims of the disaster and their families. The premiere was given by the Allegri String Quartet with the clarinettist James Campbell at the 1991 St Magnus Festival in Orkney.[39]

One of the most striking comments relayed to MacMillan from the correspondence with the mother was that a 'spontaneous keening sound rose gently from the mourners' assembled at the memorial ceremony; this sudden, unexpected expression of grief related directly to MacMillan's own interest in this area and is eerily similar to comments made by the composer regarding his earlier piece *The Keening* (see chapter one).[40] As MacMillan explains in the programme note to the work, '*Tuireadh* attempts to capture this outpouring of grief in music and makes allusions to ... various lament-forms from Scottish traditional music.'[41] The work begins with a long, repeated drone note from the clarinet, moving from an imperceptible beginning to a rasping crescendo. The third iteration of this is accompanied by repeated keening fragments in the

---

[35]   For more information on the Piper Alpha disaster and for first-hand accounts from some of the survivors see www.scotsman.com/lifestyle/the-night-the-sea-caught-fire-remembering-piper-alpha-1-1433754 (accessed 6 June 2017).

[36]   MacMillan collaborated with Taylor five years later with *Í (A Meditation on Iona)*, a work for string orchestra and percussion.

[37]   'James MacMillan talk about *Tuireadh*', soundcloud.com/hebridesensemble/james-macmillan-talks-about- tuireadh (accessed 5 June 2017).

[38]   James MacMillan, programme note to *Tuireadh*, www.boosey.com/cr/music/James-MacMillan-Tuireadh/1603 (accessed 1 June 2017).

[39]   MacMillan made a clarinet and string orchestra version of the work in 1995 that was first performed by the Gdansk Philharmonic and Karol Respondek (clarinet), with the composer conducting.

[40]   MacMillan, programme note to *Tuireadh*.

[41]   Ibid.

strings, all circling round the same pitches of D and E♭. As the clarinet becomes more agitated, so the string writing becomes more expressive (a similar device to the opening of *Isobel Gowdie*), quickly expanding to a *tremolo, fortissimo* E in unison. Simon Reade, writing in *The Observer*, asks if this opening is a 'fog horn followed by the keening of lost souls, the mewing of gulls?'[42] Though this strays into the realm of the purported flames at the end of *Isobel Gowdie*, it does highlight the continued quasi-programmatic element to MacMillan's music of this period and how it immediately conjures up images and vistas to many listeners.

The keening material continues in various guises as the piece progresses, each time returning higher in the register and more impassioned. As the music unfolds, it soon becomes apparent that *The Tryst* theme is being alluded to again, gradually being revealed in each reoccurrence of the string tableaux. The Celtic serenity of this opening is savagely interrupted at rehearsal mark F (bar 71), where dissonant, percussive stabbing chords in the strings usher in a new, more turbulent section in which the reflective music of the opening is thrust firmly into the background. In the midst of this more angular and stormy material, MacMillan introduces a quiet cadential figure that gradually becomes more pervasive as the piece progresses. This cadence is not only integral to *Tuireadh* but also to the later work *Seven Last Words from the Cross*, which uses this cadence as the opening of the piece and at other points throughout (see Example 3.4 and chapter four).

MacMillan marks the cello in Example 3.4 'crying', and this continues the lexicon of descriptive words from *The Confession of Isobel Gowdie*. Along with the 'screaming' from the earlier work, MacMillan also utilises 'violent', 'obsessive', 'harsh' and 'unconsoled' to aid the players in their delivery of the piece – this is music that wears its emotional heart on its sleeve. It is also hugely gestural music, carrying on from where the composer left off in *Isobel Gowdie*, no surprise in a piece that is constantly alluding to 'various lament-forms from Scottish traditional music'. In fact, *Tuireadh* can be reduced to a series of gestures employed by MacMillan, all of which have significance to the composer, the work and the subject matter: the drone note, the keening string material, the percussive chords, the chromatic flourishes and the lamenting cadential figure. Perhaps one of the most effective gestures in the piece is the very ending of the work where the solo viola carries on a lament figure (complete with 'crying' and 'keening' markings and microtonal slides) whilst the rest of the instruments are gradually moving towards a harmonic and

---

42   Simon Reade, 'From socialism to salvation', *The Observer* (15 August 1993).

Example 3.4   Cadential figure from *Tuireadh* (bars 92–93) and the opening of 'Father, forgive them for they know not what they do' from *Seven Last Words from the Cross* (bars 3–4)

emotional resolution (see Example 3.5). Neither music finds resolution: the D major sonority (with an added E drone) which the ensemble rests on fades away, and even the viola lament runs out of steam, leaving the violin drone to finish the work as it started.

In many ways *Tuireadh* is a deeply affecting memorial to the Piper Alpha disaster, which *The Guardian* refered to as 'a thematically terse elegy … searingly intense and precisely focussed; MacMillan has written nothing better'.[43] Certainly the work is terse, intense and focussed, but it is also a very fragmented work with many pauses disrupting the musical flow. *Tuireadh* treads on similar aesthetic ground to *The Confession of Isobel Gowdie*; however, the regular repetition of material leads to an episodic quality, not as prevalent in the preceding works. It is, however, a highly personal response to the disaster that has struck an emotional chord with audiences, like *Isobel Gowdie*, and the ending is genuinely affecting. Whether 'MacMillan has

Example 3.5   Bars 262–64 of *Tuireadh* showing viola lament gesture

---

43   Quotation taken from www.boosey.com/cr/music/James-MacMillan-Tuireadh/ 1603 (accessed 1 June 2017).

written nothing better' is a moot point, but he would rarely write pieces as emotionally charged again.

1991 saw MacMillan also complete his chamber orchestra work *Sinfonietta* (for the London Sinfonietta), a more extreme version of some of the techniques encountered in *Isobel Gowdie*, with similar savage juxtapositions of lucid, tonal material with dramatic, dissonant interjections. The work is interesting for the inclusion of a 'grotesque, quasi-militaristic central section' with a 'swaggering parody of a march'.[44] This march is a corruption of the Protestant anthem *The Sash My Father Wore* often sung by Loyalists at the Orange marches in Belfast (and other places) and MacMillan refers to its 'bigotry and triumphalism, bathed in the fading light of Britain's imperial era'.[45] The inclusion of this material continues the emergence of religious themes in MacMillan's music, here found in one of the few non-programmatic works from this period. *The Confession of Isobel Gowdie* and the *Sinfonietta* show MacMillan's religious beliefs beginning to become prominent; the work he began on the first Sunday of Advent 1991 saw them come entirely to the fore.

Veni, Veni, Emmanuel (1992)

If *The Confession of Isobel Gowdie* is MacMillan's most discussed and criticised work, then *Veni, Veni, Emmanuel* surely follows closely in second place. It is arguably his most popular orchestral piece with over 500 performances to date by many of the world's leading orchestras. It is one of a triumvirate of works (with *Isobel Gowdie* and *Seven Last Words from the Cross*) from the early 1990s on which MacMillan's compositional reputation hangs, three pieces that define him as a composer and have coloured all his subsequent work. It is as emblematic a piece as *Isobel Gowdie*, though in different ways, for if the earlier work stresses the composer's Celtic and Scottish roots (with religious influences) then *Veni, Veni, Emmanuel* shows MacMillan responding to his Catholicism in unabashed terms. It is paramount in this work and would be in many of the pieces during the remainder of the decade.

Veni, Veni, Emmanuel is a concerto for percussion and orchestra and was commissioned by Christian Salvesen PLC for the SCO, as part of MacMillan's

---

[44]   James MacMillan, programme note to *Sinfonietta*, www.boosey.com/cr/music/James-MacMillan-Sinfonietta/7163 (accessed 8 June 2017).

[45]   James MacMillan, liner notes to *The Berserking*, RCA Victor Red Seal CD, 09026-68328-2 (1996), 5.

tenure as composer in affiliation, and was first performed at the Proms on the 10 August 1992 by the SCO, with Evelyn Glennie (percussion), conducted by Jukka-Pekke Saraste.[46] Like *Isobel Gowdie*, it was an immediate success at its Proms premiere and has remained in the repertoire since. Whether this is entirely due to the quality of the music or the relative sparsity of works in this genre is a wider question, but *Veni, Veni, Emmanuel* shows no sign of relinquishing its place, nor being replaced by one of MacMillan's more recent concerti.

The work takes its title from the Latin Advent antiphon, well known to English-speaking congregations as 'O Come, O Come, Emmanuel' from *Hymns Ancient and Modern*, with its musical origins in fifteenth-century France (see Example 3.6).

MacMillan started the work on the first Sunday of Advent 1991, finishing it on Easter Sunday 1992, and thus coinciding the composition of the work with the theological journey that underpins it. As MacMillan explains in the programme note to the work:

> These two liturgical dates are important ... the piece can be discussed in two ways. On one level it is a purely abstract work in which all the musical material is drawn from the ... Advent plainchant. On another level it is a musical exploration of the theology behind the Advent message.[47]

Example 3.6   *Veni, Veni, Emmanuel* plainsong

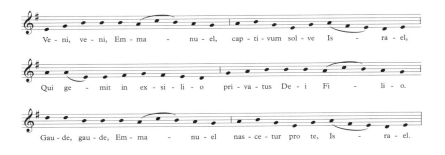

46   Christian Salvensen PLC was a Norwegian-Scottish transport and logistics organisation which had begun life as a whaling company. It ceased trading in 2007 when it merged with the wonderfully named French company Norbert Dentressangle.

47   James MacMillan, programme note to *Veni, Veni, Emmanuel*, www.boosey.com/cr/music/James-MacMillan-Veni-Veni-Emmanuel/3051 (accessed 9 June 2017).

This 'musical exploration of the theology behind the Advent message' is essentially a great longing for the Second Coming which is finally resolved in the Easter narrative and Christ's resurrection. MacMillan acknowledges this message in the programme note where he suggests 'at the very end of the piece the music takes a liturgical detour from Advent to Easter ... as if the proclamation of liberation finds embodiment in the Risen Christ'.[48] It was the first work to be openly based on a plainsong (MacMillan did not draw attention to the inclusion of the *Lux aeterna* chant in the programme note for *Isobel Gowdie*) and the first where this plainsong was both audible and arguably integral to the appreciation of the piece. It was the first in a series of Easter-inspired pieces that preoccupied the composer over the next ten years, culminating in the *Triduum* (see chapter five).

As well as being the first instrumental work to result from an openly religious inspiration, it is also the last work to have any relationship to Liberation Theology. Though MacMillan's overt interest in the movement ended with *Catherine's Lullabies*, the reference by the composer to a section from Luke 21 that proposes the liberation of man through the Second Coming has a strong resonance with his earlier interests. The text of 'O Come, O Come, Emmanuel' itself, with its reference to biblical oppression ('ransom captive Israel') and liberation through Jesus again points, obliquely, to Liberation Theology – even if the composer was beginning to distance himself from the movement, the basic principles appear to have still been important.[49]

The work is structured in an arch form of eight sections (all labelled in the score by the composer, apart from the Tempo Primo section) with an additional coda that forms the 'liturgical detour from Advent to Easter' (see Table 3.2).

The simple shape of the piece (leaving aside the theological reading) helps to make the work instantly accessible, with faster material bookending the substantial, slow 'Gaude, Gaude' section. This is the same approach as was

---

[48]   Ibid.

[49]   The section that MacMillan quotes in the programme note is: 'There will be signs in the sun and moon and stars; on earth nations in agony, bewildered by the clamour of the ocean and its waves; men dying of fear as they await what menaces the world, for the powers of heaven will be shaken. And they will see the Son of Man coming in a cloud with power and great glory. When these things begin to take place, stand erect, hold your heads high, because your liberation is near at hand.' (MacMillan, programme note to *Veni, Veni, Emmanuel*).

Table 3.2   Formal structure of *Veni, Veni, Emmanuel*

Section	Bar numbers
Introit – Advent	1–57
Heartbeats	58–126
Dance – Hocket	127–286
Transition: Sequence I	287–352
Gaude, Gaude	353–431
Transition: Sequence II	431–89
Dance – Chorale	490–564
[Tempo Primo]	565–80
Coda – Easter	581–606

successful in *Isobel Gowdie* and the *Sinfonietta*, though here found in reverse with faster music dominating (not always the case in MacMillan's oeuvre). The work begins with a *fortissimo* orchestral chord, complete with woodwind flourishes and rasping brass triplets, against which the percussionist alternates powerful tam-tam strokes and chromatic vibraphone passages. The 'screaming' strings from *Isobel Gowdie* and *Tuireadh* return, as do rhythmic hockets and long pedal notes as the orchestra winds its way to various climaxes, textures and colours. The plainchant is never far from the foreground, with the brass alluding to the tune in a dissonant chorale in bars 27–30 (see Example 3.7 – the chant is in the first trumpet in A minor).

The second section of the work, 'Heartbeats', sees the introduction of one of the key musical elements of *Veni, Veni, Emmanuel*, the 'heartbeat' motif which pervades the whole piece from this point onwards (see Example 3.8). MacMillan has stated that he 'improvised the refrain rhythm of "Rejoice, rejoice" [from the plainchant] into a "heartbeat" rhythm' and that this material has both musical and theological concerns.[50] As he clarifies in the programme

---

50   Richard McGregor, 'Transubstantiated into the musical ...': metaphor and reality in James MacMillan's *Veni, Veni, Emmanuel*', in Graham Hair, ed., *A Companion to Recent Scottish Music: 1950 to the Present* (Glasgow: Musica Scotica Trust, 2007), 23. This is an excellent analysis of *Veni, Veni, Emmanuel* which goes into detail in describing the composer's harmonic, motivic and theological workings in the piece.

Example 3.7   Allusion to 'O Come, O Come, Emmanuel' plainchant in bars 27–30 of *Veni, Veni, Emmanuel*

note: 'The heartbeats which permeate the whole piece offer a clue to the wider spiritual priorities behind the work, representing the human presence of Christ.'[51] The 'heartbeat' motif has its apotheosis in the final section of the work with the Easter material.

As the 'heartbeat' moves through the orchestra, further allusions to the plainchant can be heard in a variety of keys and rhythms before the percussionist leads the music into the third section, 'Dance – Hocket'. This section features some of the most energetic and concerted fast music that MacMillan has written, joyously filtering the plainchant through the brass, percussion and strings in a metrical fantasy. The hocket of the section title is interrupted at various points by canonic material in the upper voices and dissonant woodwind calls before swelling to a dramatic crescendo and accented, Stravinskian chords in the wind and brass that herald one of the work's two 'Transition' sections.

The 'Transition: Sequence I' sees MacMillan in familiar territory with high, keening strings, brass interjections and hockets. The percussionist takes a well-earned break as the orchestra gradually peters out to just first violins, by which time the percussionist has moved to marimba for the long solo that characterises the next section. 'Gaude, Gaude' is the emotional core of *Veni, Veni, Emmanuel*, a sustained, slow meditation on the 'Rejoice, rejoice' refrain from the plainchant, encountered in multiple keys, colours and metres against which the marimba carries out an increasingly frenetic dialogue. MacMillan

---

[51]   MacMillan, programme note to *Veni, Veni, Emmanuel*.

Example 3.8   Bars 58–62 of *Veni, Veni, Emmanuel* showing the 'Heartbeat' motif

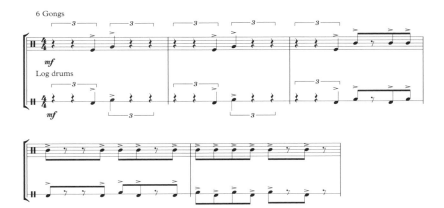

takes the four notes of the chant, with its prominent falling minor third, and uses the 'standard' harmonisation for the many repetitions that occur in this section (see Example 3.9, here in B minor).

David Wright refers to this section as a 'swelling congregational incantation' and this is an apt description; if *Isobel Gowdie* was a 'multitude of chants, songs and litanies' then this is akin to encountering a multitude of congregations, half-heard in the distance, all singing the same music in different ways.[52] MacMillan echoes this in his programme note: the music is 'evoking a huge distant congregation murmuring a calm prayer in many voices'.[53] Whether one congregation or many, it is a striking moment of reflection and repose in a hugely busy and virtuosic piece.

MacMillan also features a second chant in this section of *Veni, Veni, Emmanuel*, the Maundy Thursday plainchant *Ubi Caritas* ('Where charity and love are, God is there') which continues the theological narrative of the work (see Example 3.10).

The plainchant is found high in a solo first violin (bars 363–65) in an unabashed statement, soaring above the refrain repetitions and the declamatory marimba material. The chant returns in the final section of the work in the second violins, suggesting musical and religious resolution.

52   Wright, 'From the Heartbeat', 535.

53   MacMillan, programme note to *Veni, Veni, Emmanuel*.

Example 3.9   Bars 352–54 of *Veni, Veni, Emmanuel* showing first occurrence of 'Rejoice, rejoice' pattern

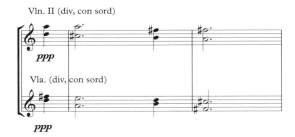

Example 3.10   *Ubi Caritas* plainsong

The 'Transition: Sequence II' follows the slow material, beginning with an E♭ pedal (recalling the similar effect in *Isobel Gowdie*) that crescendos to an episodic section recalling many of the themes and textures from earlier in the work. This then progresses to a return of the 'Dance' section, now entitled 'Dance – Chorale', in which repetitions of the hocket material from earlier provide the accompaniment to a grand statement of the *Veni, Veni, Emmanuel* plainchant (in C♯ minor) from the upper woodwind and brass (bars 546–60). MacMillan denies the chant its full resolution by not stating the final C♯ of the melody, instead reprising the opening material in a truncated fashion (bars 565–80) as a short transition to the final section, the 'Coda – Easter'. This 'Coda' finishes the journey of *Veni, Veni, Emmanuel* both musically and theologically as the 'heartbeat' motif returns ('emphatically pounded out on drums and timps') alongside further repetitions of the chant refrain in the lower voices and the aforementioned use of the *Ubi Caritas* theme in the second violins.[54] One by one the orchestra swaps its instruments for bells until the whole group is a metallic accompaniment for the solo percussionist on the

---

54   Ibid.

tubular bells, who crescendos and accelerandos on the prominent pitches from the plainchant to finish the work in a halo of resonant chimes.

Richard McGregor sees the *Ubi Caritas* plainchant as being key to understanding the theological message behind the work, as he explains, describing the 'Coda' of *Veni, Veni, Emmanuel*:

> This becomes the emotional climax of the work where the thumping heart of humanity is answered by ... *Ubi Caritas* containing within it the assurance of 'Where love and charity are, there God is', rising over the lower brass representing humanity chanting 'Rejoice, Rejoice'. This juxtaposition triggers the Easter bells which conclude the work, recalling the symbolic gesture at the *Gloria* in the Easter Vigil Mass.[55]

Certainly, the move to D major for the 'Coda' (the traditional key of religious 'rejoicing') and the statement of the *Ubi Caritas* theme in its home tonality suggests a harmonic resolution to match the theological conclusion.[56]

There is no doubt that *Veni, Veni, Emmanuel* is one of MacMillan's most popular pieces – its longevity is testament to that and the critical response to the premiere was generally positive. Whether the work's popularity stems from its easily accessible form, its use of a well-known Christmas melody, or the fact that the work is associated with the glamorous and idiosyncratic percussionist Evelyn Glennie is difficult to ascertain – perhaps it is due in part to all three. Andrew Porter, writing in *The Observer*, referred to the piece as: 'pop music – instantly appealing, referential – but a superior specimen of the genre: honestly felt, ambitious, communicative'.[57] Calum MacDonald, writing in the new music journal *Tempo*, called the work 'unexpectedly witty ... as well as beautiful and invigorating' and highlighted the 'fundamentally affirmative spirit' of the piece.[58]

Not all were quite so positive in their appraisal of *Veni, Veni, Emmanuel*. David Wright felt there was 'a lack of expressive substance that made the work a disappointing experience' and the crescendo on one pitch in the 'Transition:

---

[55]   McGregor, 'Transubstantiated into the musical ...': metaphor and reality in James MacMillan's *Veni, Veni, Emmanuel*', 30.

[56]   Johnson, 'James MacMillan', 4.

[57]   Andrew Porter, 'So many young candidates for the red-carpet treatment', *The Observer* (16 August 1992).

[58]   Calum MacDonald, 'MacMillan, Stevenson and Other Scots', *Tempo*, no. 188 (March 1994), 33.

Sequence II' was 'crude and unconvincing.'[59] Stephen Johnson questioned whether the 'quiet repetition of "Rejoice, rejoice" had to drift on so long with so little variation' and whether 'we heard the fast-dancing syncopated string version [the hocket material] of the chant once, or even twice too often?'[60] Perhaps most interestingly, Johnson asked: 'did the percussion writing prove less memorable than the orchestral ideas?'[61] This is a question posed by many commentators, and Richard McGregor wondered if the 'role of the percussionist in the work is ambiguous, if this is indeed a concerto'.[62] Certainly MacMillan's claim in the programme note that the work is for 'two equal partners'[63] suggests the piece is not following the usual concerto model, and despite several cadenza-like passages and bravura writing throughout it often feels like the percussionist is vainly searching for the musical and theological narrative that propels *Veni, Veni, Emmanuel* forward. An odd, though striking, feature is that the percussionist rarely seems to carry any of the theological argument behind the piece. Whether this is because the soloist represents humanity (with its 'heartbeat' motif) and the orchestra divinity, remains unclear, but the piece is more fascinating for the distinction.

Though MacMillan had written purely religious and religiously inspired works before, it is hard not to view *Veni, Veni, Emmanuel* as a very public declaration of faith: the musical material, the narrative, the rhetoric and the delivery all emphasise this. The work opened the door for MacMillan's Catholicism, and the outpouring of works inspired by his faith in the following years show how important *Veni, Veni, Emmanuel* was to his development.

---

[59]   Wright, 'From the Heartbeat', 535.

[60]   Stephen Johnson, 'James MacMillan: *Veni, Veni, Emmanuel*', *Tempo*, no. 183 (December 1992), 35.

[61]   Ibid., 35.

[62]   McGregor, 'Transubstantiated into the musical ...': metaphor and reality in James MacMillan's *Veni, Veni, Emmanuel*', 35.

[63]   MacMillan, programme note to *Veni, Veni, Emmanuel*.

4 | *A Different World –*
Visitatio Sepulchri, Seven Last Words
from the Cross and *Inés de Castro*

If *Veni, Veni, Emmanuel* found James MacMillan exploring the Easter narrative in his work for the first time in a substantial and meaningful fashion, the years 1993 to 1997 found him examining this event in an almost obsessive manner, returning again and again to the three days of drama, tragedy and redemption that are at the heart of Christianity. Over this four-year period, he composed at least ten works overtly influenced by the events of Holy Week, ranging from short chamber works such as *Kiss on Wood* (1993) and *Fourteen Little Pictures* (1997) to the large-scale cantata *Seven Last Words from the Cross* (1993) and the orchestral triptych *Triduum* (1996–97). As was stated in the previous chapter, MacMillan has spoken often about being 'drawn again and again to the Passion', that he seems 'to be going round and round the same three days of history' – it was no surprise he felt this following an intense period of composition on such a dramatic and personally significant event.[1] Although the Easter story has remained a powerful source of inspiration for the composer since the 1990s, it was this four-year period that saw MacMillan's most concentrated exploration of the Passion.

The years 1993 to 1997 were also some of the most successful of MacMillan's career with high-profile commissions, recordings and awards following on from the breakthrough successes of *The Confession of Isobel Gowdie* and *Veni, Veni, Emmanuel*. One of the most tangible of these saw MacMillan as the featured composer at the 1993 Edinburgh Festival, during which eighteen of his works were performed including the premieres of the one-act opera *Tourist Variations* (more of which later) and the trumpet concerto *Epiclesis* by John Wallace and the Philharmonia Orchestra, conducted by Leonard Slatkin. The exposure generated by the inclusion of MacMillan's work in the festival was both positive and negative, but it did

---

[1]   MacMillan, 'God, Theology and Music', 19.

highlight the position the then 34-year-old composer held in the Scottish musical firmament – virtually all his major works to date were featured including *Isobel Gowdie*, *Búsqueda* and *Cantos Sagrados* alongside more obscure pieces such as *Study on Two Planes*, *Beatus Vir* (both subsequently withdrawn) and *Catherine's Lullabies*.[2] The festival came hot on the heels of another significant milestone for MacMillan that year with the birth of twins (Aidan and Clare) on 10 June 1993 and a frenetic home life with three children under the age of three. MacMillan dedicated his subsequent work of the same year for the Hilliard Ensemble *... here in hiding ...* to his twins.[3]

Visitatio Sepulchri (1993)

Another substantial new work to be featured at the Edinburgh Festival that year was the 45-minute piece for soloists, narrator and chamber orchestra *Visitatio Sepulchri* (Visit to the tomb) which had its premiere at the Tramway in Glasgow earlier in the year given by the SCO conducted by Ivor Bolton. The work has variously been referred to as a 'sacred opera', 'liturgical drama' or 'music theatre' but MacMillan himself has called it a 'masque-type opera', highlighting the unusual nature and form of the piece.[4] The work is a setting of a text taken from a fourteenth-century liturgical drama from Notre Dame Cathedral in Paris along with settings of the *Victimae Pascheli laudes* and the *Te Deum* (all in Latin). *Visitatio Sepulchri* was directed by Francisco Negrin, the Mexican opera director famed for his elaborate productions of Handel, who also directed the ill-fated *Tourist Variations*.

---

[2]   *Beatus Vir* was written in 1983 and was a prize-winning piece at the Norwich Festival of Contemporary Church Music Composers' Competition in the same year (see chapter seven). MacMillan never formally withdrew the work, but it has languished in the darker reaches of his published output and had to wait until 2018 for its first commercial recording. MacMillan won £300 from the competition which he used 'to pay for my honeymoon'. Cooke, Interview with James MacMillan, 29 March 2017.

[3]   *... here in hiding ...* was also premiered at the 1993 Edinburgh Festival (on 10 August). The title is taken from the opening line of Gerard Manley Hopkins's translation of St Thomas Aquinas's *Adore te devote*, 'Godhead here in hiding, whom I do adore' and apparently has nothing to do with the composer seeking some peace and quiet away from his family.

[4]   MacMillan, as quoted in Tavener, liner notes to *Tenebrae: New Choral Music by James MacMillan*, 15.

Plate 3   James MacMillan (Photo: Peter Devlin, 1992)

Visitatio Sepulchri is an unusual work as it is both a highly original piece of ritualistic religious drama as well as a transitionary work between the Celticism of *Tryst* and *Isobel Gowdie* and the traditional vehicle of large-scale religious outpouring that can be found with *Seven Last Words from the Cross*. The work shares many of the same gestures, techniques and procedures as many pieces from this period and can be viewed as both a continuation of MacMillan's earlier successes and a prototype of the later cantata. MacMillan has stated that the libretto is 'entirely anti-dramatic' and that the initial inspiration was 'starkness, objectivity and minimal theatricality'.[5] Certainly the libretto has no dramatic or narrative devices as such, which leads to some of the issues with nomenclature for the work. Much of the drama stems from MacMillan's own decisions regarding form and repetition of text, and his music which is as vivid, colourful and powerful as any of the works that precede it. The main 'drama' of *Visitatio Sepulchri* is contained in the second movement with the appearance of three angels (taken by male voices) who utter the line: 'Quem quaeritis in sepulchre, O Christicolae?' (Whom do ye seek in the sepulchre, O followers of

---

[5]   James MacMillan, programme note to *Visitatio Sepulchri*, http://www.boosey.com/cr/music/James-MacMillan-Visitatio-Sepulchri/5913 (accessed 26 September 2017).

Christ?) in a declamatory and austere fashion. This is then answered by three female voices (representing the three Marys: the Virgin Mary, Mary Magdalene and Mary, the sister of Lazarus) in a similar manner: 'Jesum Nazarenum crucifixum, O caelicolae' (Jesus of Nazareth, the Crucified, O heavenly ones). The angels finish this momentous conversation with 'Non est hic; surrexit, sicut praedixerat. Ite, nuntiate quia surrexit.' (He is not here; he is risen, just as he foretold. Go, announce that he is risen.) Though not the most dramatic or operatic of texts, these simple lines do have an inherent gravitas and power which gives this section a narrative drive, aided by the repeating of each line and addition of cumulative material with each subsequent voice (see Example 4.1).

Alongside the trios of angels and women, there is a seventh character in *Visitatio Sepulchri*, the Cantor figure who enters the drama towards the end of the second movement (bar 216). MacMillan states that 'the Cantor acts as a "representative" of the onlookers ... he is the only figure who does not "sing" – he speaks, shouts and chants in *sprechstimme* style and he interjects questions, comments and exclaims as if from the multitude outside.'[6] The Cantor is a somewhat problematic figure: on the one hand he fulfils the 'old-fashioned device of a narrator', commenting on the development of the plot and appealing to the audience, on the other hand he anchors the work in the music theatre genre that was still in vogue in the 1990s (see the section on *Búsqueda* in chapter two) with his overly dramatic style of delivery, full of

Example 4.1   Bars 59–62 of *Visitatio Sepulchri* showing the first appearance of the Three Angels (voices only)

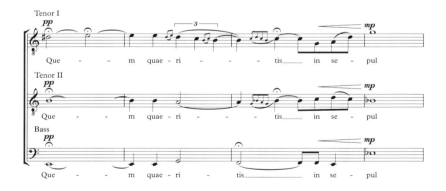

---

6   MacMillan, programme note to *Visitatio Sepulchri*.

extended vocal techniques and alien sounds.[7] The inclusion of the Cantor does accentuate the ritualistic nature of the piece and his line adds a certain vitality to the vocal parts, which often rely on the orchestral flourishes to provide necessary contrast.

The form of *Visitatio Sepulchri* (on a macro level) is unusual as the main 'drama' of the second movement is bookended by a purely orchestral first movement and a substantial final movement which is essentially a long hymn of praise and benediction with little dramatic opposition. The opening movement is very much in the mould of the orchestral works that precede it: scurrying string figures, woodwind hockets, brass crescendos and prominent percussion could all be lifted straight from *Tryst* or *Veni, Veni, Emmanuel*. The keening string motifs that open *The Confession of Isobel Gowdie* return in bars 95–137 (using the same modality, perhaps another nod in the direction of *The Tryst*) and crescendo in a similar fashion to *fortissimo* chords and gestural repeated notes. The final movement begins with material that is almost identical to the opening of *Veni, Veni, Emmanuel* with quick, scalic figures in the woodwind and rasping brass repetitions over a long tam-tam crescendo, though here we find a different plainchant featured, with the *Te Deum* harmonised in a dense fashion by the angels and women. Although much of the movement is redolent of MacMillan's music of this period, it quickly becomes more than just a guided tour of the composer's compositional techniques and mannerisms with the finale being the culmination of many of the musical strands present throughout the work. As MacMillan writes, 'this scene is devised so that a number of ideas are kept in motion at all times ... giving the impression of the same huge cyclical pattern of inevitability'.[8]

One of the musical strands that can be found throughout this movement is a deceptively simple tune that begins buried in the orchestra before reaching a full orchestral apotheosis at the end of the whole piece (see Example 4.2).

The tune is first alluded to in the violins (bars 304–13) in the midst of a busy orchestral texture and is just another strand in a densely woven passage. It is heard in full for the first time in an ornamented soprano duet (bars 395–414) accompanying the text 'Tu Rex gloriae, Christe. Tu Patris sempiternus es Filius' (Thou art the King of Glory: O Christ. Thou art the everlasting Son: of the Father). It returns in a similar duet for tenors (bars 435–54) before the female voices enter with a restatement of the opening text 'Te Deum laudamus' (We praise thee, O God) with accompanying harmonised plainchant. The cellos

---

[7]   Johnson, 'James MacMillan', 4.

[8]   MacMillan, programme note to *Visitatio Sepulchri*.

Example 4.2   Main theme from 'Movement III' of *Visitatio Sepulchri* (pitch content only)

and double basses provide a chromatic variant of the theme (bars 479–500) as accompaniment to increasingly fractured violin lines before the voices return with a dispersed, augmented version passed between them (bars 530–56) as a *Klangfarbenmelodie*. The aforementioned apotheosis occurs in bars 567–83 as the music surges into E major and MacMillan brings all the strands together with the theme powerfully stated by the brass, the sopranos and tenors reitering the *Te Deum* material. The very end of the piece sees all seven voices whispering 'In te, Domine, speravi: non confundar in aeternam' (O Lord, in thee have I trusted: let me never be confounded), gradually fading into the distance accompanied by tam-tam and *pizzicato glissandi* in the upper strings, dissipating the triumphalism of the previous section.

Visitatio Sepulchri was well received after its initial performances, with *The Independent* referring to the work as 'austere but with an impressive, ceremonial grandeur' and *The Times* stating the piece was 'as invigorating a piece of new British music ... since the last MacMillan premiere'.[9] The unusual genre of the work and the need for seven solo singers has led to it becoming one of MacMillan's least performed orchestral works from this period and it was no surprise that the composer rearranged the vocal parts for a more traditional large chorus in 2007.

Like many of MacMillan's pieces, *Visitatio Sepulchri* has provided material for future works, some in the aftermath of the 'masque-type opera', some

---

9   Michael White, 'MacMillan passes the test of time', *The Independent* (28 August 1993). Richard Morrison, 'Full of spirit in the empty tomb', *The Times* (24 May 1993).

much later in the composer's career. Even in the same 1993 Edinburgh Festival that featured *Visitatio Sepulchri* there was the premiere of a new work based entirely on material from the second scene of the larger piece – *They saw the stone had been rolled away* (1993) for brass ensemble and percussion. This six-minute work expands upon the section where the three Marys encounter the angels and the empty tomb, and alternates static material with more florid brass writing in a similar fashion to the corresponding section in *Visitatio Sepulchri*.[10] MacMillan returned to the work twice in 2010–11 to provide material for two choral pieces of a very different nature: *Think of how God loves you* (2010) and the *Missa Dunelmi* (2011). In the former, MacMillan takes the main theme of Movement III (Example 4.2) and sets it as an unassuming baptismal motet for his granddaughter Sara, complete with simple harmonies and a transparent four-part texture. In the latter, the theme appears in the Gloria firstly in a highly ornamented fashion, gradually revealed (akin to MacMillan's use of *The Tryst* in *Tryst* and other works) before a more obvious statement where the links to the previous works are evident (see Example 4.3).

The theological (and material) link between *Visitatio Sepulchri* and *They saw the stone had been rolled away* is obvious, though the link between the initial work and the later choral pieces is less so. In 2013 MacMillan referred to the inclusion of the theme in *Think of how God loves you* as a 'theological reason: *Visitatio Sepulchri* is a celebration of Easter and the risen Christ and when using it for the baptismal motet for my granddaughter, Sara, I wanted to have something of that resurrection aspect to go with her difficult life.'[11] With this in mind one can suppose the inclusion in the Gloria is a similar allusion to the resurrection or perhaps MacMillan is linking the constant stream of praise in the *Te Deum* with the similar function provided by the Gloria in the mass.

Visitatio Sepulchri feels like a transitional work between the early successes of *Veni, Veni, Emmanuel* and *Tryst* and a new period of composition begun with

---

10   *They saw the stone had been rolled away* was first performed on 27 August 1993 by the Edinburgh Festival Ensemble, conducted by Christopher Bell. The work is dedicated to Bert Richardson (see chapter one).

11   MacMillan, as quoted in Tavener, liner notes to *Alpha and Omega*, 6. MacMillan's granddaughter, Sara, was born in 2010, the first child of Catherine MacMillan. She was born with a rare condition called Dandy-Walker syndrome which led to lifetime of ill-health and she died just before her sixth birthday in 2016. A moving interview with MacMillan can be found in an article by Graeme Donohoe, 'Sir James MacMillan reveals heartbreak of losing his granddaughter to a rare condition', *The Daily Record* (26 February 2017).

Example 4.3   Bars 1–2 of *Think of how God loves you* and bars 81–83 of the Gloria
from *Missa Dunelmi*

the *Seven Last Words from the Cross*: it is full of the techniques and gestures of
the earlier works but also introduces new ideas and modes of expression that
will be developed in the later piece. Nowhere is this more apparent than in the
similarities between the opening of Movement II of *Visitatio Sepulchri* and the
third movement of *Seven Last Words*, 'Verily, I say unto you, today thou shalt
be with me in paradise'. In both pieces MacMillan builds from low bass voices
over a held double-bass pedal, gradually increasing the complexity of the voices
before interjecting an orchestral refrain, this then ushering in a new voice type
and a more animated variant on the initial idea. The refrain material in both
works may fulfil the same purpose but they are very different in style, delivery
and mood. This not only highlights the differences of the two pieces but also
MacMillan's changing aesthetic as he moved into the next part of his career.

1993 continued to be a successful year for MacMillan with further commissions, broadcasts and publications. His works also began to be recorded by some of the leading ensembles and orchestras and released on major record labels, none more so than BMG, with whom MacMillan signed a contract. An earlier recording of *The Confession of Isobel Gowdie* and *Tryst* by the BBC SSO and Jerzy Maksymiuk (who had given the premiere of *Isobel Gowdie*) on the Koch Schwann record label won *Gramophone Magazine* Contemporary Music Record of the Year at their annual awards and continued MacMillan's unlikely progression to the mainstream of not just contemporary, but of classical music as a whole.

However, all this success began to take its toll on the 34-year-old composer. His young family and the constant travel between Glasgow and Edinburgh during the festival left him exhausted and ultimately led to him crashing his car when tired at the wheel. The festival had been incredible exposure for MacMillan that few of his age and status could imagine; however, it had more detrimental effects than just the car accident, as he reminisced in 1999: 'I found that [the 1993 Edinburgh Festival] a draining experience. I dried up and it felt like a creative block.'[12] The creative block preceded his next major work, which has proved to be one of his most successful: *Seven Last Words from the Cross*.

Seven Last Words from the Cross (1993)

If there is one work by James MacMillan that is often referred to as a 'masterpiece', then that is his setting of *Seven Last Words from the Cross* from 1993, as a survey of concert brochures, CD liners or promotional materials quickly attests. But the use of this term is not reserved purely as hyperbole for commercial reasons; by the late 2000s leading critics and performers were referring to the work as a 'masterpiece of pained austerity' or a 'masterpiece of our time' – high praise indeed for a piece that was less than fifteen years old.[13] The work may not have had the exposure and dissemination of *The Confession*

---

12   Shirley Ratcliffe, 'Cantus in Choro: MacMillan', *Choir & Organ* (May/June 1999), 39.

13   Robert Stein, 'London, Barbican: MacMillan's "St John Passion"', *Tempo*, vol. 62, no. 246 (October 2008), 51. Paul Spicer, liner notes to *Seven Last Words from the Cross*, Hyperion CD, CDA67460 (2005), 8.

of Isobel Gowdie, nor the stream of high-profile performances that have greeted *Veni, Veni, Emmanuel*, but slowly and surely *Seven Last Words from the Cross* is becoming MacMillan's calling card: a work that represents the very best of him as a composer and continues to embody his compositional voice and aesthetic to the present day.

The work has aged well and continues to resonate with audiences a generation after its premiere. It has found a place in the repertoire whereas other works from the period that express similar sentiments (*Búsqueda*, *Cantos Sagrados*, *Visitatio Sepulchri*) simply have not. Whether this is due to the traditional form and genre of the work (the religious cantata, much easier to define then a 'liturgical drama') or the relatively simple instrumental forces required to stage a performance (chorus and string orchestra) is not clear, but there is a honesty, sincerity and emotional directness in *Seven Last Words* that has clearly struck a chord with audiences across the world long since its first performance. And if any of MacMillan's works set the scene (both musically and theologically) for his later oeuvre, then this is the one.

The commission of *Seven Last Words* was an unusual one: it was commissioned by BBC Television for screening during the seven nights of Holy Week 1994 (26 March to 1 April: Palm Sunday to Easter Saturday), with one movement per night. Similar to the live television broadcast of *The Confession of Isobel Gowdie* in 1990, it was incredible exposure for MacMillan, screened 'between two popular programmes, so lots of people watched it'.[14] The broadcasts were accompanied by associated visuals that have dated significantly quicker than the music, with soft-focus camerawork and an abundance of garish colours and props. The performers on the original broadcasts were Cappella Nova and the BT Scottish Ensemble, conducted by Alan Tavener, the same forces giving the first concert performance in Glasgow on 30 March of that year.

Seven Last Words from the Cross is an unusual genre of religious work and takes its title from the last seven sentences uttered by Christ as spread across the four gospels. Arguably the most famous musical setting is Haydn's 1787 instrumental meditation on the text for string quartet (though initially an orchestral piece and later becoming a choral work), but there have been settings from the Baroque to the present day. The opportunity to deliver a religious work in a serial fashion was undoubtedly what drew the BBC to suggest the text for the commission and despite initial misgivings about the

---

[14]   Mandy Hallam, 'Conversation with James MacMillan', *Tempo*, vol. 62, no. 246 (October 2008), 19.

medium, MacMillan found a text that inspired some of his most visceral and provoking music.[15]

Alongside the seven sentences that form the traditional texts, MacMillan interpolates other religious texts that form both a counterpoint and a commentary to the gospel selections (see Table 4.1). These texts are largely drawn from the Good Friday services and add to the melancholy and austerity that surround the work.

The 'creative block' that preceded the composition of *Seven Last Words* is telling, for MacMillan subsequently viewed this period of his career as particularly important, even fundamental to his future development, as he recalled in 1996: 'I had a realisation that things had to move on. Perhaps a

Table 4.1   Texts used in *Seven Last Words from the Cross*

Movement	Added Texts
I. Father, forgive them, for they know not what they do (Luke, 23, 24)	*Hosanna filio David* (Palm Sunday Exclamation); section from the Good Friday Responsaries for Tenebrae
II. Woman, Behold Thy Son! … Behold, Thy Mother! (John, 19, 26–27)	None
III. Verily, I say unto thee, today thou shalt be with me in Paradise (Luke, 23, 43)	*Ecce Lignum Crucis* (Good Friday Versicle)
IV. Eli, Eli, lama sabachtani (My God, My God, why have you forsaken me – Matthew, 27, 46)	None
V. I thirst (John, 19, 28)	Section from the Good Friday Reproaches
VI. It is finished (John, 19, 30)	Section from the Good Friday Responsaries for Tenebrae
VII. Father, into Thy hands I commend my Spirit (Luke, 23, 46)	None

---

[15]   MacMillan was insistent that there was always going to be a live performance of *Seven Last Words* and that the initial screening was 'a very incomplete and unsatisfactory way of presenting the piece' (ibid.).

"first stage" had been exhausted ... if I wanted to build on what I had achieved so far, then I had to focus very strongly on what kind of composer I was, and what I wanted to do.'[16] This self-reflection led to several early pieces being withdrawn from his catalogue and a period of 'self-analysis and self-evaluation, which I found exhausting and it stopped me writing'.[17] This introspection led to *Seven Last Words* being delivered late to the performers, but it also meant the beginning of a new period of MacMillan's compositional career, one which reflected further on the composer's faith and carried on many of themes that had propelled him to recognition in the previous four years.

One of the by-products of this 'self-analysis' and 'self-evaluation' was a further delving into the composer's earlier works for inspiration and material for current pieces and projects. As has already been shown, even in 1993 MacMillan was no stranger to reusing and recycling earlier works (whether these works had been withdrawn or not) with the large-scale borrowing of the eighth section of *Into the Ferment* in *Cantos Sagrados* and the pervasiveness of *The Tryst*, to name but two examples. Whether intentional or not, one of the ways that MacMillan overcame his creative block was to incorporate more fragments, sections and progressions from earlier pieces then he had ever done before; in doing so he not only removed the block but set the precedent for many of his works from *Seven Last Words* onwards. The three pieces that MacMillan draws on most in the cantata are *Tuireadh* (1991), *Divo Aloysio Sacrum* (1991) and *Kiss on Wood* (1993), with the last named of these almost acting as a test-bed for large sections of the larger piece.[18]

The first movement of *Seven Last Words*, 'Father, forgive them, for they know not what they do' begins with the sorrowful cadential figure first found in *Tuireadh* that characterises the mournful latter stages of that memorial work (see Example 3.4 for the comparison). Above the repeated figure the female voices gently intone Jesus's words in a soft, imitative modality with distinctive false-relations against the string accompaniment. Under this largely conjunct melodic writing MacMillan has the divided tenors then basses enter with rapid, insistent repetitions of 'Hosanna filio David' (from the Palm Sunday Exclamation) gradually building and fragmenting into impassioned cries of 'Rex Israel' alongside increasingly frenetic strings. As the music reaches almost

---

16   As quoted in Wells, 'James MacMillan: Retrospective Modernist', 153.

17   Ibid., 153.

18   For more information on MacMillan's continued 'self-quotation', see the excellent PhD thesis by Dominic Wells, 'James MacMillan: Retrospective Modernist', University of Durham, 2012.

total fragmentation a new idea is introduced with a 'plainsong monotone with the words from one of the Good Friday Responsaries for Tenebrae',[19] this continuing as the lower parts coalesce to return to the *Tuireadh* cadence, then fade to leave the unaccompanied solo sopranos and the poignant final line: 'For there was no one who would acknowledge me or give me help.'

The second movement, 'Woman, Behold Thy Son! ... Behold, Thy Mother!', includes no complementary text but has a similar tendency towards musical fragmentation that was exhibited in the first. A cadential figure is again prominent, with the gradually evolving opening outburst 'evoking memories of Bach's Passion chorales'.[20] The movement is characterised by eleven iterations of this figure (setting the words 'Woman, Behold Thy Son!'), gradually thinning and becoming more consonant as the piece progresses, though losing none of the emotional impact or drama. Here, the strings do the opposite of their vocal counterparts, moving from simple, conjunct motion into the same frenzied chromaticism of the first movement. The second movement ends with a prosaic, exhausted statement of 'Behold, Thy Mother!' by the male voices in unison as the whirlwind motion of the strings gradually dissipates.

Much of the material for this movement can be found in *Kiss on Wood*, the short violin and piano piece from earlier in 1993: in fact both the descending conjunct melody and the declamatory outbursts are present in the opening page of the previous work (see Example 4.4). The similarity can also be seen in the prominent use of silence, a characteristic trait of *Seven Last Words* and a concept MacMillan exploited further in later pieces.

The descending melody also bears a striking similarity to the repeated melodic material in the short choral work *Divo Aloysio Sacrum* which MacMillan had written for the choir of St Aloysius' Church in Glasgow two years previously (see Example 4.5). Here the melody is increased from a fifth to a seventh, but contains the same characteristic leap back to the opening pitch and shares some rhythmic similarities.

The third movement, 'Verily, I say unto thee, today thou shalt be with me in Paradise', is the most substantial and also the most discussed part of *Seven Last Words* as it contains some of the key aesthetic decisions underlying the composition of the whole piece. MacMillan reserves the words of Jesus for the very end of the movement, using the Good Friday antiphon *Ecce Lignum*

---

[19]   James MacMillan, programme note to *Seven Last Words from the Cross*, http://www.boosey.com/cr/music/James-MacMillan-Seven-Last-Words-from-the-Cross/6108 (accessed 18 October 2017).

[20]   Ibid.

Example 4.4   Similarities between melodic content in 'Woman, Behold Thy Son!
... Behold, Thy Mother!' from *Seven Last Words from the Cross*
(bars 1–3, soprano only) and *Kiss on Wood* (bars 1–11, violin only)

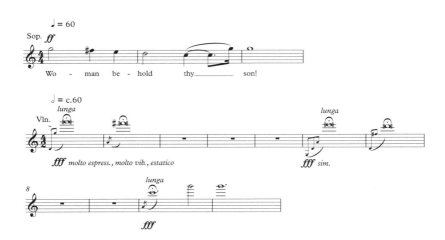

Crucis (Behold the Wood of the Cross) for the main body of the section.
Here, the antiphon is repeated three times: first by divided basses, then tenors,
then altos, each time following the duet with a refrain featuring a prominent
solo violin line. During this refrain material the divided voices sing 'Venite
adoremus' (Come let us adore him), finishing with similar liturgical chanting
to that which was utilised by the sopranos at the end of the first movement.
The choice of three repetitions, each getting progressively higher in range
and tessitura is no coincidence, MacMillan chose to do this to replicate the
Good Friday liturgy where the text is 'sung three times, each time at a higher
pitch as the cross is slowly unveiled and revealed to the people'.[21] Following
the third repetition and refrain, the strings burst into life with an impassioned
intermezzo, full of sharp dynamic contrasts and harmonic shifts, very different
in tone and mood from their earlier refrain material. After the strings have
reached their apex, divided sopranos in their highest register finally introduce
Jesus's words in a simple setting, bringing the music to a close in the F major
that has been alluded to throughout.

Much has been made of this third movement, particularly the solo violin
material in the refrain and the string interlude, critics referring to the violin

---

21   Ibid.

Example 4.5   Opening melodic phrase of *Divo Aloysio Sacrum* (bars 1–5, sopranos only)

line as 'distressingly sentimental' or 'almost indulgent'.[22] Certainly, the melody is striking and the music in general is the warmest and most alluring in the whole work: the harmonies are transparent and traditional (moving from D minor to F major), the texture simple (solo line, arpeggio accompaniment with prominent bass note) and it even finishes with a plagal cadence. The interlude has raised similar questions, particularly regarding its inclusion in not just this third movement, but in the work as a whole. In a 2007 interview, MacMillan linked the interlude to the unveiling of the cross that underpins the inclusion of *Ecce Lignum Crucis*: 'It starts off with the fundamental, there is nothing seen, then gradually ... more of what's there is unveiled. I think that is what is happening in the music, unveiling more of the ensemble and gradually adding to the ensemble.'[23] This may explain its inclusion, but does not necessarily clarify the very different character of this material from the rest of the work. The answer to this may lie in MacMillan's claim in the same interview: 'There's a liturgical detachment from the three statements previous to it and the last one, and there's a subjectivity that fills the gap.'[24] As will be shown in the final movement, MacMillan places much importance on subjectivity and objectivity in *Seven Last Words* and this is arguably the first moment in the work where this becomes apparent.

The fourth movement, 'Eli, Eli, lama sabachtani' (My God, My God, why have you forsaken me), begins with comparable low bass material to the previous movement and builds a huge arch over its ninety bars from the lowest registers to the very highest and back. As in the previous movements, the vocal

---

22   Richard Drakeford, 'Review of *Seven Last Words from the Cross*', *The Musical Times,* vol. 136, no. 1832 (October 1995), 556. Spicer, liner notes to *Seven Last Words from the Cross*, 7.

23   Hallam, 'Conversation with James MacMillan', 20.

24   Ibid., 20.

parts become progressively more animated, ornamented and rhythmic as they develop, with characteristic MacMillan *glissandi* and melodic decorations.

By far the bleakest movement of *Seven Last Words* is the fifth, 'I thirst', which interpolates a desolate section of the Good Friday Reproaches: 'I gave you to drink of life-giving water from the rock: and you gave me to drink of gall and vinegar.' It is the simplest yet most self-consciously 'difficult' section of the work as the interpolated text is chanted and whispered in an affecting and arresting fashion, not too dissimilar to techniques used by Krzysztof Penderecki in his seminal *St Luke Passion* (1966). After the final repetition of 'I thirst', the strings gradually enter on a unison G♭ before a huge crescendo erupts with the characteristic MacMillan description of 'like a violent shuddering' accompanying the ferocious *tremolandi* with semitonal cluster. No sooner has this most gestural moment of *Seven Last Words* arrived then the music fades to a solo pitch then silence: it is a dramatic and powerful moment and it is hard not to read a pictorial analogy into it, similar as this moment and material is to the unison crescendo at the end of *The Confession of Isobel Gowdie*.

The similarities with *Isobel Gowdie* continue at the beginning of the penultimate movement, 'It is finished', with the thirteen 'stabbing' chords at the start recalling the same gesture from the earlier work. The number thirteen is of great symbolic value in the Christian tradition, referring as it does to the twelve disciples and the 'false apostle' Judas, who will betray Christ. It is no great leap of the imagination to suggest that its inclusion in *Seven Last Words* and *Isobel Gowdie* (amongst other works) is MacMillan engaging in religious symbolism; in fact it is possible to read the whole of *Seven Last Words* in a symbolic fashion from the acknowledged (such as the repetitions in the third movement) to the suggested.[25] Following the disintegration of the opening chords, the choir enters with text from the Good Friday Responsories (in the upper voices) superimposed on Jesus's words in the male parts. The music returns to the *Tuireadh* material of the first movement, moving chromatically through different variations before surging to return to the initial pitches in bars 32–36 (see Example 4.6). The parts gradually drop out to leave the sopranos with their emotive final repetitions of 'Is there any sorrow like mine?', before the piercing chords from the movement's opening return to finish in an unequivocal manner.

---

[25]   Richard McGregor's paper 'Exploring Engagement and Detachment in James MacMillan's *Seven Last Words*' (University of Aberdeen, 9 February 2016) gives a reading of the symbolism in *Seven Last Words from the Cross* and shows the prevalence of the number thirteen amongst other symbols.

Example 4.6   Bars 32–35 of 'It is finished' from *Seven Last Words from the Cross* showing the return of the *Tuireadh* cadential material

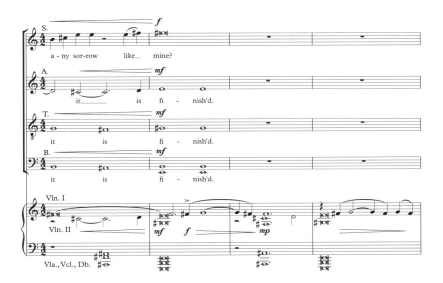

The final movement, 'Father, into Thy hands I commend my Spirit', returns to the declamatory outbursts of the second movement, with anguished cries of 'Father' punctuated by long silences. The third repetition (perhaps more symbolism) again sees the material return to the *Tuireadh* cadence for the final line of text, 'into thy hands I commend my spirit', at which point the voices fall silent and the string orchestra carries out an expressive postlude to finish the work. The ending of the piece is of great personal significance to MacMillan, and his comments about it are telling:

> On setting such texts it is vital to maintain some emotional objectivity in order to control musical expression in the way that the Good Friday liturgy is a realistic containment of grief ... In this final movement, with its long instrumental postlude, the liturgical detachment breaks down and gives way to a more personal reflection: hence the resonance here of Scottish traditional lament music.[26]

---

26   MacMillan, programme note to *Seven Last Words from the Cross*.

Here we find MacMillan returning to the objectivity/subjectivity dialectic that was first encountered in earnest in the third movement, with his own personal subjectivity emerging from the 'liturgical detachment' of the rest of the piece. The 'Scottish traditional lament music' that ends *Seven Last Words from the Cross* is as personal as *The Tryst* or the modality of the opening of *The Confession of Isobel Gowdie* (all in the same mode) and the expressive melodic lines serenely weave their way to the very highest registers to leave a virtually inaudible F♯/G dyad, perhaps a symbol of Christ's final breaths, or perhaps the last word in non-resolution.

Whether *Seven Last Words from the Cross* is James MacMillan's masterpiece or not will only be decided by the passing of time, though its increasing and consistent relevance to audiences and performers makes it a clear candidate as one of the composer's most important artistic statements. Whereas one can view the continued success of *Veni, Veni, Emmanuel* as being partly due to the lack of available vehicles for solo percussionists (and the increase of virtuoso players looking to perform with orchestra) the same cannot be levelled at *Seven Last Words* – even in a growing secular age cantatas, oratorios and other large-scale religious works continue to be composed, the longevity of MacMillan's work is testament not only to the quality of the music but to the conviction of the composer's religious beliefs and the directness of his emotional language.

Inés de Castro (1991–95, rev. 2014)

Following on from the 'music theatre' of *Búsqueda* and the 'liturgical drama' of *Visitatio Sepulchri* it seemed a natural progression for MacMillan to move into the operatic world proper, and this duly occurred with his first full-scale opera *Inés de Castro* which was premiered at the Edinburgh Festival in 1996 by Scottish Opera. However, this was not the composer's first foray into opera: this had occurred three years earlier with the one-act comic offering *Tourist Variations* that was premiered at the 1993 Edinburgh Festival amongst the many works of MacMillan's performed that year.

Tourist Variations was a collaboration between Francisco Negrin, MacMillan and the Glaswegian playwright Iain Heggie (famed for his idiosyncratic and vernacular work) and was a comic tale exploring the philosophy of tourism. The work was instantly dismissed by both critics and composer alike and was one of the first pieces to be culled by MacMillan following his post-Edinburgh Festival creative silence. The reviews were harsh ('frantic, dense and cynically verbose' stated *The Independent*) but MacMillan has been even more critical of the work, referring to it as 'a match made in hell' and a 'terrible miscalculation'.[27] The speed at which MacMillan disowned *Tourist Variations* suggests a venture that bore no fruit of any artistic worth and in candid fashion he stated in 2017 that he tried to recycle the material in later works but 'there was nothing worth keeping'.[28]

Whatever the relative merits of *Tourist Variations*, it is safe to assume that *Inés de Castro* represents MacMillan's first acknowledged opera and therefore has coloured all his operatic repertoire (*Parthenogenesis*, 2000; *The Sacrifice*, 2005–06; and *Clemency*, 2010) since its composition.[29] The opera is an adaptation of Jo Clifford's play of the same name from 1989, which MacMillan had seen at that year's Edinburgh Festival, and he was drawn to the work from the outset, as he explains: 'I was immediately struck by its operatic potential, and I spoke to the author about it that same night.'[30] The work recounts the story of Inés de Castro, the fourteenth-century Spanish (Castilian) mistress of Pedro the Crown Prince of Portugal (later King Pedro or Peter I) during a period of strife between the two nation states. As the conflict becomes more intense, the king (under the influence of the scheming advisor Pacheco) sends Pedro to the front line where it is presumed he will be defeated and die. When he unexpectedly returns to court victorious, he finds Inés and their two children have been murdered despite his desperate rush back to be with them. Following the king's death, Pedro is crowned alongside the exhumed Inés in full queen's regalia and he orders his subjects to kiss her decaying hand, taunting them for their rejection of her. Pacheco's scheming is short-lived, as he dies in a brutal fashion, described in a macabre manner in one of the opera's most notorious sections, the Executioner's Song.

[27] Michael White, 'MacMillan passes the test of time', *The Independent* (28 August 1993). Phillip Cooke, Interview with James MacMillan, University of Aberdeen, 16 November 2017.

[28] Ibid. MacMillan is surprisingly candid about works he is ashamed of: 'I am embarrassed about it, there are only two pieces that I am embarrassed about and that's one of them! The other one is a piece for choir which I've more or less managed to hide called *Ruin*.'

[29] *Parthenogenesis* returns to the more 'fluid' dramatic genres of *Búsqueda* and *Visitatio Sepulchri* and is referred to as both 'music theatre' and a 'dramatic scena'.

[30] David Kettle, programme note for Scottish Opera's production of *Inés de Castro* (2015), 12. There may be some confusion as to the playwright in question, earlier sources referring to John Clifford and later ones to Jo Clifford. These are the same person, with Jo Clifford coming out as transgender in 2005 after the death of her partner.

The premiere of *Inés de Castro* was given by Scottish Opera on 23 August 1996, directed by Jonathan Moore and conducted by Richard Armstrong. However, the links between the company and MacMillan went as far back as the mid-1980s. Scottish Opera commissioned the piece in 1991, though composition in earnest took place between 1993 and 1995, and became an all-encompassing project for the composer, MacMillan stating 'for a work like this, it seems like I have to give my whole life to it for that period of time'.[31] With the success of MacMillan's earlier work for other major artistic bodies in Scotland (the SCO, the BBC SSO and the Edinburgh Festival) it seemed a natural progression that he would write for the nation's premiere opera company at some point, and *Inés de Castro* followed hot on the heels of the composer's most successful early works. However, the link between MacMillan and Scottish Opera was much more long-standing than this first collaboration: some of his earliest, formative musical experiences were trips to see the opera in Glasgow in the 1970s (see chapter one), conducted by Alexander Gibson, in whose memory the work is dedicated.

One of the major factors that makes *Inés de Castro* different to the earlier dramatic works is its relationship to operatic tradition. It is a work that is indebted to previous operatic models and relies on this relationship to give the piece its *raison d'être*: its scope, its form and its narrative. As MacMillan commented: 'I can feel Wagner, Strauss, Berg and other composers in *Inés de Castro*, and I didn't shy away from allowing that tradition to be present in what I was writing.'[32] A term that is often used to describe the work is 'grand opera', suggesting not only a link to the composers MacMillan mentioned but also to a tradition of opera from Donizetti to Verdi, a tradition of large casts, orchestras and choruses, lavish scenography and stage effects, and narratives derived from dramatic historic events: *Inés de Castro* certainly fits this description. The work has seven main roles (eight including the double role of nurse and old woman), a large orchestra featuring the characteristic MacMillan arsenal of percussion and a substantial part for the chorus: it is a big-boned operatic tragedy much in the mould of Verdi's *Macbeth* and other similar works. The links to grand opera continue in the smaller-scale forms MacMillan uses throughout: there are set-piece arias (such as the aforementioned Executioner's Song, Act II Scene 3), a love duet (between Pedro and Inés, Act I Scene 13) and an 'almost Verdian quartet' (between Pedro, Inés, the king and Pacheco) that brings the

31   Ibid., 13.
32   Ibid., 12.

first act to an end.[33] *Inés de Castro* revels in its relationship to tradition and its place in a continuum of musical history, it is as far removed from *Búsqueda* and the other earlier dramatic works as it is possible to be within the same, loosely defined genre.

That being said, *Inés de Castro* does bear some similarities to the earlier forays into the operatic world, particularly the static ritualism of *Visitatio Sepulchri*. MacMillan binds the first act together with a setting of the *Stabat Mater* (in Latin) as a counterpoint to Clifford's libretto. The text begins in the chorus basses in long, low notes of similar construction to the beginning of the second movement of the earlier work and gradually moves through the chorus, becoming more animated and more prominent. Its initial appearance accompanies a religious procession as the 'ordinary people' carry aloft a statue of the Virgin Mary, praying for intercession from the threat of their neighbours. It disappears shortly afterwards, but returns again in the penultimate scene to underpin the dramatic quartet that finishes Act I. The ritualistic associations of the *Stabat Mater* are enhanced when it appears for the final time in Scene 4 of Act II, now acting as the herald of the grisly coronation that is the denouement of the opera.

The gruesome final scene is the culmination of the theme of horror and revulsion that permeates *Inés de Castro* from beginning to end, and it is one of the elements that most critics drew upon. From Blanca's (Pedro's wife) detailed description of her miscarriages through to Pacheco's revelling in the murder of Inés's children, blood and gore is never far from the narrative and MacMillan was well aware that this divided opinion: audiences 'found the Grand Guignol aspect of it too much, the eerie, dark spectacle of it too ripe'.[34] The opera is almost unceasing in its portrayal of the darker aspects of humanity and even those characters who aren't obviously malign are deeply flawed and capable of dubious deeds. Again, MacMillan was aware of this facet of *Inés de Castro* and embraced it in characteristic fashion: 'there's a case to be made that when artists deal with the most unsettling aspects of evil, it's an attempt to transcend that evil, to find some kind of redemption beyond it'.[35] This links the opera to much of MacMillan's work of this period: *The Confession of Isobel Gowdie*,

---

[33]   Ibid., 16. The scenes relate to the revised version of *Inés de Castro* that MacMillan made in 2014, which removes the initial third scene.

[34]   Ibid., 14. The Grand Guignol was a Parisian theatre specialising in horror shows. Its name has since become a generic term for any sort of graphic horror entertainment.

[35]   Ibid., 14–15.

Cantos Sagrados and *Tuireadh* for example, all feature redemption as the final goal of the narrative and the musical discourse.

Perhaps what is unusual about *Inés de Castro* is that this redemption is not necessarily achieved through religious means, in fact the opera is not as obviously influenced by Catholicism, as is much of MacMillan's music from this period. The use of the *Stabat Mater* and the set-piece religious processions certainly show the composer's keen interest in the sacred, but Inés the ghost's final words to a young girl (who is the only person who can see the ghostly Inés) are more human than sacred in their redemptive power and hope: 'They'll tell you that they have to kill, that they cannot avoid committing crimes. Do not believe them. Do not believe them. Do not believe them for a moment. Remember, remember there is another way.' Certainly, the links to the Passion narrative are strong and obvious, but *Inés de Castro* is also linked to MacMillan's political works of the 1980s. Although the political message is not overt, it is easy to make comparisons between fourteenth-century Portugal and events in our time: betrayal, torture and suffering have become all too commonplace. But MacMillan has been quick to distance himself from contemporary issues: 'I don't think the essence of the piece is about getting a message across. It's sheer coincidence that it touches on contemporary resonances.'[36] Sheer coincidence or not, it is difficult to avoid parallels.

As with many of MacMillan's works from *Seven Last Words from the Cross* onwards, *Inés de Castro* finds the composer reusing and recycling material, in this case to draw out strong themes in his oeuvre. One of the most striking self-quotations in the opera is from MacMillan's setting of William Soutar's 'The Children', which was initially composed in 1984 as part of *Songs of a Just War* for soprano and ensemble, but arranged for voice and piano in 1995. The text of Soutar's poem is bleak and uncompromising, describing the death of children at the hands of the Luftwaffe during the Spanish Civil War, and although separated by hundreds of years, the links between the events in the poem and Clifford's libretto are stark. MacMillan uses a quotation from 'The Children' twice in *Inés de Castro*, first in Pacheco's aria in Act II Scene 1 where he describes the butchery of his own family, particularly his baby sister, by Spanish soldiers (see Example 4.7).

Its second appearance is at the very end of the opera when a little girl converses with the ghost of Inés following the crowning of Inés's corpse. Here, the childlike quality that MacMillan alludes to in the performance direction for 'The Children' becomes apparent as the little girl intones: 'I'm just a little girl.

---

36   Ibid., 15.

Example 4.7   Opening from 'The Children' (bars 1–2) and quotation in Act II
Scene 1 of *Inés de Castro* (bars 306–08)

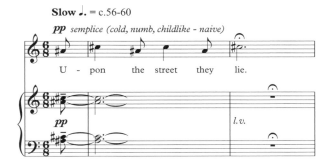

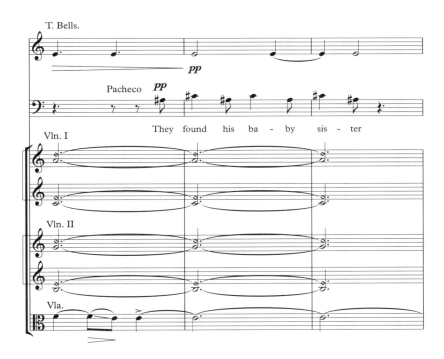

I am on my way home. Are you a ghost?' with the repeating minor third figure arresting in its simplicity and naivety.

Unfortunately for MacMillan, *Inés de Castro* was the first of his major works to meet with largely negative criticism (on a greater scale than *Tourist Variations*), particularly from the English press who were savage in their disapproval of the work. *The Independent* likened the opera to 'a precociously ambitious child, it can't help showing off everything the composer can do, as well as several things he can't.'[37] *The Daily Telegraph* dismissed it as 'too ambitious, too grandiose, too much', whilst the *The Financial Times* referred to it as 'less than a success ... an assembly-line opera ... just not the real thing'.[38] By far the most cutting criticism was in the *Evening Standard*, which found little to commend in a 'medieval hokum' full of 'shlock horror' and 'unconvincing drama'.[39] The reception was more positive in Scotland, with *The Scotsman* opining that 'the music is MacMillan's masterpiece, economical, stinging', and *The Herald* describing *Inés de Castro* as 'a big boned piece with moments of intimacy, both tender and fierce'.[40]

The criticism of *Inés de Castro* was a difficult pill for MacMillan to swallow, particularly for a composer who had only recently come to national prominence and was still relatively young. The criticism of the opera had the opposite effect on MacMillan than was the case with *Tourist Variations*, with the composer choosing to revise the work in 2014, rather than expunging it from his creative output. A new production of the work was given by Scottish Opera in 2015, conducted by the composer, with several changes made to the original score, the most substantial being the omission of Act I Scene 3. This scene, a dialogue between Inés and her nurse, was omitted by MacMillan for dramatic and pacing reasons: 'In retrospect it seemed rather static – I thought I had to be brutal, and you can afford to be brutal when you're a different person – or an older person.'[41]

---

[37]   Anthony Peattie, 'Opera Premiere: Inés de Castro', *The Independent* (26 August 1996).

[38]   Rupert Christiansen, 'Portuguese promise of greater things', *The Daily Telegraph* (26 August 1996). Richard Fairman, 'James MacMillan's first full-length opera', *The Financial Times* (27 August 1996).

[39]   Tom Sutcliffe, 'Overdoing the shlock horror', *Evening Standard* (28 August 1996).

[40]   Mary Miller, 'MacMillan poses dark dilemma', *The Scotsman* (24 August 1996). Michael Tumelty, 'Inés de Castro', *The Herald* (25 August 1996).

[41]   Kettle, programme note for *Inés de Castro*, 16.

Inés de Castro was MacMillan's last foray into large-scale, 'grand opera' until *The Sacrifice* in 2005–06 and only his second venture into the medium. Other operatic works have appeared since, though smaller in scope and ambition and perhaps without the commotion that greeted the arrival of the Scottish Opera commission. Dramatic vocal works have remained at the heart of MacMillan's oeuvre since *Inés de Castro*, though arguably pieces for choir have replaced opera as the composer's preferred vehicle for this exploration.

5 | Changed – Triduum and Quickening

If the years from *The Confession of Isobel Gowdie* to *Inés de Castro* were MacMillan's first period of sustained success, one that announced him firmly to the country's musical consciousness, then the years from 1996 to 2000 were years of consolidation: a steady building on what he had achieved and a continued affirmation of all that had made him successful to that point. They were years of plenty, with a substantial increase in the amount of works produced, the quality of performers that the composer was working with, and exposure and dissemination of his work to a larger and more diverse audience. The backbone of MacMillan's output from this period rests on orchestral pieces: a standalone concerto (*Ninian*, for clarinet, 1997), a string orchestra work (*Í – A Meditation on Iona*, 1996), a piece for chamber orchestra (Symphony No. 2, 1999) and the monumental orchestral triptych, *Triduum* (1996–97).[1] It also saw an increase in chamber and instrumental works, and perhaps most importantly (for future developments), a marked increase in vocal and choral pieces, including the substantial song cycle *Raising Sparks* (1997) and culminating in the 50-minute oratorio *Quickening* for solo vocal quartet, choirs and orchestra in 1998.

It also saw the first major retrospective of MacMillan's work in England, with the 'Raising Sparks' festival at the South Bank in London running from 28 September to 26 October 1997. This featured many of MacMillan's key works from the past decade including *Veni, Veni, Emmanuel* and *The Confession of Isobel Gowdie*, the London premieres of pieces such as *Búsqueda* and *The Berserking* and, presented as its centrepiece, the first full performance of the entire *Triduum* including the world premiere of the third part, Symphony: 'Vigil', in the opening concert. 1997 also found MacMillan as the featured composer at the Bergen Festival in Norway and saw the 100th performance of

---

[1]   MacMillan also revised the 1993 trumpet concerto *Epiclesis* in 1998.

Veni, Veni, Emmanuel, an incredible feat in British contemporary music for a work that had only been premiered five years earlier in 1992.[2]

This increase in productivity was not without its side-effects as MacMillan recalled before 'Raising Sparks', suggesting his home life was suffering under the increased workload: 'She's [MacMillan's wife, Lynne] been very concerned over the last year, because I haven't been sleeping well. I decided it was time to recharge my batteries, so I'm going on a retreat to a Benedictine monastery ... I think I've also got to learn how to smile at my kids again.'[3] This characteristically honest quote from MacMillan not only highlights the strain his compositional activities were placing on domestic life, but is also one of the first mentions of the composer's trips to the Benedictine monastery at Pluscarden in north-east Scotland, where regular visits have aided MacMillan's creativity and provided spiritual nourishment and solace.[4]

Triduum I: The World's Ransoming (1996)

The major output of this period of consolidation was the Easter triptych *Triduum* that MacMillan composed for the London Symphony Orchestra (LSO) between 1995 and 1997 and which was the culmination of the intense exploration of Holy Week that had arguably begun with *Veni, Veni, Emmanuel* in 1992. *Triduum* comprises three interrelated works, which share material, ideas and concepts, but are all individual pieces: *The World's Ransoming* (1996), Cello Concerto (1996) and Symphony: 'Vigil' (1997). The word 'Triduum' refers to the period in Catholic liturgy of the three key days of the Easter period: Maundy Thursday, Good Friday and the Easter Vigil, and this provides the narrative arc for the *Triduum* as a whole. *The World's Ransoming* is the first of the triptych, as MacMillan explains in the programme note to the work: '*The World's Ransoming* focuses on Maundy Thursday and its musical material includes references to plainsongs for that day ... as well as a Bach chorale which I have heard being sung in the Eucharistic procession to the altar

---

[2]   In fact, *Veni, Veni, Emmanuel* was performed 'over 30 times around the world in the 1995–96 concert season alone' (Unknown author, 'Scots Firebrand', *The Economist*, 1 November 1997).

[3]   Stephen Johnson, [untitled], *The Independent* (25 September 1997).

[4]   For more information, see *The South Bank Show: James MacMillan*, presented by Melvyn Bragg, directed by Robert Bee, series 26, programme 8, aired on ITV, 5 January 2003.

of repose.'[5] The piece is a concertante work for cor anglais and orchestra and was first performed by the LSO, with its dedicatee Christine Pendrill as the soloist, conducted by Kent Nagano in November 1996.

The title of *The World's Ransoming* is taken from St Thomas Aquinas's hymn *Pange lingua,* which MacMillan uses substantially in the piece, with its vivid description of Christ's Passion:

Excerpt from *Pange lingua*, by St Thomas Aquinas (1224–74)

Of the glorious Body telling,
O my tongue its mysteries sing
And the Blood, all price excelling,
Which the world's eternal King,
In a noble womb once dwelling,
Shed for the world's ransoming.

Pange lingua (see Example 5.1) is one of the plainsongs for Maundy Thursday mentioned above, as is *Ubi caritas* (Where charity and love are, God is there), which MacMillan had used memorably in *Veni, Veni, Emmanuel* (see Example 3.10).

To this characteristic mix of plainsongs MacMillan adds the Bach chorale 'Ach wie flüchtig, ach wie nichtig' (Ah how fleeting, ah how futile) that Bach used in his cantata BWV 644 of 1724 (see Example 5.2).[6]

These 'borrowed' materials form the conceptual and theological framework for *The World's Ransoming*, but also provide much of the musical material on which the piece is constructed. The opening cor anglais melody (following a brief woodwind flourish that introduces the work) is a plangent melodic elaboration of the opening phrase of *Pange lingua*, transposed to an expressive, modal C♯ minor, a favoured key of MacMillan's (see Example 5.3).[7]

[5] James MacMillan, programme note to *The World's Ransoming*, http://www.boosey. com/cr/music/James-MacMillan-The-World-s-Ransoming/281 (accessed 6 March 2018).

[6] McGregor notes: 'In the score MacMillan refers to this text as "Ach wie nichtig" and it is sometimes so referenced, but that is the second phrase of the text.' (McGregor, 'A Metaphor for the Deeper Wintriness: Exploring James MacMillan's Musical Identity', 34.)

[7] It is used throughout his oeuvre, though perhaps most strikingly in final statement of the plainchant in *Veni, Veni, Emmanuel* and large sections of the *Sinfonietta* (a work with which *The World's Ransoming* shares several similarities).

Example 5.1   *Pange lingua* plainsong

Example 5.2   Chorale 'Ach wie flüchtig, ach wie nichtig' by J. S. Bach

The first appearance of the Bach material occurs shortly afterwards (following the first section of melodic activity from the cor anglais) in a rhythmically augmented, funereal chorale in the upper brass (see Example 5.4). As with other works from this period, MacMillan introduces the quotation quietly at first, marking the brass *pp*, 'lontano' (distant) and with mutes, giving the impression the Bach is half-heard and drifting into the orchestral texture from another time or place. Again, C# minor is the prevailing key (though the surrounding instrumental groups do their best to subvert this) with the majority of the opening third of the work coloured by this melancholy hue.

Example 5.3   Opening melodic phrase of the cor anglais in *The World's Ransoming*
(bars 6–15)

Example 5.4   Bars 77–82 of *The World's Ransoming* showing Bach quotation in brass

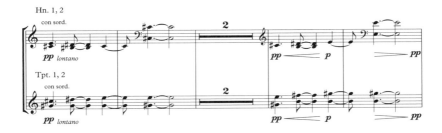

Similarly to MacMillan's use of pre-existing musical material in *Veni, Veni, Emmanuel* and *The Confession of Isobel Gowdie*, he juxtaposes the assembled plainsongs and chorale throughout *The World's Ransoming*, particularly in the final quarter of the piece as the work reaches its climax. Richard McGregor refers to this juxtaposition as 'thematic strands ... deployed together creating an Ivesian texture of competing tonalities (or atonality against tonality)'.[8] Certainly MacMillan has no qualms about colliding his borrowed material together for dramatic effect, with the Bach often pounded forth by the brass with plainsong interjections in the upper woodwind and strings; the resolution (or perhaps, non-resolution) of these strands in a powerful apotheosis is an archetypal MacMillan finale to a major work from this period.

The form and shape of *The World's Ransoming* are interesting, with MacMillan drawing attention to this in his programme note: 'Although the

---

8   McGregor, 'A Metaphor for the Deeper Wintriness: Exploring James MacMillan's Musical Identity', 35.

music is through-composed and seamless, a series of trios emerge to carry the music forward.'[9] The first trio involves the highly ornamented and filigree cor anglais pitted against a pair of bassoons (bars 136–41) before the strings and percussion envelop the dialogue in a rich G♯ minor. The second (bars 158–69) finds two agile solo cellos passing semiquaver material between themselves with a rasping cor anglais almost an onlooker to this conversation. The third (bars 194–210) sees the cor anglais sailing above staccato horns, whilst the fourth (bars 229–46) features an agitated soloist accompanied by timpani and tubular bells with dramatic orchestral interjections. The cor anglais acts as the counterpoint to a pair of accented piccolos in the fifth trio (bars 341–52) before it briefly entertains two solo violins in a descending chromatic sequence (bars 359–63). MacMillan adds these changes of emphasis and texture to a broad arc-shape form (another traditional form such as used in earlier orchestral works) with the opening cor anglais and then woodwind flourish returning at the end of the piece, before a short, theatrical coda.

Ronald Weitzman refers to these trios as the piece's 'imposing self-restraint upon itself', perhaps suggesting they are moments of textural and emotional clarity in a work of such lamenting orchestral drama: certainly the change of focus gives the piece new impetus in what might be viewed as a work of subtly changing colours.[10] The similarity in musical material throughout *The World's Ransoming* arguably comes from two sources: the relationship between the solo instrument and the orchestra, and the nature of the solo line itself. As a concertante work (or a work for orchestra with obbligato instrument) the cor anglais writing was always likely to be less virtuosic and rhetorical than in a standard concerto (such as the companion Cello Concerto from the same year) and the work does not feature a cadenza or any such moments of individual brilliance and flair.[11] MacMillan tends to have the cor anglais more as an animated onlooker, commenting and improvising on material from the orchestra, often in an elaborate, ornamented fashion replete with the grace-notes and flourishes that had become a mainstay of his musical language in the past decade. Although the tempo alters at various points (what MacMillan refers to as 'metric gear-changes') the pulse remains the same throughout

---

9   MacMillan, programme note to *The World's Ransoming*.

10   Ronald Weitzman, 'Triduum: MacMillan's Easter Triptych', *Tempo*, no. 204 (April 1998), 32.

11   'Indeed the soloist in the premiere of *Ransoming*, Christine Pendrill, insisted on sitting among her colleagues.' (Daniel Jaffé, 'James MacMillan' http://www.compositiontoday.com/articles/james_macmillan_interview.asp (accessed 15 March 2018).

(unusually for a work from this period) leading to much of the cor anglais's material sounding similar.[12] This is compounded by the closely controlled intervallic content of the solo instrument, full of semitone movement and lamenting falling minor ninths. The overall effect is one of sustained melancholy, by no means a literal depiction of the events of Maundy Thursday, but with a powerful and uniform meditation on the theme present.

The very end of *The World's Ransoming* is perhaps the most striking and divisive part of the piece as it represents much of what makes MacMillan's work appealing to some and abhorrent to others: the striking of a large plywood cube in a declamatory and symbolic fashion to finish the piece.[13] As the cor anglais winds its way to its final note, the struck cube continues to interrupt the line with sudden crescendos and interjections before continuing alone for eight bars, moving with an ominous tread to its chilling denouement at its loudest dynamic (see Example 5.5). It is hard not to read the symbolism of this moment in the Easter narrative and it is one of MacMillan's most gestural moments, akin to the thirteen repeated chords of *The Confession of Isobel Gowdie* and the 'violent shuddering' of 'I thirst' from *Seven Last Words from the Cross*. If for the most part *The World's Ransoming* has been 'a passionate rhapsody, inspired by Maundy Thursday, yet universalised in grief', then it takes a sinister and more individualistic turn at its very end, leaving none in doubt as to what will come next.[14]

Triduum II: Concerto for Cello and Orchestra (1996)

If *The World's Ransoming* is an essay in sustained melancholy, a poignant representation of all Maundy Thursday signifies for Christians, then the Cello Concerto is a bleak but multi-facetted response to Good Friday and the apex of the Christian year. For if *The World's Ransoming* is a 'passionate rhapsody' then the Cello concerto takes the same strands but weaves a fabric that is much

---

[12]   MacMillan, programme note to *The World's Ransoming*.

[13]   The cube used is often referred to as an 'Ustvolskaya Cube' after the Russian composer Galina Ustvolskaya (1919–2006) who used the instrument in a variety of works. For more information see http://ustvolskaya.org/eng/precision.php (accessed 9 March 2018). MacMillan has spoken warmly about Ustvolskaya's work throughout his career.

[14]   Nicholas Williams, 'Acts of Grace', *The Musical Times*, vol. 140, no. 1866 (Spring 1999), 45.

Example 5.5   Bars 434–38 of *The World's Ransoming* showing final phrase of cor
anglais with accompanying large plywood cube

more detailed, more colourful and more dramatic. It is the 'emotional heart of the triptych', an emotive and personal take on Good Friday which MacMillan imbues with his own reading and the significance of the events portrayed.[15] The work was first performed by the LSO, with the celebrated Russian cellist Mstislav Rostropovich (the work's dedicatee) as soloist, conducted by Colin Davis at the Barbican, London, in October 1996.

How the commission of the Cello Concerto came into being is an interesting story, as it shows how quickly MacMillan had become an international figure and how much of this was on the back of the continued success of *Veni, Veni, Emmanuel*. It was during MacMillan's visit in 1994 to Washington for the US premiere of the percussion concerto that the composer first met Rostropovich, who was conducting the work. As MacMillan recalled in 1999: 'I didn't know anything about him ... I just assumed that he would behave like a big star and wouldn't be very interesting. But from the first second I met him I could feel this huge kind of personable warmth ... he was friendly, took us to his house ... and shared lots of fascinating memories with insights about his time in the Soviet Union.'[16] This convivial evening shaped the composition of *Triduum*, as Rostropovich finished the meal by stating 'I'd like you to write me not just a piece but two pieces' and from this came commissions that resulted in the Cello Concerto and the last work of the triptych, Symphony: 'Vigil'.[17]

---

[15]   Weitzman, 'Triduum: MacMillan's Easter Triptych', 33.

[16]   Jaffé, 'James MacMillan'. It's not clear from this interview whether MacMillan actually meant 'wouldn't be very interesting' or 'wouldn't be very interested': it is hard to believe that an artist of the calibre and experience of Rostropovich, who had worked with composers such as Prokofiev, Shostakovich and Britten and had lived through Stalinist Russian 'wouldn't be very interesting'.

[17]   Ibid.

The Cello Concerto is the most intense part of the *Triduum*, as to be expected when dealing with the dramatic and emotional highpoint of Holy Week, but it does not deal with the related events in the same monothematic way as in *The World's Ransoming*, rather here MacMillan features some of the most diverse and characterful music of the whole triptych. The expressive palette is varied, moving from grief to surprising optimism though moments of fragility, irony and devotion, it is also the work that pays the greatest homage to other composers and to MacMillan's extant compositions. It takes the musical ideas and techniques espoused by *The World's Ransoming* but fashions them into something more vivid, powerful and theatrical: it may not be a literal representation of Good Friday, but it is a work bound up in the significance and spectacle of that day.

Like many of MacMillan's later concerti, the Cello Concerto is in a three-movement form and was composed in full recognition of traditional models and attributes. Whereas *The World's Ransoming* questions the relationship between solo instrument and orchestra, the Cello Concerto is a bravura, virtuosic vehicle for its star soloist and is as indebted to its Romantic predecessors as *Inés de Castro* was to Verdi and Wagner. The first movement of the concerto is entitled 'The Mockery', taking its title from the derision of Jesus by Roman soldiers after his condemnation by Pontius Pilate and the similar events that occurred during the crucifixion.[18] The 'mocking' of the title is translated into an unusual musical atmosphere, as MacMillan describes in his programme note: 'the material ... is modelled on the comic songs of the Music Hall tradition, though the humour is predominantly black and sardonic in tone'.[19] The first occurrence of this 'black and sardonic' humour is in the allegro section (beginning at bar 34) with material marked *burlando* (mocking) and 'grotesque'; here MacMillan employs an orchestral combination of staccato piano, snare drum and muted brass (using the prominent 'wah-wah' mute which can create a sound not too dissimilar to a chorus of laughter) to accompany the agitated solo cello. Alongside this a rasping E♭ clarinet (the most piercing member of the clarinet family) sneers a countermelody 'bringing to mind the jeering expressions on the faces of Christ's tormentors

---

[18]   The mocking is mentioned in the Gospel of Luke: 'The soldiers also came up and mocked him. They offered him wine vinegar and said, "If you are the king of the Jews, save yourself."' (Luke 23:36–37, New International Version).

[19]   James MacMillan, programme note to the Cello Concerto, http://www.boosey. com/cr/music/James-MacMillan-Cello-Concerto/2478 (accessed 12 March 2018).

in Grünewald's great painting *Verspottung Christi*.[20] This opening allegro finds MacMillan reworking material from the Executioner's Song (Act II Scene 3) of *Inés de Castro*, with the parallels between tormenter and the tormented instantly apparent.

MacMillan draws on material from *Inés de Castro* at several points in the Cello Concerto, using not only the Executioner's Song, but also Pacheco's aria in Act II Scene 1 and the ironic waltz that grief-stricken Pedro enacts for the coronation of Inés's corpse in Act II Scene 4. In many ways it is no surprise that music from MacMillan's most substantial work at that time should seep into the *Triduum*, as the composition of the triptych followed hot on the heels of the opera. But MacMillan's inclusion of these self-quotations is not purely a by-product of intense composition, but rather making direct links between events and emotions portrayed in the two works. The parallels between the crowds who had mocked Inés at an earlier part of the opera and those who mocked Christ are obvious and MacMillan emphasises this by including a short waltz section, quoted directly from *Inés de Castro* (see Example 5.6).

The deeply ironic tone of 'The Mockery' brings to mind Dmitri Shostakovich at his most biting, and the prominent piano part and muted trumpets all nod towards the Russian composer. In an interview in 1998 MacMillan made a telling comment about Shostakovich: 'In many ways he's a traditional composer; he works with sonata form and sonata-type forms ... but there's something of his music that stares into that abyss.'[21] The idea of 'the abyss' is something MacMillan returns to again and again in interviews and has obvious religious connotations regarding the underworld or hell, however his reference to Shostakovich and the abyss suggests something more secular, perhaps referring to the evil the composer was subjected to during the Stalinist period.[22]

Like *The World's Ransoming*, the Cello Concerto relies on plainsongs associated with the day to provide the theological underpinning to the work, in 'The Mockery' MacMillan uses the chant *Crucem tuam adoramus* (O Lord,

---

[20]   Weitzman, 'Triduum: MacMillan's Easter Triptych', 33. Matthias Grünewald's work *Die Verspottung Christi* (The Mocking of Christ, 1503–05) is housed in the Alte Pinakothek in Munich.

[21]   Interview with James MacMillan, during the Second Annual Vancouver New Music Festival, 1998.

[22]   For more information on MacMillan and 'the abyss' see McGregor, 'James MacMillan: a conversation and a commentary', 97.

Example 5.6   *Inés de Castro* (bars 1147–52, Pedro and violin parts only) and
quotation in the Cello Concerto (bars 122–27, violin parts only)

your cross, we adore and glorify), an antiphon sung during the Mass of the
Presanctified on Good Friday (see Example 5.7).

The plainsong is featured throughout the first movement, often in an
ornamented, rhythmically diverse variant of the chant in the solo cello, similar
to the opening cor anglais melody and its relationship with *Pange lingua* in
The World's Ransoming. Although the plainsong can often be found in the
solo instrument, MacMillan also reserves this material for 'fragments of a full-
throated chorale' in the brass which disrupt the cello line with dramatic force
towards the end of the movement.[23] The final interjection of the chant finds a
fortissimo climax before the cello is left swirling over a low double-bass pedal,
repeating and fading into the distance.

The second movement, 'The Reproaches', is the most emotional but
universal part of the concerto and finds MacMillan at his most radiant and
heartfelt, in a very traditional slow movement. Again, a plainsong features at
the core of the music, here the chant of the movement's title, with its stark
opening lines: 'My people, what have I done to you? How have I offended
you? Answer me!' Unlike the opening of 'The Mockery', MacMillan offers the
chant with very little elaboration, accompanied by *tremolando* violins, celeste
and harp: it is unabashed and presented without substantial commentary and

---

23   MacMillan, programme note to the Cello Concerto.

Example 5.7   *Crucem tuam adoramus* plainsong

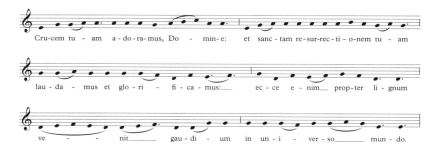

is the most earnest of MacMillan's plainsong quotations in the entirety of the *Triduum*. Although the *Reproaches* forms the theological underpinning to the second movement, it is the inclusion of a second quotation that gives this music its human and most poignant element. MacMillan includes the Scottish Presbyterian hymn-tune *Dunblane Cathedral*, known more widely as the hymn 'Far round the world thy children sing their song' (see Example 5.8), firstly in the horns (bars 64–73) in the middle of a busy orchestral texture, before a chromatic variation marked 'tutti feroce e ardente' (everyone fiercely and with passion, bars 105–16) heralds a return to the opening instrumentation and sonorities as the movement ends.[24]

The inclusion of a hymn-tune is not too dissimilar to that of a plainsong (though from a different Christian tradition) and the transformations to which MacMillan subjects his borrowed material is no different to similar procedures in this work and others. However, it is the inclusion of this particular tune and the significance of both the tune's title and associated words that gives the movement its poignancy and contemporary relevance. On 13 March 1996 (during the composition of the *Triduum*) a local man, Thomas Hamilton, entered Dunblane Primary School and shot dead sixteen children and a teacher before killing himself. It remains to this day the deadliest mass

---

[24]   *Dunblane Cathedral* was written by Dr Archie Fairbairn Barnes (1878–1960) who spent time as headmaster of Queen Victoria School in Dunblane, Stirlingshire in the early twentieth century (for more information see https://hymnary.org/tune/dunblane_cathedral, accessed 27 March 2018).

Example 5.8   *Dunblane Cathedral* hymn-tune

shooting in British history and led to two new Firearms Acts banning the majority of private ownership of handguns. The tragedy left an indelible mark on MacMillan and resulted not only in the inclusion of this hymn-tune in the Cello Concerto, but also *A Child's Prayer* (1996), one of MacMillan's most performed choral works.

In the programme note to the Cello Concerto, MacMillan mentions the inclusion in an understated fashion with no reference to any extra-musical significance: it is at odds with his description of his plainsong usage, which he describes in detail with all its associations and implications. Whether in 1996 it was too raw for the composer to go into any detail about this event, or whether it was seen as bad taste is unclear, but there is no doubt as to the importance of this material being including in the concerto. MacMillan emphasises the link with the massacre by alluding to similar themes from his earlier work, in this case Pacheco's aria from Scene 1 Act II of *Inés de Castro*, which itself was a quotation from MacMillan's setting of William Soutar's 'The Children' (see Example 4.7). The quotation is reserved for the glockenspiel (an instrument associated with childhood music-making in Britain and with obvious timbral similarities to a children's music box), accompanied by harp and celeste, providing a heart-wrenching accompaniment to the final iteration of the plainchant and the end of the movement.

The third movement, 'Dearest Wood and Dearest Iron', takes its title from the plainsong on which the music is based, *Crux fidelis* (Faithful Cross) with its final lines of 'dearest wood and dearest iron, dearest weight is hung on thee'. The *Crux Fidelis* is sung during the ceremony of the Adoration of the Cross on Good Friday, immediately after the *Reproaches*, and directs the worshippers to the cross in commemoration of the Lord's Passion (see Example 5.9).

As with *The World's Ransoming*, MacMillan alludes to the shape of the work in the programme note, stating: 'The skeleton of the structure is a strict series of episodes with the plainsong providing a recurring refrain.'[25] The movement covers similar ground to its predecessors with the solo cello's opening line recalling its first appearance in 'The Mockery', though now in longer note-values accompanied by a portentous orchestration of thundersheet, piano clusters and *col legno* (played with the back of the bow) lower strings. Akin to the previous movements, MacMillan reserves a full statement of the plainsong for the climax of the work: as the solo cello reaches one of its highest notes (bar 142) the orchestra responds with a full-bodied rendition of the chant, *fortissimo* and dramatic.[26] As the drama subsides and the opening sonorities return, MacMillan reintroduces the large plywood cube from *The World's Ransoming*, but now accompanied by a large metal bar – if the corresponding passage in the earlier piece was a suggestion of what was to come, this gesture in the concerto leave little doubt to the events that have occurred. The cello ends the work beyond its highest register, whirling round a repeated figure, improvising in a fleeting fashion, quickly dissipating and disappearing.

Triduum III: Symphony: 'Vigil' (1997)

The final work in the *Triduum* is the most substantial, the most dramatic and possibly the most bewildering of the triptych, dwarfing the other two in terms of its length, scope and ambition (it runs to nearly 50 minutes in performance). It is the work that relates to the Easter Vigil (the ceremony that is the culmination of Holy Week and is held in the hours of darkness between sunset on Holy Saturday and sunrise on Easter Day) and by its very nature deals with the journey from darkness to light which the service traditionally represents. Although the Cello Concerto might contain some of the bleakest moments of the *Triduum*, the Symphony undeniably is the darkest, most sombre and most unforgiving work, using its extensive canvas to explore these shadowy hues to its fullest. It is a work that is full of questions, but one that gives few answers, and, for a piece that deals primarily with the resurrection, there is little in the way of continued celebration or optimism. The Symphony

---

25   MacMillan, programme note to the Cello Concerto.

26   Weitzman refers to this moment in the orchestra as 'like the yelling of a mob at a football match'. (Weitzman, 'Triduum: MacMillan's Easter Triptych', 34.) Perhaps not the most appropriate metaphor, but no doubt one that MacMillan would approve of.

Example 5.9   *Crux Fidelis* plainsong

was commissioned by the LSO and first performed by them at the Barbican, London, in September 1997, conducted by Rostropovich.

Weitzman refers to the Symphony as 'the most intentionally unrefined part of the triptych', and there is certainly something unrestrained if not prolix about the work with its Mahlerian dimensions and ambition.[27] The first movement is entitled 'Light', though paradoxically (according to the composer) 'it's actually about 95% dark ... it's only towards the end that there are these flickers of light'.[28] It is the most concise of the Symphony's three movements (and the shortest) and has a singularity of mood and design that is perhaps missing in the later sections. The title of the movement comes from the Easter Vigil, as the ceremony is often referred to as 'The Service of Light' (though, strictly speaking, that is the first part of the service only), with fire being an important aspect of the service, through the lighting of the Easter fires and the blessing of the Paschal candle. MacMillan stresses the importance of these aspects in his programme note to the work: 'The initial inspiration for Symphony: "Vigil" came through the potential interplay of elements of fire and water, which are central to the liturgy of the Easter Vigil.'[29] It is a movement that begins in absolute darkness (which MacMillan tellingly refers to as a 'sepulchral dark') with divided lower strings setting the tone for a striking introduction, and murky instrumental colours dominating the opening

---

[27]   Weitzman, 'Triduum: MacMillan's Easter Triptych', 34.

[28]   Johnson, [untitled], 30. MacMillan has also referred to the movement as being '99% dark' (Johnson and Sutton, 'Raising Sparks: On the Music of James MacMillan', 32).

[29]   James MacMillan, programme note to Symphony: 'Vigil', http://www.boosey.com/cr/music/James-MacMillan-Symphony-Vigil/771 (accessed 26 March 2018).

section (in fact the violins are not present in 'Light' at all).[30] The darkness that MacMillan envisages for the opening of the Symphony is all-pervasive, as he reiterated in 2010: it is 'about making a dark, dark world palpable in sound, and the dark world in that symphony is certainly the world of death, the world of a tomb'.[31]

As the culmination of the *Triduum* (both musically and theologically), MacMillan alludes to the previous two works in 'Light' so as to emphasise their importance in the Easter narrative: the cor anglais enters in bar 52 with the same phrase from *The World's Ransoming* (bars 8–20, see Example 5.3) now accompanied by quiet, staccato chords from the low woodwind and brass. The solo cello from the concerto enters to duet with the cor anglais in bar 58 and both reprise earlier material against ominous percussion and piano effects (see Example 5.10).

It is following the duet that the first piece of plainchant is heard in the Symphony, this time a tiny but significant two-note motif known as *Lumen Christi* (Light of Christ) which is sung three times during The Service of Light as the Paschal candle proceeds through the church.[32] MacMillan chooses to have this chant performed by an off-stage brass quintet, in a free tempo, quiet and distant (see Example 5.11). It is performed twice in 'Light', firstly in slowly moving chords, secondly with characteristic MacMillan ornamentation, with the third iteration saved for the second movement.

The 'flickers of light' that MacMillan refers to at the end of the movement are provided by the piano (then moving to celeste), flutes and metallic percussion which begin their material in bar 99. This new instrumental group does provide a textural and timbral contrast to the music that has preceded it, and, if not giving a radiant and pervasive light, they do give the first suggestion of some hope and some sense of light in the all-encompassing darkness.

The second movement takes its title from the Easter Proclamation, Exsultet, which is the culmination of The Service of Light, here MacMillan borrowing the final line 'Tuba insonet salutaris' (sound the trumpet of salvation). The movement has a theatrical element, with the previously off-stage brass quintet moving to the auditorium at five different locations, 'representing the trumpets of salvation' and repeating a simple rising figure three times that is

---

30   McGregor, 'James MacMillan: a conversation and a commentary', 85.

31   Ibid., 85.

32   MacMillan wrote a short piano 'sketch' for the Symphony entitled *Lumen Christi* in 1997. This material, based on the eponymous chant, found a home in the celeste solo at the end of the second movement.

Example 5.10   Duet between cor anglais and solo cello in Symphony: 'Vigil' (bars
                    58–61, cor anglais and solo cello only)

Example 5.11   *Lumen Christi* plainchant and first quotation in off-stage brass quintet
                    (bars 82–84)

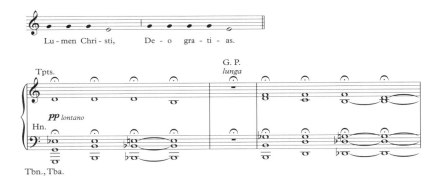

answered by swirling woodwinds and fierce orchestral brass.[33] The movement
features much 'senza misura' or free-time material (which apparently caused
Rostropovich some issues[34]) with choirs of brass, woodwind and percussion
all jostling for prominence (MacMillan continues to omit strings, with the
violas and cellos now joining the violins on the sidelines). The most striking
moment of the movement is the very end, where after a dramatic full-orchestral

---

33   MacMillan, programme note to Symphony: 'Vigil'.

34   'There are in fact things in it [the Symphony] that he [Rostropovich] maybe felt
slightly uneasy about – you see it was the first time he had ever seen senza misura
markings, and having to give cues to off-stage brass.' (Jaffé, 'James MacMillan').

crescendo a solo celeste is revealed, giving the third iteration of the *Lumen Christi* material, instructed to 'fade away to nothing like a child's musical box.'[35] In true MacMillan fashion, this material is savagely interrupted three times by grotesque orchestral chords (including the previously off-stage brass) before leaving the lone celeste to finish its forlorn epilogue to the movement. The similarity in design to the end of 'The Reproaches' from the Cello Concerto is obvious, with the loss of innocence suggested by both the musical material and the instruments of the earlier work, replicated here for all to see.

Weitzman is critical of 'Tuba insonet salutaris', referring to is as 'uneven and undeniably perplexing', though he does not go into any great detail. Certainly there is a rough-hewn element to the movement, with great blocks of sound colliding, with hocketing woodwind often interspersed with free-time brass chords and percussion episodes. The omission of the majority of the string section gives the movement a more abrasive texture and the music is often reminiscent of great twentieth-century sacred works such as Stravinsky's *Symphony of Psalms* (1930) and Messiaen's *Et exspecto resurrectionem mortuorum* (1964). There is, perhaps, less subtlety in the movement than in the previous one, with each gesture seeming more extreme than at any other point in the *Triduum*, with the final *Lumen Christi* appearance the most pronounced.

The final movement of the Symphony is entitled 'Water' and is the most substantial of the three, being longer than the previous two combined. The water of the title comes from the final part of the Easter Vigil service, as MacMillan confirms: 'There's a baptismal aspect to the vigil and a sense of new life beginning which I wanted to capture.'[36] MacMillan emphasises the 'baptismal aspect' by including the antiphon associated with this section of the vigil, *Vidi aquam* (I saw water) and reintroduces the strings, particularly the violins, which have a long introductory section in their highest register, representing a new sound and a new beginning. For MacMillan this movement is the climax of the journey from darkness to light which this symphony represents, with the culmination of the work being the 'idea of new life, the dying of one thing, the beginning of something else and the transformation of one thing into another'.[37] This eucharistic element is nothing new in MacMillan's work – *The Confession of Isobel Gowdie* and *Veni, Veni, Emmanuel* deal with similar themes in different ways – but here, at the conclusion of the *Triduum*, it is of utmost importance and is what the previous two hours of

---

[35]   Taken from the score of Symphony: 'Vigil', published by Boosey & Hawkes.

[36]   Johnson and Sutton, 'Raising Sparks: On the Music of James MacMillan', 23.

[37]   Ibid., 23.

music have been moving towards. The Symphony ends with celestial sounds and radiant sonorities, with high string chords gradually thinning to leave a single pitch accompanied by antique cymbals and triangle, these finally surrendering to silence and the promise of what is to come.

The *Triduum* is possibly the highpoint of James MacMillan's orchestral composition: certainly he would never cover such thematically related material on quite such a broad canvas again. It is the apex of MacMillan's exploration of the Passion, and though he returned to this narrative again and again over the next twenty years, it was never in the detail and drama of the triptych, and never at such length. It is worth remembering how unusual it was for such a relatively young composer to be given such an orchestral opportunity in the late 1990s. Few British composers could hope to have had the exposure that was granted to MacMillan and the possibility to work on a personal project in such a fashion. The *Triduum* is a work of consolidation and culmination: the end of one period of composition, but suggesting the beginnings of something new. Although the Cello Concerto and the Symphony have extra-musical programmes (and these are totally explicit), the very fact that they have generic titles points towards a change of direction in MacMillan's orchestral work in the new millennium and the move toward greater abstraction in his oeuvre.

Quickening (1998)

By far the most substantial work to follow straight after the *Triduum* was the oratorio *Quickening*, a joint commission from the BBC and the Philadelphia Orchestra in the United States that MacMillan wrote in 1998. *Quickening* is a 48-minute piece for orchestra, large symphony chorus, children's choir and solo vocal quartet that formed 'easily the most ambitious' of the new commissions for the 1999 BBC Proms.[38] The work was first performed in September of that year at the Royal Albert Hall in London by the Hilliard Ensemble, the trebles of Westminster Cathedral Choir and the BBC Symphony Chorus and Orchestra, conducted by Sir Andrew Davis.

Quickening was the second time that MacMillan had collaborated with English poet Michael Symmons Roberts (1963–), the first occasion being the song cycle *Raising Sparks* that MacMillan had composed for the Nash Ensemble the previous year. The two men first met in 1995 whilst Symmons Roberts had been a producer for the BBC's religious broadcast department

---

38   Andrew Clements, 'Composition by numbers', *The Guardian* (7 September 1999).

and had interviewed MacMillan for a documentary entitled 'Contemporaries of Christ', which featured artists 'who were around the same age as Christ at the time of his crucifixion, to get their take on the story of the Passion'.[39] They quickly formed an enduring partnership, built round similarly held beliefs and passions, but one focussing primarily on a shared Catholic faith. MacMillan had been searching for a new source of texts, as he commented in 1999: 'The choice of text is very important to me. I seem to have been seeking a kind of textural anchor. I feel Michael is just that and it is a very important development.'[40] Symmons Roberts has provided the text for several high-profile works, including the operas *The Sacrifice* (2005–06) and *Clemency* (2010), the dramatic scena *Parthenogenesis* (2000) and two substantial choral works, *The Birds of Rhiannon* (2001) and *Sun-Dogs* (2006) – it is a lasting and powerful collaboration that has characterised MacMillan's output in the first decade of the new millennium.

Quickening sets four poems from a five-poem sequence entitled 'Quickening' from Symmons Roberts's 1997 collection *Raising Sparks* – 'Incarnadine', 'Midwife', 'Poppies' and 'Living Water' (another sequence entitled 'Smithereens' from the collection formed the text for the earlier song cycle). The oratorio is an exploration and celebration of birth, new life and new beginnings and sprang from the shared event of fatherhood that both MacMillan and Symmons Roberts had recently experienced, as MacMillan confirmed: 'Michael and I realised that there wasn't a lot in our culture which marked parenthood ... an overwhelming, transformative experience'.[41] The title of the work refers to the stage in pregnancy where a woman can first feel the movements of the foetus, 'the quickening seed that will become ripe grain' as the composer recalled in 2005.[42] Symmons Roberts's poems 'juxtapose mysticism and hyper-realism', moving swiftly from a dense, vivid language of metaphor and allusion to stark descriptions of human events and existence, all against the backdrop of a rich Christian narrative.[43] The sacred aspect of the work, though present from the

---

[39]   Rhiannon Harries, 'How We Met: James MacMillan & Michael Symmons Roberts', *The Independent* (12 April 2008).

[40]   Shirley Ratcliffe, 'Cantus in Choro: MacMillan 2', *Choir & Organ* (July/August 1999), 39.

[41]   Lynne Walker, programme note to *Quickening*, *Darkness into Light: The Music of James MacMillan*, (accompanying brochure to BBC Festival, 2005).

[42]   Ibid.

[43]   Paul Spicer, programme note to *Quickening*, http://www.boosey.com/cr/music/James-MacMillan-Quickening/3599 (accessed 27 March 2018).

outset, is really only explicit in the final movement, 'Living Water', with its Baptismal and Pentecostal associations brought to the fore. MacMillan has been coy as to whether the work is sacred or secular, referring to the 'universality' of the text: 'the words are flexible and each time people will come to them in different ways as I did'.[44] Certainly the 'universality' that MacMillan refers to is played out through a broader concern than the subject matter: *Quickening* deals with struggle, war and ultimately death in its four movements and the final music is as redemptive as any MacMillan had composed to that point.

The first movement, 'Incarnadine', is the most mystical of the four and the 'love's alchemy' of conception calls for a striking orchestration of steel drums and tuned gongs to enhance the divided cellos, piano and harp. The chorus enters with the Lord's Prayer in Aramaic, chanted quietly in free time, a distinct representation of the 'Babel songs which none can recognise' that features in Symonns Roberts's poem.[45] In the first three movements, the vocal quartet perform separately to the chorus, accompanied by the children's choir, a chamber organ and reduced orchestration (one of many nods to Benjamin Britten's *War Requiem*); a more intimate sound-world to accentuate the change from third- to first-person in the poem.

The second movement, 'Midwife', finds the piece lurching to a very different mood and emphasis, with the pains and worries of childbirth brought to the fore. There is a repetitiveness to MacMillan's text-setting (both for the chorus and quartet) with key phrases such as 'she washes the hands' and 'frogs' legs cocked to jump' reiterated obsessively as if to sooth the nerves of the would-be father. The biblical allusions are clearer, with the final lines comparing a midwife's act with both Pilate and Herod, giving a chilling sense of foreboding to the end of the movement.

The third movement, 'Poppies', is the dramatic heart of *Quickening*, Symmons Roberts choosing to move his analogy to war and the battle between life and death. MacMillan returns to *burlando* material not too dissimilar to passages in *Inés de Castro* and the Cello Concerto which bear the same description, and the movement has a violence and drive not present in the previous movements. MacMillan continues the self-quotation and self-recycling that had characterised his works since *Tryst* by including a short

---

44   Ratcliffe, 'Cantus in Choro: MacMillan 2', 40.

45   According to the then chorus master of the BBC Symphony Chorus, Stephen Jackson, MacMillan had heard the Lord's Prayer in Aramaic 'on a Radio 1 documentary on world music and had taken it down phonetically' (Ratcliffe, 'Cantus in Choro: MacMillan 2', 41).

section of the recent anthem *A New Song* (1997, see chapter seven). This setting of Psalm 96 ('O sing unto the Lord a new song'), with its references to 'salvation', 'judgement' and 'righteousness', chime with the emotional kernel of *Quickening* and Symmons Roberts's striking lines 'Before the dead turn cold, the quickening has struck fields red and women heavy' (see Example 5.12).

The final movement, 'Living Water', begins with the soft hum of temple bowls, returning the piece to the mysticism of the opening, suggested by Symmons Roberts's lines 'It is a charmer's gift ... to stroke a bowl's bronze rim ... until a clear note rises from the hum.' Now, the vocal roles are switched with the quartet taking centre stage and the chorus adopting the first-person voice, entering with vivacity and exuberance with the lines 'we dance to its resonance' as the movement heads towards its climax. Following a thrilling orchestral crescendo, the chorus returns to the babbling of 'Incarnadine', now representing the 'dumb choirs at Pentecost', this material passing to the children's choir as the temple bowls and steel drums return for a characteristic, mesmeric MacMillan ending.

Quickening owes much to the *War Requiem* (as do most late-twentieth-century works in this mould), not only in the use of spatial and vocal effects and the delineation of voices and 'characters', but in the very ambition and scope of the work. It deals with weighty subject matter that is at the heart of our very existence, it is a work that asks difficult questions and urges the audience to engage fully with this discussion. It owes much to the 'safe 20th-century styles' of not just Britten, but of works ranging from Walton's *Belshazzar's Feast* (1931) and Tippett's *A Child of Our Time* (1941) through to Penderecki's *St Luke Passion* (1966) with its babbling, mummering, shouting and multiple vocal groups.[46]

Quickening also received the mixed critical response that had greeted MacMillan's work since *Inés de Castro*, particularly in the English press. Though there were largely positive reviews from *The Independent* ('a brilliant, dancing evocation of the Pentecost') and *The Telegraph* ('this is another superbly composed score from one of our most ardent musical communicators'),[47] there was a torrent of scorn and derision from *The Guardian* and *The Times* with any shackles the reviewers may have kept on following *Inés* now firmly off.

---

46   Johnson, 'James MacMillan', 2.

47   Keith Potter, 'MacMillan's thriller', *The Independent* (8 September 1999). David Fanning, 'The whistling of temple bowls', *The Daily Telegraph* (6 September 1999). Potter has been a long-time admirer of MacMillan's music since his 1990 article in *The Musical Times* onwards.

Example 5.12 Similarities in material from *Quickening* (bars 98–102, chorus parts only) and *A New Song* (bars 55–59, choir parts only)

Andrew Clements, writing in *The Guardian* was by far the most vehement, referring to the work as 'a ragbag of grandiloquent gestures, academic choral writing and kitschy effects', 'second-hand atmospherics'; the piece was 'a massive disappointment'.[48] His final sentence was perhaps the most cutting: 'When MacMillan gets back to writing what he really feels, rather than what

48   Clements, 'Composition by numbers'.

he thinks the audience will lap up most eagerly, maybe he'll become a serious composer again.'[49]

The suggestion that MacMillan was pandering to the audience is an *idée fixe* amongst critics, one that continues to the current day, an assumption that continued success breeds a familiarity and contempt for originality and innovation. Though there are plenty of moments in *Quickening* that are warmer, more accessible and easier to understand than in works such as *Tryst* or *The Confession of Isobel Gowdie*, it is hard to imagine the oratorio as a work an 'audience will lap up'. Both the words and the music have jagged edges throughout, with the middle two movements generating much discomfort and anxiety. It seems that MacMillan was damned if he did and damned if he didn't: *Inés de Castro* was panned for being too grotesque and brutal, with little in the way of light and shade, whereas *Quickening* finds the critics bemoaning MacMillan's drive for audience approval over compositional integrity. Certainly, *Quickening* is not a work without issues, but it hardly warranted the chorus of disapproval that the English press gave it, suggesting a deeper, more subjective narrative at play. Much of this may be due to 'too much, too soon', with new commission after new commission reaching the critics' ears from all the major orchestras and ensembles, leading to a sense of 'MacMillan fatigue', or the assumption that the composer was being commissioned too much, at the expense of other (perhaps English) composers. However, some of the particular vitriol against MacMillan and *Quickening* may have been a direct result of the composer's foray into the religio-political sphere, with a talk he had given at the Edinburgh Festival a month earlier: his infamous 'Scotland's Shame' lecture.

---

[49]   Ibid.

6 | *Raising Sparks* – 'Scotland's Shame', Politics and *A Scotch Bestiary*

'My three kids were so terrified by the sequence of sullen visitors, they were packed off with the childminder' wrote James MacMillan in 2006, a stark reminiscence by the composer of the eye-of-the-storm that had greeted the MacMillan family in August 1999 after the speech he had given at the Edinburgh Festival days earlier.[1] This speech, entitled 'Scotland's Shame', is one of the most decisive events in MacMillan's career and one that defines him as much, if not more, than *The Confession of Isobel Gowdie* or *Seven Last Words from the Cross*: it was a watershed moment in the composer's career and one that has had a direct influence on the music he has written and the political opinions he holds in its aftermath. But what was quite so incendiary about the speech and why have its repercussions continued to be felt in MacMillan's work to this day?

In the loosest terms, 'Scotland's Shame' highlights the sectarianism in modern-day Scotland and the discrimination and prejudice against Catholics in many walks of everyday life. It is a passionate but reasoned polemic suggesting that the age-old Protestant–Catholic tensions that existed in Scotland since the Reformation were still very much present at the turn of the new millennium. The speech deals head on with anti-Catholicism and suggests that 'Scotland is guilty of "sleep-walking" bigotry' in a more pluralist and secular age.[2] His speech covers what would become familiar political ground for MacMillan, including faith schools, nationalism (particularly the Scottish National Party, which later became a *bête noire* for the composer) and the growing secularisation of society. Along with a startling analogy between

---

[1] James MacMillan, 'How I rattled the deniers', *The Guardian* (7 August 2006).

[2] James MacMillan, 'Scotland's Shame', in Tom Devine, ed., *Scotland's Shame? Bigotry and Sectarianism in Modern Scotland* (Edinburgh: Mainstream, 2000), 15. MacMillan's speech and a collection of essays in response by many of Scotland's leading academics and sociologists was published here, highlighting the impact 'Scotland's Shame' had in certain Scottish circles and the debate that ensued.

the Reformation and the Cultural Revolution in China, MacMillan suggests the issue is 'as endemic as it is second nature' and places the problem across all areas of society including the sporting arena and the media. It is perhaps the reference to the latter that caused the greatest consternation and explains why the reaction to 'Scotland's Shame' rumbled on for weeks in the Scottish broadsheet newspapers.[3]

Certainly, the speech opened up a Pandora's box that many Scots either presumed or hoped had been shut by previous generations, and it was not helped by having the issue discussed in such a public (and international) forum, meaning the subject could not easily be sidestepped or dismissed. To this end, the speech was a success, but as the quote from MacMillan at the beginning of this chapter illustrates, it was not without its personal toll on the composer. MacMillan's 2006 article in *The Guardian*, 'How I rattled the deniers', is full of colourful recollections of what was no doubt a difficult and turbulent period that saw the composer move from the arts section of the national newspapers to the front page, with loaded references to 'Catholic Street Marches' and 'giving succour to the IRA'.[4] If MacMillan's relationship with his homeland had blossomed since his return in 1988, then it took a turn for the worse in August 1999, the resonances of which are still being felt in both his politics and compositions.

Perhaps one of the issues with 'Scotland's Shame' was that no one was expecting a composer to have such a strident opinion, certainly on a subject that was outside the usual remit of what an artist might say. Even in an age of decreased exposure of serious classical music, a composer might still be given a soap-box every so often to discuss relevant issues, and in this respect MacMillan was following an illustrious line of British composers including Ralph Vaughan Williams, Benjamin Britten and Peter Maxwell Davies. The key difference is the subject concerned: one might regularly find Maxwell Davies discussing music education in schools or cuts to arts funding, but rarely a topic that affected wider society, and even more rarely on a contentious and sensitive subject with such potential ramifications. MacMillan has certainly spoken often on music-related issues, but he has equally regularly had his say on larger national and social matters including sectarianism in Scottish football (2009),[5] the Papal

---

3   Ibid., 15.

4   MacMillan, 'How I rattled the deniers'.

5   A large portion of 'Scotland's Shame' explains the problems of sectarianism in Scottish football, particularly regarding the heated relationship between Glasgow Rangers and Glasgow Celtic (the team that MacMillan supports). Rangers are

visit of Pope Benedict XVI (2010), more of which in chapter ten, and the Scottish Independence Referendum (2014). It is a mark of the high esteem in which MacMillan was held by the Scottish establishment that he not only was given the platform to deliver the speech, but that his words carried so far and with such potency.

However, 'Scotland's Shame' was not without precedent in MacMillan's career: he had been politically active since his mid-teens ('I joined the Young Communist League in 1974, when I was just 14') and had been chairman of a local Labour Party branch in his early twenties.[6] By the time he was reaching national attention in the late 1980s and early 1990s he was regularly defined by his 'socialist political commitment', his 'passionate devotion to the far left' or his 'strong left-wing political convictions'; for his first period of success these monikers greatly outweighed any references to his faith.[7] These political influences were felt in his compositions as well, most noticeably with the trio of works inspired by Liberation Theology (see chapter two): *Búsqueda* (1988), *Cantos Sagrados* (1989) and *Catherine's Lullabies* (1990). However, MacMillan had first sought to express his politics in music during his student days with the now withdrawn work *Songs of a Just War* (1984) for soprano and small ensemble.[8] This work set texts by Chilean poet Pablo Neruda, three 'ballads' by Chinese poet Tsou-ti-fan (both in English translation) and 'The Children' by William Soutar (see chapters three and four), and was first performed in May 1986. In MacMillan's PhD commentary he explains his thoughts behind the piece:

> The work ... is a setting of texts by three poets from different parts of the globe, but all writing from similar experiences of the tragedy of war and from a shared conviction in the necessity of fighting injustice or oppression. Therefore this

---

traditionally seen as the Protestant club of Glasgow with Celtic as the Catholic. Though most large cities have fierce football rivalries based on economic or political grounds (such as Everton and Liverpool or Atlético and Real Madrid) few have one based on a religious divide.

6   James MacMillan, 'Unthinking dogmatism', *The Spectator* (January 2008), 47.

7   Reade, 'From socialism to salvation'; Greenfield, 'An echo of the pure sound of prayer'; Purser, *Scotland's Music*, 274.

8   MacMillan withdrew *Songs of a Just War* in 1993, later referring to the work as 'too unwieldy, just an awful lot packed into it, it was nearly 30 minutes' (Cooke, interview with James MacMillan, 29 March 2017).

work is political in the sense that the three poets were associated with 'The Left' in their respective countries.[9]

MacMillan here clearly identifies himself with 'The Left' in his discussion and sows the seeds of his Liberation Theology works by suggesting that the very idea of a 'just war' leads 'one's thoughts ... inevitably ... to central America and South Africa'.[10]

One of MacMillan's most politically charged but least-known works is the wind band piece *Sowetan Spring* that he wrote in 1990 for the wind section of the Royal Scottish National Orchestra (RSNO). The work is political for two reasons: firstly because it was written to celebrate future South African leader Nelson Mandela's release from prison in February 1990, and thus incorporates fragments of the African liberation anthem *Nkosi Sikelel' iAfrika*; and secondly because the work is inspired by the techniques of Dutch composer Louis Andriessen, whose strong left-wing politics have been present in many of his mature works. In many ways *Sowetan Spring* is the most overtly political of MacMillan's works: both the title and the programme note are more explicit than any of the Liberation Theology pieces (which include politically engaged texts) and it is arguably the zenith of MacMillan's expression of his political views through music.

Dominic Wells breaks down MacMillan's works from this period into 'politically engaged' or 'politically themed' music, defining the former as 'music ... governed by a political commitment ... to actively promote social consciousness' and the latter as 'music which has a political subject, but ... has *not* been organised according to the political subject'.[11] In this distinction, *Songs of a Just War*, *Sowetan Spring* and the Liberation Theology works fall under the first category, and many of MacMillan's successful early-period, 'Scottish' pieces such as *Tuireadh* and *The Confession of Isobel Gowdie* come under the second; there is an extra-musical political element to these pieces, but the listener need not be aware of this element in order to appreciate the work. MacMillan has always been keen that his works do not seek to proselytise and has regularly written about music's need for autonomy from exterior forces, even if (ironically) a large portion of his published work has extra-musical subject matter or influences.

---

9   MacMillan, 'Music Composition', 33.

10   Ibid., 34.

11   Wells, 'James MacMillan: Retrospective Modernist', 347, 353.

The early 1990s was the apex of MacMillan's left-wing politics and politically themed music; from the middle of the decade onwards the political was replaced by the religious to the point where articles seldom mention anything to do with the composer's socialism or Marxism. There has been a sea-change in MacMillan's politics in the first decade of the twentieth-first century that has seen him move from the left to the right, often railing against many of the bodies and organisations that he had previously held in high esteem. The move from left to right is not unusual, even in the most vociferous of left-wing artists: as they become older, richer and more established, the transformation begins.[12] This change was forcefully revealed by MacMillan in a 2008 article in the right-wing magazine, *The Spectator*, entitled 'Unthinking dogmatism', in which he vehemently debunks his previous beliefs and associations.[13] Here he argues against the Labour Party, progressive liberalism, the left-wing media and the arts, with the last of these coming under the fiercest criticism. The main theme of 'Unthinking dogmatism' is a perceived attack on traditional and religious values by the left-leaning metropolitan artistic classes, with their 'destructive atheistic iconoclasm' opposed to 'traditional family and education, sexual mores, artistic aspirations [and] religious beliefs'.[14] The article is much more incendiary than 'Scotland's Shame' (though operating in a far less public arena) with MacMillan not mincing his words at any point, likening the left-controlled media and arts to a totalitarian state creating a 'secular priesthood.'[15] This was not the aim of old-style socialism, he argues, which tended to be morally and culturally conservative. The article is intended to shock (like many MacMillan articles from this period, particularly those he had previously written for the left-wing *Guardian*) and to rid the composer of an unwanted label, the final sentences making his stance clear:

> The destruction visited on schools and universities, the degradation of the media, the vulgarisation of culture, the deliberate and planned dismantling of

12   Although this is the case with many composers, it should be noted that other British composers of MacMillan's generation who shared similar left-wing ideals, such as Mark-Anthony Turnage (1960–) and Steve Martland (1954–2013) did not relinquish the political stance of their formative years.

13   The fierceness of MacMillan's tone in the article is striking, as fellow *Spectator* columnist (and Catholic) Damian Thompson put it: 'In person, MacMillan is gentle, but in print he can be ferocious.' ('MacMillan's loyalty', *The Spectator*, December 2010).

14   MacMillan, 'Unthinking dogmatism, *The Spectator* (January 2008), 47.

15   Ibid., 47.

the family – all of this is a result of liberalism, not socialism. I hope to God that
I don't see myself described as a liberal left-winger again.[16]

The question that springs from 'Unthinking dogmatism' is: what caused this
political volte-face? What caused a composer so closely associated with the left
to be criticising it in such a violent fashion? The answer is nuanced, and relates
to a variety of life events that MacMillan experienced in the period from
1995 to 2008, but forefront amongst these is the reaction in his homeland
to 'Scotland's Shame', quite possibly the catalyst to MacMillan's political
transformation in the early 2000s.

It is telling that in 'Scotland's Shame' in 1999 MacMillan refers to the
artistic world in positive terms, stating it 'is one arena where I have never
encountered anything approximating the visceral anti-Catholicism which so
disfigures many other walks of life in our society'.[17] By 'Unthinking dogmatism'
in 2008 this has changed entirely, with MacMillan asserting his 'revulsion'
for the same artistic circles with their 'eager acceptance of the new hectoring
political puerilities'.[18] His relationship with the arts had soured completely in
a nine-year period, with this relationship breakdown mirroring his political
conversion. In 2007 MacMillan suggested that 'Scotland's Shame' had 'divided
opinion about me in Scotland … to the extent that some people have a severe
dislike and regard me as a troublemaker rather than a composer'. He also
mentioned for the first time that his family were considering moving away from
their homeland (which, in the event, they never did).[19] Certainly the backlash
from the Edinburgh Festival speech hurt MacMillan deeply, but rather than
spurring him to compose political pieces in response, he sought to express his
faith in stronger and stronger terms, with the reaction to 'Scotland's Shame'
appearing to be more of an attack on the composer's religion, rather than on
him as an artist. If MacMillan's work from 1992 to 1999 had seen a gradual rise
in religious pieces and an increased commitment to religious concerns, by 2008
his output was almost entirely related to his faith (see Table 6.1).

Wells refers to MacMillan's change in politics as a shift from 'the
communist-inflected Christianity of his formative years' to 'a fervent advocacy
of the Catholic Church', and it is hard to disagree with this distinction. Few
artists or public figures have been as unequivocally supportive of the church

16   Ibid., 47.

17   MacMillan, 'Scotland's Shame', 14.

18   MacMillan, 'Unthinking dogmatism', 47.

19   Hallam, 'Conversation with James MacMillan', 28.

Table 6.1   Increasing use of religious themes in MacMillan's music after 'Scotland's Shame'

1999	Cello Sonata	No stated religious inspiration
	The Company of Heaven	A setting of *The Company of Heaven* by John Bell of the Iona Community
	Cumnock Fair	No stated religious inspiration
	Fanfare for the Reopening of the Scottish Parliament	No stated religious inspiration
	Heyoka Te Deum	Setting of *Te deum laudamus* in Latin and Lakota native Indian text
	Magnificat	Setting of Luke 1:46–55
	Symphony No. 2	No stated religious inspiration
2008	*Pascha nostrum immolatus est*	Communion motet for Easter Day
	Lux aeterna	Section of the *Missa pro defunctis*
	O	Advent antiphon
	Padre Pio's Prayer	Prayer attributed to Padre Pio (adapted by the composer)
	The Song of the Lamb	Setting of Revelation 15:2–4
	Lament of Mary, Queen of Scots	Robert Burns
	Os mutorum	Medieval chant from the Inchcolm Antiphoner
	Walfrid, On His Arrival At The Gates of Paradise	Relating to Celtic Football Club*
	Piano Concerto No. 3	Structure based on the Rosary

*   'Paradise' in this context is not related with the Christian heaven, but with the entrance to Celtic Park, the home of Celtic Football Club. Brother Walfrid (a Marist brother) was the founder of the club and MacMillan wrote this music for the unveiling of a statue.

as MacMillan (his devotion to his faith led to him being hailed 'Catholic of the year' in 2015 by *The Catholic Herald*).[20] Though it is wrong to suggest that MacMillan's faith was of secondary importance in his early years as a composer, it has certainly become exponentially more important as the composer's reputation has increased; whether this is due to a change in personal circumstances, or in society, is hard to ascertain, but MacMillan's 'fervent advocacy' of the church is in strong contrast to early interviews and articles which mention it fleetingly, if at all.

A Scotch Bestiary (2004)

When asked in 2007 whether 'Scotland's Shame' had affected his artistic process at the time, MacMillan replied: 'I don't think so, no ... apart from one piece that grew out of it'.[21] That piece was the organ concerto *A Scotch Bestiary*, which was commissioned for the inauguration of the new organ at the new Walt Disney Concert Hall in Los Angeles. This set of 'Enigmatic variations on a zoological carnival at a Caledonian exhibition' (as MacMillan subtitles the work) is one of the most colourful, humorous and baffling of MacMillan's pieces, but also one of the most satirical, responding in no uncertain terms to both 'Scotland's Shame' and the change in political views that crystallised in 'Unthinking dogmatism' four years later. The work was first performed in July 2004 by the Los Angeles Philharmonic, with Wayne Marshall as soloist, conducted by Finnish composer-conductor Esa-Pekka Salonen.

The unusual subtitle is explained by MacMillan in the programme note to the work: it 'follows in a tradition of musical portraiture set by Elgar, Saint-Saëns and Mussorgsky'.[22] The piece is a set of eight 'character portraits' of 'human archetypes and personalities encountered in Scottish life over the years', with the link to Elgar's *Enigma Variations* (1899) instantly apparent.[23] However, whereas Elgar's work was dedicated 'to my friends pictured within',

20   'The Holy Warrior with a baton', *The Catholic Herald* (17 December 2015).

21   Hallam, 'Conversation with James MacMillan', 27.

22   James MacMillan, programme note to *A Scotch Bestiary*, http://www.boosey.com/cr/music/James-MacMillan-A-Scotch-Bestiary/15163 (accessed 17 April 2018).

23   Ibid. It is worth noting that MacMillan had already composed his own 'pictures at an exhibition' in 1990 with the chamber ensemble piece ... *as others see us* ..., featuring 'sound paintings' of seven portraits hanging in the National Portrait Gallery in London, including Henry VIII, William Wordsworth and T. S. Eliot.

A Scotch Bestiary is far less friendly and flattering, depicting a grotesque set of characters (some human, some animal), all 'either directly or indirectly related to the sectarianism in Scotland debate'.[24] The work is a much more savage representation of animal species than Saint-Saëns's *The Carnival of the Animals* (1886), with MacMillan's assorted 'menagerie' given negative and derogatory characteristics such as 'The red-handed no-surrender, howler monkey' and 'The Reverend Cuckoo and his Parroting Chorus'. The link to Mussorgsky is clear from the onset, with the 'Promenade' from *Pictures at an Exhibition* (1874) being adapted by MacMillan to form the recurring refrain that features in the first of the work's two movements (see Example 6.1).

Whereas in *Pictures at an Exhibition*, Mussorgsky imagined himself touring a gallery of portraits, in *A Scotch Bestiary* MacMillan imagines the listener (or the composer) leafing through a book of zoological specimens, no doubt repulsed by the collection of ungainly creatures pictured within. The choice of the 'Promenade' theme is unusual: though the theme is stripped of its original pitch content, MacMillan keeps the rhythm and metre (although, as Example 6.1 shows, he amalgamates the two bars into one) thus making the original always evident to the listener. The refrains are in stark contrast to the kaleidoscopic episodes, full of verve and rhythmic vitality: they are mainly homophonic, understated and sound like a half-heard, muffled performance of Ravel's orchestration of *Pictures at an Exhibition*.

A Scotch Bestiary is in two parts, the first entitled 'The Menagerie, Caged', the second 'The Menagerie, Uncaged', with the first part featuring the bestiary of creatures in portrait, as the work's title suggests. MacMillan's variations differ from Elgar's in that MacMillan does not give any indication as to who the different animals represent: each has a cryptic title but does not feature the initials or pet-names of the *Enigma Variations*. However, as the years have passed the composer has given more information as to the identity of each caricature, and with each revelation *A Scotch Bestiary* becomes more and more a reaction to the controversies regarding 'Scotland's Shame'. The two variations that MacMillan has publicly revealed are the third, 'Her Serene and Ubiquitous Majesty, Queen Bee' and the seventh, 'The Reverend Cuckoo and his Parroting Chorus'. In an article in *The Spectator*, long-time MacMillan stalwart Damian Thompson 'outed' these as Scottish journalist and television presenter Kirsty Wark (well known to British audiences as the presenter of BBC Television's flagship current affairs programme, *Newsnight*) and 'Bishop Richard Holloway and his politically correct sycophants' (Holloway was former Primus of the

---

24   Wells, 'James MacMillan: Retrospective Modernist', 73.

Example 6.1   'Promenade' theme from Mussorgsky's *Pictures at an Exhibition* and
the opening of *A Scotch Bestiary* (bar 2, organ part only)

Scottish Episcopal Church and liberal in his views on both church and state).[25]
MacMillan's issue with Wark stems largely from her pejorative views on
Catholic schools which were aired in the early 2000s; MacMillan responded to
this in print in an article entitled 'Dangers of Wark's Whinge' in *The Scotsman*
in 2005 (the year after the first performance of *A Scotch Bestiary*) in which he
covers similar ground to 'Scotland's Shame'.[26]

Some of the episodes are less specifically identifiable, such as the more
general second and fourth movements, 'Reptiles and Big Fish (in a small pond)'
and 'Scottish Patriots'. The former may well refer to the Scottish media and
political classes, though the same may apply to the latter, which features 'a
discarded fanfare for the opening of the new Scottish Parliament'.[27] The final

---

25   Thompson, 'MacMillan's loyalty', 32.

26   James MacMillan, 'Dangers of Wark's Whinge', *The Scotsman* (6 February 2005).

27   MacMillan, programme note to *A Scotch Bestiary*. The fanfare was written in 1999,
though withdrawn shortly afterwards.

caricature, 'Jackass Hackass', is less opaque, being an open attack on the Scottish media which MacMillan fell foul of following his 1999 speech. The percussion section for this episode is augmented by two typewriters (which MacMillan asks to be 'noisy' in the score), leaving little doubt as to the composer's intentions. When asked in 2007 as to the meaning of this caricature he was explicit: 'A couple of Scottish journalists whose faces I would never tire of hitting.'[28]

The fourth episode, 'The red-handed, no-surrender, howler monkey', is perhaps the most obviously linked to the sectarianism described by 'Scotland's Shame', with the 'red hand' being a reference to the 'Red Hand of Ulster' and its Loyalist connotations. The Red Hand is inextricably linked with the Orange Order, a Protestant organisation based primarily in Northern Ireland, but with strong links in Scotland, the 'no-surrender' of the title being one of the slogans associated with the order. This link to sectarianism is enhanced by MacMillan quoting one of the most well-known Loyalist anthems, *We are the Billy Boys*, a song regularly sung by Glasgow Rangers fans to stress their Protestant affiliations (see Example 6.2).[29]

MacMillan had made reference to sectarianism in his music before, in the early 1990s, most prominently in the *Sinfonietta*, with its inclusion of another Loyalist anthem *The Sash My Father Wore* (see chapter three), and MacMillan's treatment of both anthems is similar. In the programme note to the *Sinfonietta*, MacMillan refers to the inclusion of the anthem as 'bigotry and triumphalism, bathed in the fading light of Britain's imperial era',[30] and this was not the only time MacMillan sought to pass comment on imperialism, doing so again three years later in 1994 with the orchestral overture *Britannia*.

Britannia was commissioned by British Telecommunications plc (BT) as a concert overture for all the major UK orchestras to perform during their 1994–95 season, and went on to have over thirty performances during that period. As MacMillan states, it is a 'ten-minute orchestral fantasy based on "patriotic themes"', with these 'patriotic themes' including *Rule Britannia*, *God Save the Queen* and the music-hall favourite *Roll Out the Barrel*.[31] To these diverse sources MacMillan adds the march theme from Elgar's *Cockaigne*

[28]   Hallam, 'Conversation with James MacMillan', 28.

[29]   The 'Fenian blood' of the song relates to the Fenians, an Irish Independence movement in the nineteenth and early twentieth centuries. The term is used today in a purely sectarian way to denote both Scottish and Irish Catholics.

[30]   MacMillan, Programme note to *Sinfonietta*.

[31]   James MacMillan, programme note to *Britannia*, http://www.boosey.com/cr/music/James-MacMillan-Britannia/3918 (accessed 16 April 2018).

Example 6.2   Loyalist anthem *We are the Billy Boys*

Overture (1901), which MacMillan refers to as Elgar's 'imperial theme', and juxtaposes them all with 'an Irish reel ... other march tunes and a hazy Celtic modality'.[32] *Britannia* is 'politically themed', with MacMillan seeking to make 'an extra-musical point about imperialism, nationalism, smugness and xenophobia', simultaneously celebrating yet mocking British music and its perceived self-importance.[33] Though *Britannia* (like *A Scotch Bestiary*) is a largely humorous piece, it is not without its dark side (unsurprisingly for a MacMillan work) with the divided strings and portentous timpani strokes at the very end of the piece subverting much of the verve and vibrancy of what had preceded it.

The second part of *A Scotch Bestiary*, 'The Menagerie, Uncaged', saw MacMillan pull together many of the strands he had introduced in the first, referring to this as a 'freewheeling, through-composed fantasy on all the major ideas from the first movement'.[34] To his menagerie, MacMillan adds 'elephants, horses, cows, dogs and more birds', but the chaos never reaches any recognisable order, rather continuing in its chaotic fashion to the very end. To emphasise these newly acquired animals with their 'added grunting and rooting', MacMillan nods in the direction of other canonic orchestral composers with a prominent *Herdenglocken* (a rack of elevated Alpine cow bells), alluding to both

---

[32]   Ibid. Elgar famously dedicated *Cockaigne* to my 'many friends, the members of British orchestras', this no doubt influencing MacMillan's choice of 'imperial' material. The 'hazy Celtic modality' rather amusingly features a quotation from *The Confession of Isobel Gowdie*.

[33]   Johnson and Sutton, 'Raising Sparks: On the Music of James MacMillan', 18.

[34]   MacMillan, programme note to *A Scotch Bestiary*.

Strauss's *Eine Alpensinfonie* and Mahler's Symphony No. 6, to which are added snatches of Wagnerian Valkyries and Messiaen's birds.[35]

A Scotch Bestiary is one of MacMillan's most humorous pieces (the title and subtitle suggest a lighter touch from the composer than usual) and it is in sharp contrast to some of the large-scale works he had composed in the years preceding it, such as the angular *A Deep but Dazzling Darkness* (2002) for violin, tape and orchestra and the dramatic *Birds of Rhiannon* from 2001. The humour is not purely for audience enjoyment, with the tone of the piece being very much a mix of savage parody and satire, with an undercurrent of resentment. In 2005, MacMillan referred to the work as having 'a bitterness' to it: some listeners had commented about the 'bitterness of the piece'.[36] Certainly, behind the colourful, Disneyesque façade is something much darker, with the composer trying to come to terms with a sense of isolation and alienation from his homeland and the artistic circles within which he had moved. Though working in a different political sphere and for different political ends, *A Scotch Bestiary* asks many of the same questions as the Liberation Theology works, as MacMillan stated in the same interview: 'I'm sort of the angry young man [who] has become a grumpy old goat in recent years, but there's still a compulsion to confront the world, to engage with the world and to colour it in a musical way.'[37] Though *A Scotch Bestiary* was largely well received by the critics (with *The Guardian* publishing an article entitled 'At last post-devolutionary Scotland has the subversive music it merits'[38]), the Scottish press have not been given the opportunity to opine on a Scottish performance: as yet, the work has not been performed in MacMillan's homeland.

MacMillan's relationship with his homeland will always be a problematic love–hate relationship; as Dominic Wells puts it, 'half-shame, half pride'. 'Scotland's Shame' did little to repair that relationship, and it is testament to the strength of MacMillan's ties to his country that he did not leave in the early 2000s, particularly as he had been appointed the composer–conductor of the Manchester-based BBC Philharmonic in 2000 with regular commitments with the orchestra.[39] However, despite all the anxiety and heckling that

---

35   Ibid.

36   McGregor, 'James MacMillan: a conversation and a commentary', 85.

37   Ibid., 85.

38   Hywel Williams, 'At last post-devolutionary Scotland has the subversive music it merits', *The Guardian* (29 December 2004).

39   Wells, 'James MacMillan: Retrospective Modernist', 80.

MacMillan's speech engendered, there have been several positive outcomes amidst the recrimination. In a follow-up to 'Scotland's Shame' that MacMillan wrote in 2000, entitled 'I Had Not Thought About It Like That Before', the composer sets a reasonably conciliatory tone, even going as far as regretting his 'clumsy and lame attempt at humour in comparing Knox with Mao'.[40] Although dismayed by some reactions from politicians, MacMillan does tell of his 'encouragement' that the Scottish Executive (the recently created devolved Scottish government) 'appear to have taken seriously the comments I made in August 1999'.[41] By the time of 'How I rattled the deniers' in 2006, MacMillan was able to say: 'The debate has ebbed and flowed since, developing in fascinating and fulfilling ways. The wounds of religious sectarianism are being cleansed ... official and unofficial initiatives point to a growing resolve to remove this blight from Scotland's reputation.'[42] A year later MacMillan reflected that Scotland is 'still a racially fraught place, but we've given ourselves the kind of cultural and intellectual facility to deal with a problem which could be used to great benefit ... fingers crossed, anyway'.[43]

Whatever the outcome for wider society that may have resulted from 'Scotland's Shame', the speech did little to affect MacMillan's standing as a composer of international reputation, and commissions have continued to flow from across the world, including both sides of the English–Scottish border. If anything, the speech enhanced MacMillan's status as an artist of integrity and substance, one with important things to say who did not shy away from tackling society's injustices. It is because of this that 'Scotland's Shame' is as important to the ongoing narrative of James MacMillan's career as any of the musical works on which his professional reputation is based. It has shaped his subsequent music inextricably.

---

[40]   James MacMillan, 'I Had Not Thought About It Like That Before', in Devine, ed., *Scotland's Shame? Bigotry and Sectarianism in Modern Scotland*, 269.

[41]   Ibid., 269.

[42]   MacMillan, 'How I rattled the deniers'.

[43]   Hallam, 'Conversation with James MacMillan', 29.

7 | *A New Song – Mass* and MacMillan's Choral Renaissance

'I don't really regard myself as a church composer and I don't really see myself doing too much of it' exclaimed James MacMillan in 1998, in an interview with Helen Burrows for a PhD thesis entitled 'Choral Music and Church of England: 1970–1995'.[1] In a chapter titled 'James MacMillan: Tackling the Divine in Music', MacMillan makes various statements about his disillusionment with the state of contemporary Catholic liturgical music (as he would at various points over the next two decades) and his own views on the role of the composer working in this arena. Burrows, despite being somewhat harsh on MacMillan's congregational mass settings – she refers to the 'paucity of ideas' in the works and bemoans the 'self-conscious use' of the 'Scotch Snap'[2] – carries out a fair survey of his sacred choral works up to 1995 and includes substantial pieces such as *Cantos Sagrados* and *Seven Last Words from the Cross* as well as shorter anthems and motets. What is most striking about the chapter are her thoughts on the public awareness of MacMillan's sacred choral works, with Burrows asserting 'although most of MacMillan's compositions have been critically acclaimed his sacred choral music has largely escaped attention'. She continues: 'MacMillan's choral music has never attained the popularity of his instrumental works.'[3] There is more than a grain of truth to her assumptions, since as of 1998 none of MacMillan's work in this genre had achieved anywhere like the public exposure and dissemination of *The Confession of Isobel Gowdie* or *Veni, Veni, Emmanuel*, and his published choral works (both sacred and secular) at the time amounted to less than a quarter of his output. However, fast-forward ten years and choral music dominates the works MacMillan is writing, to the point where it dwarfs the orchestral and instrumental music, in number if not scope. Writing for choirs has moved from being a secondary part

---

[1]   Helen Jane Burrows, 'Choral Music and the Church of England: 1970–1995' (PhD, University of East Anglia, 1999), 239.

[2]   Ibid., 240.

[3]   Ibid., 231.

of the composer's oeuvre to one of his primary concerns, and shows no sign of relinquishing this position. But what exactly caused this 'choral renaissance' for MacMillan, what caused this resurgence in a genre that the composer did not see himself 'doing too much of'? How did it move to become such an integral and substantial part of MacMillan's published work?[4]

MacMillan went some way to answering this in an interview for another doctoral thesis in 2015, when asked about the changing landscape of contemporary music. He spoke of:

> the emergence, or re-emergence of choral music as an important part of contemporary music ... a number of composers in the last few decades have come forward and have made choral music their speciality and priority ... In a sense I've been able to stop hiding my guilty secret. I love choirs so I'm delighted that choirs are being rediscovered by composers.[5]

The quote above is telling and reflects a growing movement in contemporary music in the new millennium towards a softer, more traditional, tonal language, possibly as a reaction to the high modernism of the 1960s–1980s that MacMillan and many other composers studied at university. This 'rediscovery' of tonality resulted in a whole new generation of composers for whom writing for choirs was as natural as writing for any other ensemble and did not require a substantial change in style or technique. In many ways, MacMillan has ridden on the crest of this wave: as equally respected writing for choirs as for ensembles and orchestras.

Certainly, choral music had always been a vital part of MacMillan's musical life, with his earliest pieces being sacred choral works (see chapter one); however, there is a marked hiatus between those early works (from 1977 to 1981) and *Cantos Sagrados* in 1989, and it was not until the end of the 1990s that MacMillan composed multiple works for choir in a single calendar year. His reference to a 'guilty secret' is interesting, for on more than one occasion he has referred to the disjunct between choirs and composers in the 1980s, with the latter suffering from a 'macho modernism that didn't really rate

---

[4]   As Table 6.1 shows, choral music has proliferated in MacMillan's output, in this instance as a snapshot showing 1999 (the year after Burrows's interview) to 2008 (in the midst of MacMillan's choral revival).

[5]   As quoted in Bethany Alvey, 'Spirituality and Scottish Identity in Selected Works of James MacMillan' (DMA, University of Miami, 2016), 170–71.

choral music'.[6] As the musical climate changed, so did the vehicle for musical expression, with many composers more likely to write for choirs than for cutting edge new-music groups or music theatre ensembles.

MacMillan's choral renaissance also goes hand-in-hand with two key factors: the election of Cardinal Joseph Ratzinger to Pope Benedict XVI in 2005 and his continued personal reaction to 'Scotland's Shame', MacMillan's Edinburgh Festival speech in 1999. One of Benedict's early reforms brought a change of liturgy, the reintroduction of the extraordinary form of the Roman Rite (which is also referred to as the Tridentine Mass), the mass used before the Second Vatican Council (Vatican II) introduced the ordinary form in the 1960s. This move, which sought to re-establish a more traditional form of worship, appealed greatly to MacMillan, who had previously referred to Vatican II as 'de-poeticisation, de-sacralisation, and general dumbing down of the Church's sacred praise', and called Benedict's change a 'gift' to the 'wider church [and] to its grateful musicians'.[7] With Papal encouragement now evident, MacMillan threw himself into the tradition with a flurry of motets, chants, psalms and other liturgical works.

As shown in chapter six, MacMillan's shift in politics from the left to the right in the early 2000s resulted in a stronger affirmation of his faith and the move to a fiercer adherence to the church. With MacMillan's adoption of a new political stance, governed by traditional Christian values and ethics which rejected liberalism and secularisation, it is no surprise that the amount of religiously inspired works increased (see Table 6.1). It was only natural that this should include setting more religious texts and working with greater frequency with church choirs and associated organisations. It is perhaps serendipitous that MacMillan's avowal of faith through sacred choral music coincided with the election of a pope who strongly believed in the power of music as part of the traditional liturgy.[8]

The final possible reason for MacMillan's choral resurgence is more mundane and earthly: the growing importance and popularity of *Seven Last*

---

[6]   Cooke, Interview with James MacMillan, 30 November 2015. He repeated this to Alvey: 'When I was twenty-something, yes there were choirs, but the composers didn't really seem to involve themselves as much with choirs as they did with instrumentalists.' (Alvey, 'Spirituality and Scottish Identity in Selected Works of James MacMillan', 170).

[7]   As quoted in Wells, 'James MacMillan: Retrospective Modernist', 130–31.

[8]   Ratzinger had put forward his views on liturgical reform (including the role of Gregorian Chant and Renaissance polyphony) in a book entitled *The Spirit of the Liturgy* in 2000, before he became pope.

Words from the Cross, particularly in the USA, was leading to more commissions and more links with the choral world. As the work was disseminated across the globe, so new opportunities were presented at the same time as the composer was changing his politics and prerogatives. By the end of the 2000s, MacMillan was regularly writing for choirs on both sides of the Atlantic (and further afield), with many prestigious commissions, recordings and residencies.

It is somewhat ironic that one of the first pieces that brought MacMillan any national recognition was a choral work, his setting of *Beatus Vir* that won the 1983 Norwich Festival of Contemporary Church Music, Composers' Competition. This distinctive, if difficult, piece bears few similarities to MacMillan's mature choral works, though does share technical and stylistic elements with the ensemble works he was composing at the time (such as *The Road to Ardtalla* and *Three Dawn Rituals*). *Beatus Vir* is a setting of Psalm 112 (though omitting three of the verses) and is an interesting amalgam of many of MacMillan's youthful influences, and much of the prevailing modernism that was the lingua franca for young composers.[9] In the work's six-minute duration MacMillan includes hocketing, multiple metre changes, shouting and highly dissonant and declamatory organ writing, all of which contributes to a powerful and volatile setting of a well-worn text.

Beatus Vir begins with imitative choral entries leading to a strident, dissonant, contrapuntal six-part texture, punctuated by heavy, dramatic organ chords (which vary between ten, eleven and twelve-note clusters) often placed at irregular and unpredictable moments, gradually moving closer together. Following a more turbulent transition section with many changes of metre, there follows softer material with a lyrical solo soprano line accompanied by hushed choir and organ pedals. The turbulent material returns before a lesser doxology recaps the opening polyphony, leading to a forceful final Amen.

Though *Beatus Vir* appears on the surface to be a product of its time, it does still point in the direction of MacMillan's later choral works, particularly his most substantial work for choir from the 1980s, *Cantos Sagrados*. The agitated delivery of text in the first movement, 'Identity', with its rapid-fire, staccato phrases mingling with shouted exclamations, all taking place amidst changing metres and dissonant organ interjections, are redolent of the earlier piece (see

---

9   Burrows states that the 'harmonically-enriched triads of the central section evoke both Igor Stravinsky and Olivier Messiaen – particularly Messiaen's *O sacrum convivium*, a work that MacMillan conducted frequently as a student.' (Burrows, 'Choral Music and the Church of England: 1970–1995', 232.). The influence of Andriessen is again present.

Example 7.1). The middle movement of *Cantos Sagrados*, 'Virgin of Guadalupe', also has some similarities to *Beatus Vir*: the characteristic MacMillan device of two oscillating chords that is prominent in this movement is similar to the lyrical material in the motet, as is the soprano-dominated texture and low organ writing. Though similarities exist between these two works, it should be noted that by *Cantos Sagrados* MacMillan is using the techniques, textures and harmonies in a more subtle fashion, with warmer sonorities and softer edges – these two works highlight the aesthetic transformation that had occurred in MacMillan's work during the 1980s.[10]

Much of MacMillan's growing success as a choral composer rests on three short works for choir written during his most accomplished period of orchestral writing in the mid-1990s: *Christus Vincit* (1994), *A Child's Prayer* (1996) and *A New Song* (1997). These three pieces form the backbone of his performed choral output, with countless performances in concerts and services across the globe. They also represent the compositional blueprint to much of the work that followed with the success of these compositions codifying a MacMillan 'choral sound', and paving the way for many future commissions. These pieces find MacMillan at his most transcendent, his most heartfelt and his most accessible, it is no surprise they have become some of his widest-reaching repertoire.

Christus Vincit (Christ Conquers) was commissioned by the Musician's Benevolent Fund for the annual St Cecilia's Day service, and was first performed by the combined choirs of St Paul's Cathedral, Westminster Abbey and Westminster Cathedral at St Paul's in November 1994. Of the three pieces, it is the most radiant and numinous and finds MacMillan as close to the voguish 'mystic minimalism' of the 1990s as he ever would be, with the work's simple, unchanging metre, entirely diatonic harmony and repeated phrases.[11] The text is

---

[10]   MacMillan referred to *Beatus Vir* in an interview in 2017: 'It is probably the most difficult piece I've written … it has been published, but it isn't performed … it's real "new music", more in a rhythmic way than anything else.'(Cooke, Interview with James MacMillan, 29 March 2017.) It has had sporadic performances since its premiere, with the first professional recording being released in 2018 when recorded by the Salzburg Bach Choir, conducted by Wolfgang Kogert.

[11]   The term 'mystic minimalism' refers primarily to the music of Arvo Pärt (1935–), Henryk Górecki (1933–2010) and John Tavener (1944–2013) whose hypnotic, religiously inspired music became both fashionable and incredibly successful in the 1990s. The work that arguably created this phenomenon was the 'rediscovery' of Górecki's Symphony No. 3 (1976) in 1992, and its sustained exposure on Classic FM, a newly formed British commercial classical music radio station.

Example 7.1   Bars 15–16 of *Beatus Vir* and bars 19–21 of 'Identity' from *Cantos Sagrados* showing similarities in organ texture

taken from the *Worcester Acclamations*, a tenth-century Latin text used primarily for Ascension Day, with its simple but powerful message of 'Christ conquers, Christ is King, Christ is Lord of All'.[12] Many commentators have referred to the Celtic elements of the work: MacMillan's imitative polyphony seems to suggest Gaelic psalm-singing amongst its numerous Scottish-inspired elements, Patrick Russill poetically rhapsodising that 'it seems to breathe the open air of Celtic Christianity, something heard in the wind at Iona perhaps'.[13] Burrows suggests that the piece is 'based on an archetypal Gaelic phrase ... though one probably written by the composer'. She is partly correct: the opening melodic material of *Christus Vincit* is the Scottish lament tune *Great is the Cause of My Sorrow* that MacMillan first appropriated in 1987 for the orchestral work *The Keening* (see Examples 1.1 and 1.2), now elongated and prolonged to capture the full resonance of St Paul's Cathedral (see Example 7.2).

In true MacMillan fashion, the recycling of material does not end with the folksong quotation: much of *Christus Vincit* appeared earlier in the year in the short string quartet *Memento* that was first performed by the Kronos Quartet in New York, the month before the premiere of the choral piece. *Memento* was written for a memorial concert for David Huntly, the American representative of MacMillan's publisher Boosey & Hawkes, so it seemed entirely appropriate that MacMillan turned to a lament tune for this occasion. In the programme note to *Memento* MacMillan explains: 'The music is slow, delicate and tentative and is based on the modality of Gaelic lament music and the Gaelic heterophony

Example 7.2   Appropriation of *Great is the Cause of My Sorrow* in bars 1–22 of *Christus Vincit* (see Example 1.1 for the original tune)

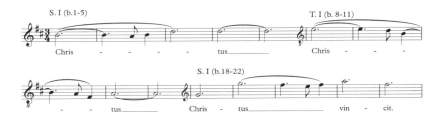

---

12   Patrick Russill suggests that the *Worcester Acclamations* are 'known in France as the acclamations of the Emperor Charlemagne' and are 'designed to be sung by an army on the march' (Russill, 'Cantos Sagrados', 36).

13   Ibid., 36.

of psalm-singing in the Hebrides.'[14] But there is no mention of a particular tune, nor of *Great is the Cause of My Sorrow*. Like MacMillan's own 'Tryst' theme, the weaving of this lament through his oeuvre is both conscious and subconscious, it is embedded in the very core of the composer's musical language.

If *Christus Vincit* is a 'delicate, slowly lilting cat's cradle of polyphony',[15] then *A Child's Prayer* is much more homophonic and in keeping with the majority of contemporary choral music from this period and beyond. As was mentioned in chapter five, the work was written in response to the Dunblane massacre of 13 March 1996 and it is dedicated to the dead of this tragedy. It was premiered in a service of remembrance in July of that year given by the Choir of Westminster Abbey, conducted by Martin Neary. The text of the work is simple and heartfelt and is actually a reminisce of something MacMillan learned as a child, as he recollected in 2015: 'The text is probably the earliest prayer I remember ... I remember being taught it at school ... by nuns who were preparing me for my first communion, and it's stayed in my mind ever since.'[16] MacMillan emphasises the link with childhood and innocence by having the main melodic material of the opening section given to two solo trebles who softly repeat the line 'Jesu, Deep in my soul forever stay' in consonant, always rising conjunct lines (see Example 7.3). Underneath these floating voices, MacMillan has a repeated three-chord pattern in the rest of the choir (featuring an inverted Celtic drone, on F♯), quietly reciting the word 'welcome' as the soloists wind towards the apex of their line.

This is followed by a contrasting section on the word 'Joy', where the whole choir take part in a heterophonic exchange, with highly ornamented phrases quickly climaxing in an ecstatic *fortissimo*. Burrows suggests that this section is 'reminiscent of the natural vocal inflections of laughter', and although this may seem a little fanciful, there is something earnestly optimistic about this section which lingers long after the work has faded into silence.[17] In other hands, *A Child's Prayer* could have been overly sentimental and mawkish, but the simplicity and sincerity of MacMillan's setting negates this and creates a heartfelt memorial to one of the darkest days in Scotland's recent history.

---

[14]   James MacMillan, programme note to *Memento*, http://www.boosey.com/cr/music/James-MacMillan-Memento/3747 (accessed 7 June 2018).

[15]   Russill, 'Cantos Sagrados', 36.

[16]   As quoted in Alvey, 'Spirituality and Scottish Identity in Selected Works by James MacMillan', 144.

[17]   Burrows, 'Choral Music and the Church of England: 1970–1995', 243.

Example 7.3   Bars 7–10 of *A Child's Prayer* showing rising solo treble lines and accompanying chords in choir

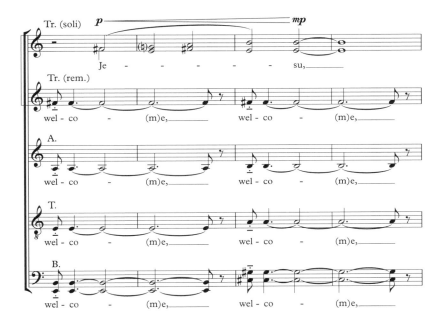

A New Song finds MacMillan returning to the psalms, but in a very different fashion to *Beatus Vir*, here setting Psalm 96 though again cherry-picking the verses to suit the mood and tone of the work (he sets verses 1, 2 and 13 only). The piece is the most strident of the three, accumulating texture and emotional power as it progresses to its thrilling organ coda and ecstatic ending. Like *Christus Vincit* and *A Child's Prayer* it is simple in design with an easily identifiable verse and refrain structure until the final organ interjection. As in the previous pieces, the Gaelic and Celtic influences are never far from the surface: alongside drones and 'scotch snaps', MacMillan peppers his verse material with turns and trills and many other forms of ornamentation, leading to extremely filigree, contrapuntal lines swirling above the ethereal organ figures. Again, many have referred to the work's similarity to Gaelic psalm-singing, though in *A New Song* this may be more pertinent and fundamental than in other pieces: there is a definite feeling of cantor and congregation in the refrain and verse material, with the simple, unadorned lines of the refrain leading to a wash of polyphonic music in the subsequent verses.

As shown in chapter five, MacMillan reused material from *A New Song* in the third movement of his oratorio *Quickening* in 1999 (see Example 5.12), though in time-honoured fashion, *A New Song* is actually a recycling of an even older work, the *Advent Antiphon*, which dates from the early 1990s. There is little information about this work, though in a 2011 interview MacMillan recalled: 'It might be as much as twenty years old, it prefigures *A New Song* and I re-used the melody for that as it was just lying there!'[18] This simple antiphon for cantor, congregation, male voices and organ follows the same verse and refrain pattern as the psalm setting, with an elaborate tenor cantor role (performed by the composer in early service use) alternating with more conjunct congregation parts and associated choir drones. As has been shown, and will be shown again, much of MacMillan's choral music is fertile ground for compositional ideas and fragments, many of which take root in much larger and more substantial pieces.

Though MacMillan may have not regarded himself as a 'church composer' (in a later interview he reiterated this by stating 'I don't think of myself as a "liturgical" composer'[19]), he soon found himself writing some substantial liturgical works, with a *Magnificat*, *Nunc Dimittis* and *Te Deum* all appearing in the next four years. By far the most ambitious and the most personal of these was his setting of the *Mass*, which was a millennium commission for the choir of Westminster Cathedral and first performed by it in June 2000 on the Feast of Corpus Christi.

Mass (2000)

The *Mass* was MacMillan's fourth setting of the Eucharist, following on from the *Missa Brevis* (1977, though published in 2006), the *St Anne's Mass* (1985) and the *Galloway Mass* (1996), and the first for a 'professional' choir of some repute. It was also the first time that MacMillan had set the mass in his 'mature' compositional voice, one honed from his successes in the late 1980s onwards.[20] The *Mass* is an uncompromising and individual setting,

---

[18]   MacMillan, as quoted in Rebecca Tavener, liner notes to *Who Are These Angels: New Choral Music by James MacMillan*, Linn CD, CKD383 (2011), 10.

[19]   Roderic Dunnett, 'Subtle Celebration', http://www.mvdaily.com/articles/2000/07/macmill1.htm (accessed 20 June 2018).

[20]   The *Missa Brevis* is a juvenile work, whereas the settings from the 1980s and 1990s are both congregational settings and thus have different aesthetic considerations.

featuring some of MacMillan's most memorable and striking choral writing in an organic and surprisingly taut setting which must rank amongst some of the composer's finest achievements in this medium. James Whitbourn refers to the work as 'an extraordinarily complete one, not only because he writes music for elements other than the Ordinary, but because it has a mysterious sense of the physical presence of the body of Christ, which is at the heart of the Eucharistic celebration.'[21] Whitbourn is right: the work is 'extraordinarily complete' with MacMillan setting the Ordinary (though omitting the Credo), the associated Alleluias and Amens and many of the of interactive sections that occur in the service between priest, choir and congregation. It leads to the setting being entirely holistic and coherent, with the composer actively shaping all the musical decision-making of the whole service. Whitbourn's suggestion of the 'mysterious sense of the physical presence of the body of Christ' is again apposite – the *Mass* is a beguiling mixture of the divine and the corporeal, as much relating to the contemporary as to the everlasting: it is the embodiment of MacMillan's own relationship with the Eucharist and his own brand of Catholicism.

MacMillan repeats this and explains the concept behind his setting in a programme note for the first performance:

> The movements of the *Mass* are crafted like a musical journey which mirrors the progression of mood, emphasis and poetic tension in the liturgy. From the Penitential Rite to the joyous hymn of the Gloria, to the mysteries of the Consecration through to the reflective ambiguities of the Agnus Dei, the music moves from clarity to a sense of uneasy resolution. Even though this is a work which explores the eternal mysteries of the Catholic faith, it is written through the experience of the tragedies and uncertainties of our own age. It is inevitable that a contemporary celebration of Divine Love would be shrouded in the doubts and fears which characterise our time.[22]

MacMillan's assertion that his setting of the mass would be 'shrouded in the doubts and fears which characterise our time' is entirely typical, and follows firmly in the mould of *Seven Last Words from the Cross* which brought a gritty realism to Jesus's suffering amongst the more celestial and angelic moments of the cantata. He reiterated this in an interview in 2004 when he stated: 'To me, the very sense of the sacred ... is rooted in the here and now, in the joys and

---

21   James Whitbourn, liner notes to *MacMillan: Mass and other sacred music*, Hyperion CD, CDA67219 (2001), 3.

22   As quoted in Whitbourn, liner notes to *MacMillan: Mass and other sacred music*, 4.

tragedies of everyday life, in the grit and mire of human existence.'[23] The *Mass* has its moments of radiant hope and heavenly praise, but it is a work entirely preoccupied with 'doubts and fears'; from the unsettling organ figure that begins the work to the almost inaudible low clusters that finish it, it is suffused with ambiguity and uncertainties, more so than any of MacMillan's other mass settings and his liturgical works in general.

The coherence of the *Mass* is achieved through the work's different sections being 'linked in a through-composed flow' from the cantor's initial statement to the end of the Agnus Dei.[24] The opening phrase of the cantor provides much of the melodic, harmonic and intervallic material for the whole setting (see Example 7.4) and it is this reuse and revisiting of ideas that gives the work its organic and lucid structure.

The opening fragment of the above example with the rising fifth and falling semitone, all coloured by a Lydian modality, informs much of the music in the *Mass*, and it can be traced throughout the Ordinary sections as well as much of the congregational material. This particular motif is seemingly of great personal significance to MacMillan, not only because of the important role it plays in the *Mass*, but because he also chooses to give prominence to a very similar motif in the *Magnificat* of 1999 and in the Kyrie from the *Missa Dunelmi* of 2011 (see Example 7.5). It is almost as if this particular motif is in some way directly related to his process of writing liturgical music: as if it were a personal leitmotif that MacMillan feels he must work into these compositions as a show of faith.

MacMillan's decision to through-compose the *Mass* is not unique in his output: the same technique is found (with varying degrees of sophistication) in the two earlier, congregational mass settings and the later setting the *Mass of Blessed John Henry Newman*. In fact, in many ways the earlier mass settings act as a test-bed for the *Mass*, since many ideas found in the later work have their seeds in the congregational pieces. There are similarities in the formal schemes of the mass settings: all three omit the Credo; the first Amen is taken from the Gloria; the Agnus Dei includes material reworked from the Kyrie.[25] The idea of blending cantor and congregational sections is first exhibited in

---

23   As quoted in Spicer, liner notes to *Seven Last Words from the Cross*, 5.

24   As quoted in Whitbourn, liner notes to *MacMillan: Mass and other sacred music*, 4.

25   MacMillan explained his decision not to include the Credo in 2000: 'As with the old *Missa Brevis*, so too nowadays it's not strictly necessary to set the Credo to fresh music. It's one of the sections of the Ordinary of the Mass which the congregation needs to join in: often in Catholic Church they sing it to traditional plainsong.' As quoted in Dunnett, 'Subtle Celebration'.

Example 7.4   Bars 2–4 of the Kyrie from the *Mass* showing opening cantor phrase
as material for the whole work

Example 7.5   Similarities between motifs from the Kyrie from the *Mass* (bars 2–3),
the *Magnificat* (bars 28–29) and the Kyrie from *Missa Dunelmi*
(bars 15–16)

the *Galloway Mass*. That these pieces might all share material is strange, as the
simple homophony of the *St Anne's Mass* is completely removed from the florid
polyphony of the *Mass*; however, as has been shown, MacMillan is no stranger
to reusing quite often the simplest fragments and ideas to inform a new work,
even one in the same genre, with the same text.

The Kyrie finds some of the most agile contrapuntal writing in the *Mass*,
with the long melismatic lines unfolding over a shimmering organ figure –
marked *prestissimo possibile*, as fast as possible, by MacMillan – grounded
by the sixteen-foot pedal. Of all the movements in the *Mass*, this is the most
directly influenced by the opening cantor material, with the modality lingering
until the final organ embellishments and dissipation of energy. The Gloria is
perhaps where we find the clearest example of MacMillan's 'doubts and fears':
following a strident beginning with many variants of the opening fragment, the
music becomes suddenly more reflective as altos, tenors and basses interject a
new *pianissimo* theme. This theme (for the words 'receive our prayer') is taken

directly from the Agnus Dei, there found with the text 'have mercy upon us'. It is no coincidence that this material is placed in the middle of the Gloria, for MacMillan is choosing to echo the final ambiguous sentiments of the Agnus Dei at the moment when the liturgy is at its most triumphant. MacMillan emphasised this in 2000: 'If anything the mood in my setting is to understate, I wanted to fashion music that was more subtle in celebration ... to include lots of shade and intimacy, to offset the more celebratory moments.'[26]

The Sanctus follows on the dark hues of the Gloria, building from the lowest register of the organ in a slow, foreboding tread until the full choir are revealed in a bi-tonal climax. This unleashes a whirlwind, *fortissimo* setting of 'Hosanna in the highest' replete with dramatic organ flourishes and spectacular choral polyphony. Following another declamatory 'Hosanna', the music gradually thins, slows and quietens to return to the opening pitches: a simple formal design, but one executed with unerring skill.

The Agnus Dei continues the uncertain, questioning mood, with MacMillan choosing to stress the reflective ambiguities present in this text – the composer himself referring to it as 'the most mysterious and intimate of the movements'.[27] Though this final movement does dwell on ideas and motifs from earlier in the piece it is in no way the culmination of what has gone before, rather, a moment of concentrated tension in the work: it is as if all the insecurities and conflicts from earlier movements are collected and magnified in this moment. Nowhere is this more apparent than in the final bars with the closing repetitions of the word 'peace'. Here a simple, falling motif suggests a resolution; however, MacMillan introduces a new sonority, a distant, dark rumbling from the organ in its lowest register, a chromatic cluster totally unrelated to the warm modality of the voices and hinting at something much darker (see Example 7.6). It is as if one moment of peace and resolution is clouded by the 'doubts and fears' that have haunted this setting of the *Mass*, the 'tragedies and uncertainties' that MacMillan referred to coming to the fore in the final supplication of the liturgy.

Like *A New Song*, the *Mass* has been recycled in a later work, this time in the virtuoso choral piece *Sun-Dogs* from 2006. Here MacMillan transforms the celebrant material from the Eucharistic Prayer section of the *Mass*, with its free tempo and static organ accompaniment, into a corresponding section in the fourth movement of the later work with a smaller chamber choir accompanied by the remaining singers, rapidly intoning a complementary Latin text. It is interesting that MacMillan refers to the text of *Sun-Dogs* (written by Michael

---

26   As quoted in Dunnett, 'Subtle Celebration'.

27   Ibid.

Example 7.6   Final bars of the Agnus Dei from the *Mass* (bars 72–75)

Symmons Roberts) as 'terrifying one minute, radiant and ecstatic the next' – this has clear parallels with the composer's thought-processes behind his setting of the mass.[28] MacMillan chooses to use this quotation from the *Mass* to emphasise the quasi-Eucharistic links in Symmons Roberts's poem, with the chamber choir taking the lines 'One offers bread, part chewed, soft with saliva'. MacMillan affirms this in his programme note, referring to the fourth movement of *Sun-Dogs* as a 'sensual and bestial Eucharistic scene'.[29]

The *Mass* can be viewed as a transition piece between MacMillan's harder-edged large-scale works of the 1990s and the softer harmonies of his choral output in the new millennium: often the two musical mindsets seem at odds with each other. There is an inherent modality to much of the choral writing in the *Mass*, but the organ often seeks to disrupt or disturb this music with an intentional clash of sonority and delivery. MacMillan has referred to the work as a 'gradualist piece ... you can feel some of the new simplicities and modalities of the choral music, but the organ part is virtuosic and more angular'.[30] Certainly the organ gives the work a more dazzling and modernist veneer and changes the tone and aesthetic of the piece throughout. But it is not just the organ that

[28]   James MacMillan, programme note to *Sun-Dogs*, http://www.boosey.com/cr/music/James-MacMillan-Sun-Dogs/45441 (accessed 14 June 2018).

[29]   Ibid.

[30]   Cooke, Phillip, Interview with James MacMillan, Eton High Street, 22 May 2018.

stands out: the *Mass* is a bravura choral showpiece, far more advanced than much of the weekly fare that even a choir of Westminster Cathedral's standard would expect to perform.[31]

MacMillan revised the *Mass* in 2012 for the new English translation of the Roman Missal that came into use in 2011, and this new adaption is considerably less 'complete' than the original, with MacMillan omitting the whole Eucharistic Prayer section.[32] He referred to this decision in 2018: 'I read somewhere (by one of Pope Benedict's acolytes) that composers really shouldn't be setting this [the Eucharistic Prayer] and it should be left to simple Roman chants that exist already, so when we came to republish it in the new version, I didn't put any chants in it.'[33] However, both versions of the work are still in use, giving potential congregations the opportunity to experience one of MacMillan's most personal and all-encompassing sacred works.

The Strathclyde Motets (2005–10)

If one work embodies James MacMillan's choral renaissance in the new millennium, then it is the collection of fourteen pieces that comprise *The Strathclyde Motets*, MacMillan's most prolonged and substantial offering of sacred choral works, written between 2005 and 2010 (see Table 7.1). This group of works, mainly settings of Communion motets appropriate for the associated feast day in the Catholic Church calendar (otherwise known as the 'Propers' of the Mass), show MacMillan's willingness to throw himself into writing liturgical music and the wholehearted embracing of the choral medium as an important vehicle for compositional expression.

The idea behind *The Strathclyde Motets* was both theological and practical. MacMillan wanted to write works that were both liturgically appropriate for the Catholic Church in the new era of Pope Benedict XVI, and that were also

---

31   Martin Baker, the Master of Music at Westminster Cathedral (and conductor of the first performance of the *Mass*) revealed to Dominic Wells how difficult the work was to rehearse stating that this explained the 'relative infrequency with which we sing it. This is often the case with commissions: they can turn out to be "occasion" pieces that need a disproportionate time for rehearsal.' As quoted in Wells, 'James MacMillan: Retrospective Modernist', 128.

32   MacMillan also revised the *St Anne's Mass* of 1985, adding a Gloria, but chose not to adapt the 1996 *The Galloway Mass* to the new translation.

33   Cooke, Interview with James MacMillan, 22 May 2018.

Table 7.1   Contents of *The Strathclyde Motets*, set out as in published scores, not chronologically

Book One (2005–07)	Book Two (2007–10)
Data est mihi omnis potestas (2007)	*Benedicimus Deum caeli* (2010)
Dominus dabit benignitatem (2006)	*The canticle of Zachariah* (2007)
Factus est repente (2005)	*Lux aeterna* (2008)
Mitte manum tuam (2006)	*O Radiant Dawn* (2007)
Sedebit Dominus Rex (2005)	*Os mutorum* (2008)
In splendoribus sanctorum (2005)	*Pascha nostrum immolates est* (2008)
Videns Dominus (2005)	*Qui meditabitur* (2010)

performable by 'good church choirs or good amateur concert choirs ... without causing them too much stress'.[34] The initial impulse for the works came from discussions between MacMillan, Alan Tavener (the conductor of Glasgow-based choirs Cappella Nova and the Strathclyde University Chamber Choir) and Brendan Slevin, the Catholic Chaplain at Strathclyde University, concerning a group of new works that would beneficial to the chaplaincy, the choir and the composer. MacMillan had worked with Tavener for many years, from the first concert performance of *Seven Last Words from the Cross* in 1994, and the MacMillans had been regular worshippers at the university chaplaincy: the collaboration on these motets seemed a logical product of these relationships.

Subsequent events meant that much of the composition and conception of *The Strathclyde Motets* became bound up with MacMillan's role as the choirmaster at St Columba's Church, Maryhill, in Glasgow, where he had an active role in the musical provision for the congregation from 2005 until his move from Glasgow in 2015. MacMillan assumed the role at St Columba's when the Dominican Order, which was responsible for the chaplaincy at Strathclyde University, was invited by Archbishop Mario Conti (then Archbishop of Glasgow) to run the church in Maryhill. Both composer and the ongoing motet project followed, and this new environment and relationship shaped the later pieces in the collection. MacMillan's time at St Columba's is one of the most pivotal in his career and one of the most unusual: for a

---

[34]   MacMillan, as quoted in Tavener, liner notes to *Tenebrae: New Choral Music by James MacMillan*, 6.

composer of international standing to be writing religious works for amateurs and non-musicians on such a regular and sustained basis is almost unheard of, and MacMillan's ongoing commitment to the church and its music influenced his compositions during this period.

Maryhill is a traditionally working-class area of Glasgow, and although it has seen some investment in recent years it still bears the scars, like many post-industrial, inner-city areas, of poverty, drug and alcohol issues and general depopulation. The arrival of a group of 'middle-class, academic-minded people moving in with some of the poorest people in Glasgow' led to suspicion and concern from the congregation and, as MacMillan recalled: 'they thought we were a cult'.[35] Whatever the initial misgivings may have been, MacMillan quickly set about transforming the music provision at the church, creating a choir from the community and composing simple, memorable works for them: 'Every week I would write a new responsorial psalm ... and teach it to them just before Mass began.' It was a labour of love that had a direct impact on the amount of choral works MacMillan was producing and the level of performer ability that he had in mind.[36] MacMillan found his time at St Columba's edifying and inspiring: 'I loved it and it really energised me ... I thought about it right through the week, planning the music.'[37] Although the earliest motets from the collection were premiered at the Strathclyde University Chaplaincy Centre, all the later pieces were first performed at St Columba's, mainly by the university choir as part of Mass.

In 2007, to accompany the first recording of Book One of *The Strathclyde Motets*, MacMillan made a telling statement about the thought-processes behind the works: 'there's a kind of suspended animation about them ... they don't seem to go anywhere, they kind of float as an entity, and there are one or two ideas that sort of ease into being and just exist, and then it stops.'[38]

---

[35]   Cooke, Interview with James MacMillan, 22 May 2018.

[36]   James MacMillan, 'James MacMillan in Scotland', https://jamesmacmillaninscotland. wordpress.com (accessed 16 June 2018). MacMillan wrote an intermittent blog entitled 'James MacMillan in Scotland' for eighteen months from June 2010 to January 2012, where he covered a variety of topics from the 2010 Papal visit to football and snoring. There is no indication as to why the blog was discontinued, but like many of MacMillan's forays into social forums (like social media sites) it was no doubt accompanied by strong reactions and vigorous discussion.

[37]   Cooke, Interview with James MacMillan, 22 May 2018.

[38]   MacMillan, as quoted in Tavener, liner notes to *Tenebrae: New Choral Music by James MacMillan*, 7.

Many of the motets follow the shape described by MacMillan, with simple but striking material presented and passed throughout the choir before the introduction of a second idea, in some cases, for a similar process before the work ends. The motets have a homogeneity about them (certainly in Book One) with invariably slow tempi, largely homophonic textures, plainchant-derived melodies and characteristic MacMillan ornamental passages. There is a sense of something mystical and otherworldly about the pieces, feeding into MacMillan's idea of 'suspended animation'; there is an introspective quality throughout, perhaps entwined with the Communion aspect of the motets, the most personal and numinous moment of the whole mass.

Although *The Strathclyde Motets* are conceived for 'good church choirs or good amateur concert choirs', they still require a level of technical ability that would place them in the 'more challenging repertoire' category for many groups: the more filigree rhythmic passages and sustained, divided *pianissimo* material suggesting choirs experienced in either MacMillan's music or contemporary choral music in general. The exceptions to this rule are the two works composed specifically for the choir of St Columba's: *In splendoribus sanctorum* (2005) and *O Radiant Dawn* (2007). *In splendoribus sanctorum* (Amidst the splendours of the heavenly sanctuary) is one of the most arresting motets of the whole collection and highlights the technical level of performer that MacMillan was working with – it is some of the simplest and most modest music in the fourteen pieces, with unassuming lines of plainchant unfolding over bass drones and parallel fifth harmonies. The work is enlivened by the addition of a solo trumpet (one of two works in *The Strathclyde Motets* to feature an accompanying instrument) that interjects more animated flourishes at the end of each choral phrase, using the full range of the instrument to contribute an entirely different sonority to the understated material from the choir. Though the choral writing undeniably reflects the quality of performer MacMillan had at his disposal – 'they could hardly sing ... many of them could hardly read music'[39] – the blending of the repeated sections of choir material with the elaborate trumpet quickly takes on a mantra-like effect, full of reflection and mystery that seems wholly appropriate for a Communion motet for Midnight Mass on Christmas Eve, the Nativity.

O Radiant Dawn (one of only two pieces in English in *The Strathclyde Motets*) was written two years after *In splendoribus sanctorum* but illustrates how more technically able the St Columba's choir had become under MacMillan's directing: the work is recognisably in four parts with traditional part-writing

---

[39]   Cooke, Interview with James MacMillan, 22 May 2018.

and voice leading and has a natural ebb and flow commensurate with church music of the sixteenth and seventeenth centuries. MacMillan strengthens the links with music of the previous generations in the very first bars of *O Radiant Dawn*, with an opening phrase highly redolent of Thomas Tallis's *O nata lux* of c.1575 (see Example 7.7).

Though there are differences of pitch and modality, the same melodic contour and individual part direction still remain: it is hard not to listen to the opening of *O Radiant Dawn* without the Tallis instantly coming to mind, and MacMillan's work must surely be a homage to his Tudor forebear. MacMillan has never publically stated whether this is a conscious or subconscious appropriation of *O nata lux* (such as with *Great is the Cause of My Sorrow* in *Christus Vincit*) and with the composer's continued borrowings from both art and traditional music showing no sign of ceasing, it becomes part of a wider aesthetic and conceptual framework.

The second book finds MacMillan varying not only the textures, forces and atmosphere of the motets, but also the liturgical function, with three of the works being settings other than Communion texts. There is more stylistic diversity to the group, with three works in particular suggesting a divergence from the norm established in Book One: *The canticle of Zachariah* (2007), *Lux aeterna* (2008) and *Os mutorum* (2008). *The canticle of Zachariah* finds MacMillan setting a text associated with Lauds, the early morning service of the Catholic Church, and from this he conjures a largely homophonic and often irregular setting, replete with false relations and metric shifts. As Rebecca Tavener suggests, 'the chord sequences and rhythms ... evoke the English carol' and there is something of the early twentieth-century settings by Peter Warlock or Herbert Howells that springs to mind, with the peculiar mixture of expressive dissonance and melancholy that characterised that period.[40] Unusually for MacMillan (and without exception in *The Strathclyde Motets*), the Doxology is set as a unison chant, as if to wrench this homage to an earlier period back into the 'suspended animation' that characterised the first book of motets.

Lux aeterna shows MacMillan referencing previous musical epochs in a different, technical way, with the whole motet based around an existing *cantus firmus*, the *Lux aeterna* plainsong, which the altos sing throughout (see Example 3.2a). As has been shown in previous chapters, MacMillan is partial

---

[40]   Tavener, liner notes to *Who Are These Angels: New Choral Music by James MacMillan*, 5. The opening of *The canticle of Zachariah* bears a striking similarity to the opening narrator chorus material in the *St John Passion* (2007), a work that was written at the same time as the motet.

Example 7.7   Opening bars of *O Radiant Dawn* and similarities with the opening of *O nata lux* by Thomas Tallis

to including plainsong across his oeuvre; however, he rarely uses it in such a complete and unadulterated fashion. He stresses the links with earlier *cantus firmus* motets, by Josquin and Ockeghem for example, by writing the alto line in long, unchanging note values, very different to the shifting polyphony that circles around it.

Os mutorum (Mouth of the dumb) is one of the more distinctive of *The Strathclyde Motets*, as it not only features an accompanying instrument (a medieval harp), but it is also the only motet to be scored for reduced choral forces, in this case just for soprano voices. It is a setting of a characterful text from the Inchcolm Antiphoner (a fourteenth-century manuscript from Inchcolm Abbey in the Forth of Firth, one of the few existing examples of Celtic plainsong) and was first performed by Canty, a Scottish early-music ensemble, at St Columba's in 2008. Like many of the motets, it adheres to MacMillan's assertion of 'one or two ideas that sort of ease into being and just exist', the ideas in this case being a reduced intervallic pallet of thirds, fifths and octaves in the voices alternating with arpeggiated harp phrases, outlining the modality of the work (see Example 7.8). The arpeggio material then passes to the voices for a brief antiphonal section before the return of the opening textures to finish the piece.

Not all of *The Strathclyde Motets* are as simple and accessible as *O Radiant Dawn* or *Os Mutorum*, there are more challenging works in both books with the final motet of the collection, *Qui meditabitur* (He who meditates) arguably

Example 7.8   Opening bars of *Os mutorum* illustrating harp writing and intervals in soprano parts

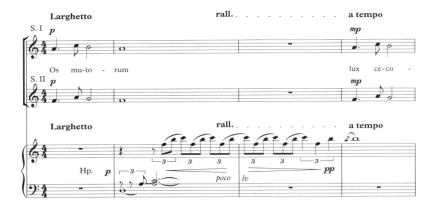

the most challenging. MacMillan certainly wrote more difficult, more thought-provoking and possibly better choral pieces during the period in which he composed *The Strathclyde Motets* (such as the *Tenebrae Responsories* of 2006 or the *Miserere* of 2009), but the prolonged composition of the collection and the period in MacMillan's career in which they appeared make them of true significance to the composer's development. In 1998 he may not have regarded himself 'as a church composer' and may have not seen himself 'doing too much of it', but it has since become of one of MacMillan's calling-cards and he is as well known today for his short, sacred choral works as he is for *Veni, Veni, Emmanuel* or the *Triduum*.[41] Calling it a 'choral renaissance' may be a little

---

[41]   In 2010 MacMillan was a featured composer in the BBC's *Sacred Music* series in an episode entitled 'Searching Out the Sacred' (BBC TV, 30 July 2010, directed Andy King-Dabbs), which featured MacMillan (alongside John Tavener and John Rutter) as a composer giving 'a special insight into the challenges and rewards of writing sacred music in the twenty-first-century'. The programme also featured performances of MacMillan's music (including *A Child's Prayer* and *Dominus dabit benignitatemn* from *The Strathclyde Motets*) in performances by long-term MacMillan advocates The Sixteen, with conductor Harry Christophers. The programme shows MacMillan conducting the choir at St Columba's (including his wife and daughter) in the 2009 work *Serenity*. MacMillan later stated that the exposure led to the choir 'gaining a few more members' (jamesmacmillaninscotland.wordpress.com/).

overblown, but it is as important to understanding MacMillan's music as his stylistic shift in 1987 or his return to Scotland in 1988. The choral works did not stop in 2010, and *The Strathclyde Motets* have become another thread in the tapestry of MacMillan's compositional career.

8 | *After Virtue* – Symphony No. 3, *The Sacrifice* and the *St John Passion*

The first decade of the new millennium saw James MacMillan firmly recognised as one of the country's leading artists, with major commissions, broadcasts, recordings and festivals devoted to his music. The sense that MacMillan was becoming part of the musical establishment was cemented in 2004, when he was made a Commander of the Order of the British Empire (CBE) by the Prince of Wales in a ceremony at Buckingham Palace, London. Although the fall-out from 'Scotland's Shame' rumbled on in his homeland, it did little to affect his standing in the rest of the UK or further afield and MacMillan's composing and burgeoning conducting career took him to all corners of the globe, to work with many of the world's leading orchestras. In 2005 the BBC devoted a whole weekend to MacMillan's work with the festival 'Darkness into Light: The Music of James MacMillan', which featured twenty-three of his works including the London premieres of *Parthenogenesis*, the orchestral version of *Cantos Sagrados* and the motet *Laudi alla Vergine Maria*. Amongst various talks, film screenings (including Scottish Opera's 1998 performance of *Inés de Castro*) and a late night ceilidh, MacMillan himself conducted the BBC Philharmonic and Symphony Orchestras in his own works, the Violin Concerto by his former tutor John Casken and Harrison Birtwistle's seminal *Exody*.

He was also featured in the long-running British television arts programme *The South Bank Show* in 2003 (directed by Robert Bee) which followed MacMillan's composing and conducting life in the latter half of the previous year, with some personal material including MacMillan playing folk music, attending a Glasgow Celtic football match and memorably accompanying a mobile phone ringtone at the piano.[1] Much of the documentary focussed on MacMillan's relationship with the BBC Philharmonic – he had been appointed composer–conductor in September 2000 – and the programme shows him recording several works including *The Birds of Rhiannon* and the orchestral

---

[1] *The South Bank Show: James MacMillan*, presented by Melvyn Bragg, directed by Robert Bee, series 26, programme 8, aired on ITV, 5 January 2003.

version of the *Magnificat* with the orchestra. The association with the BBC Philharmonic lasted ten years, although MacMillan wrote comparatively little for the orchestra, the only world premiere being *The Birds of Rhiannon*, followed by two UK premieres: the Third Symphony (2002) and *A Scotch Bestiary* (2004).[2] However, like his time as director of the Philharmonia's *Music of Today* series, MacMillan was involved in multiple projects with the orchestra, including working with young composers and conducting pieces by HK Gruber, Kalevi Aho and Peter Maxwell Davies (himself a former composer–conductor of the BBC Philharmonic). As MacMillan recollected in 2018: 'I was able to do a lot of new music during those ten years and the orchestra enjoyed it, and I think they enjoyed me being in charge.'[3]

MacMillan's conducting career has taken him further than just performing his own pieces (although that still represents the majority of his engagements) and has been an important strand to his work since the early 1990s. Like many composers, MacMillan has conducted his works in some fashion since the very early days – in fact the first acknowledged performance of one of his works, the Sanctus from the *Missa Brevis*, was conducted by the composer in March 1977 – and this continued throughout the 1980s including important premieres such as *Búsqueda* and *Into the Ferment*. Much of his reputation as a conductor stems from a 1991 performance of *The Confession of Isobel Gowdie* where MacMillan stepped into the breach the week of the performance with the Philharmonia to replace Giuseppe Sinopoli, as he recalled: 'I had never been in the Royal Festival Hall, I had never stood in front of a professional orchestra, so I was just thrown into it … it gave me a taste for it and gradually other things emerged.'[4] The exposure led to MacMillan joining the musical agency Intermusica as a conductor and composer, and forthcoming engagements followed quickly.

Little is written about MacMillan the conductor, but it has been an ongoing element of his career that arguably reached its zenith in his years with the BBC Philharmonic, when he also guest-conducted with other orchestras such as the Los Angeles Philharmonic, the Rotterdam Philharmonic and the City of Birmingham Symphony Orchestra. He was candid about his experiences in

---

2   Although he wrote few new works for the orchestra he did record five CDs on the Chandos Records label, including recordings of *Into the Ferment*, *The Confessions of Isobel Gowdie* and *Quickening*.

3   Cooke, Interview with James MacMillan, 22 May 2018.

4   Ibid.

Plate 4   James MacMillan in rehearsal with the BBC Philharmonic
(Photo: Sisi Burn, 2001)

2018: 'I did a kind of apprenticeship in the late 1990s and early 2000s ... I was sent off to orchestras in France and Portugal ... it became clear that I needed to do a bit of remedial work and to gain confidence out of the public glare.'[5] He was equally honest that much of his conducting work was 'a way of making money', with MacMillan's conducting career being at its most demanding in the years 2010–15 when the composer's granddaughter Sara was born and her healthcare needs necessitated an increased financial commitment from her grandparents. Following Sara's death in 2016, and the family's relocation to Ayrshire, MacMillan relinquished many of his conducting responsibilities, although it still remains an active part of his career.[6]

Symphony No. 3: 'Silence' (2002)

MacMillan's reputation as an orchestral composer rests on his early orchestral tone-poems such as *Tryst* and *The Confession of Isobel Gowdie*, and a series of colourful concerti including *Veni, Veni, Emmanuel*, *The World's Ransoming* and *Epiclesis*: it is probably safe to say that his symphonic works have not reached the same level of public appreciation as their orchestral counterparts. However, MacMillan's symphonies are an important and ever-expanding part of his oeuvre from Symphony: 'Vigil' in 1997 to the Fourth Symphony in 2015: this shows no sign of waning, with a Fifth Symphony planned for his sixtieth year in 2019. For all the positivity and high regards that these four symphonies have garnered, they have not stuck in the contemporary repertoire like the previously mentioned works, with *Isobel Gowdie* and *Veni, Veni, Emmanuel* (which achieved its 300th performance in 2003, the year of the Third Symphony's premiere) still his most performed and most discussed orchestral pieces, some twenty-five years or more since their first performances. However, the four symphonies are significant, serious statements, each emphasising a diverse facet of MacMillan's compositional persona, each with something different and important to say, the Third Symphony being arguably his most succinct and thought-provoking essay in the genre.

The Symphony No. 3: 'Silence' was composed in 2002 for a joint commission from the NHK Symphony Orchestra and the BBC Philharmonic, with the premiere being given by the NHK, conducted by Charles Dutoit,

---

[5]   Ibid.

[6]   Ibid.

at the NHK Hall in Tokyo in April 2003. The subtitle of the symphony, 'Silence', refers to Japanese writer Shūsaku Endō's (1923–96) 1966 novel of the same name, a powerful declaration of Catholic faith set in seventeenth-century Japan, where Portuguese Jesuit missionaries try to reach an apostate former priest during a period of religious persecution. As MacMillan states in the programme note to the work: 'His book asks profound philosophical questions and resonates with one of the most anguished questions asked 2000 years ago "My God, my God, why have you abandoned me?" Endō's "silence" is the silence of God in the face of terrible events springing from the merciless nature of man: torture, genocide, holocaust.'[7] Although seventeenth-century Japan may be an unusual source for inspiration for MacMillan, critic Robert Stein summed up the work succinctly: 'Struggle, hope, grace, martyrdom, defeat. MacMillan's devotees will recognise his trademarks in a dramatic new piece, albeit one whose narrative is more oblique than *Isabel* [sic] *Gowdie* or *Veni, Veni, Emmanuel*.'[8] The central tenet of both book and symphony is that the 'silence' of the title is not the absence of God, but rather His presence: a pervasive deity choosing to suffer with humanity rather than to ameliorate the suffering. When viewed through that prism, the work becomes less location-specific and more in the trajectory of works that includes the prayers of the Mothers of the Disappeared in *Búsqueda* and the 'Requiem that Isobel Gowdie never had' in his 1990 breakthrough work.

Nevertheless, the location of Endō's novel has more of a bearing on the symphony then just continuing a global search for Catholic persecution: Japanese musical influences can be felt throughout the piece, sometimes at the surface, sometimes buried deep in a complex texture. Like Britten's appropriation of Japanese Noh drama in *Curlew River* (1964), MacMillan treads a careful line between homage and cultural tourism, but like his predecessor the end result is an earnest influence rather than exotic tokenism. The east Asian influences can be felt most in the small sextets that occur towards the beginning and end of the piece, where three flutes, including the plaintive alto flute which is asked to 'play and sing the same note at unison pitch simultaneously', accompanied by *tremolo* marimba and two solo cellos,

---

[7]   James MacMillan, programme note to Symphony No. 3: 'Silence', http://www.boosey.com/cr/music/James-MacMillan-Symphony-No-3-Silence/15181   (accessed 21 June 2018).

[8]   Robert Stein, 'London, Royal Albert Hall Proms 2003: MacMillan, Adams, Kancheli', *Tempo*, vol. 58, no. 227 (January 2004), 52.

Example 8.1   Bars 70–72 of the Symphony No. 3: 'Silence' showing Japanese musical
influences

playing entirely in harmonics, weave an 'expressive and melancholy line, tinged
with influence of the Japanese shakuhachi' (see Example 8.1).[9]

Conceptual and theological 'silence' may be at the heart of the Symphony
No. 3, but musical silence plays an important role as well, not least with the
prominent empty bars that begin and end the work. MacMillan punctuates
the first part of the symphony with silent bars and pauses that disrupt the
musical flow, causing the narrative to begin again in what often feels like a
futile effort; the material is constantly interrupted and fragmented. As the
work progresses, the silences become shorter and occur closer together as
the symphony begins to grow in 'scope, density and drama'[10] as more of the
MacMillan thumbprints from his earlier scores begin to pierce the sustained

---

9   MacMillan, programme note to Symphony No. 3: 'Silence'. The shakuhachi is a
traditional Japanese bamboo flute associated in the western world with exotic, east Asian
sounds.

10   Ibid.

eastern sonorities: hocketing, heterophonic modality and a low brass chorale. A change of direction is felt at bar 265 where a pair of solo violas introduce a dance-like theme in an irregular metre accompanied by woodwind and piano flourishes and the low chorale (like *The World's Ransoming*, the vast majority of the symphony is in a regular 4/4 metre which is unusual for a contemporary work of this scale). This material then begins to fragment as the music moves towards what MacMillan refers to as an 'inevitable crisis-point', a moment in the work when all the narrative strands are torn and the process of reweaving must begin: a characteristic MacMillan formal device that is used successfully in many of the mature orchestral works.[11]

As the symphony begins its return (both musically and conceptually) to its opening sonorities, MacMillan introduces a new scherzo section with the marking 'like a dance' (bar 399) which heralds a sudden change in direction and impetus. However, this new material is something of a red herring – no sooner has the piece reached another climax than the orchestration thins, firstly to just upper woodwind, then to a low C pedal in the double basses, retreating to their quietest dynamic. From this, MacMillan introduces a whole new conceptual idea, a 'slow and stagnant section'[12] entitled 'The Swamp' in which forlorn horn calls echo amidst the murky wastes, as contrabassoon and contrabass clarinet thicken the double-bass pedal. 'The Swamp' is a direct reference to an idea in Endō's novel. The author 'deploys the image of a swamp to emblematize the incompatibility of Christianity with Japanese culture', many times in *Silence* Endō refers to Japan as 'waterlogged and cloaked in mist, a constant reminder of decay and impermanence'.[13] MacMillan had alluded to this moment earlier in the symphony – the piano was marked 'watery' (bars 310–12), the string *glissandi* as 'weeping' (bars 350–51) and the long descending *pizzicato* section as 'like falling rain' (bars 323–33). However, this swamp is not the end of life in its entirety, but rather a 'new world emerging from the depths and darkness'.[14] This hope is suggested by the direct allusion to the opening of Wagner's *Das Rheingold* with the pedal notes, the horn calls and the tonality all redolent of the German composer's awakening of life (see Example 8.2).

As the new life emerges, the music swells to a characteristic string threnody which eventually fades to leave the Japanese-inspired sextet, which

---

[11]   Ibid.

[12]   Ibid.

[13]   John T. R. Terry, 'Shūsaku Endō's Swamp', https://www.firstthings.com/web-exclusives/2016/12/shsaku-ends-swamp (accessed 2 July 2018).

[14]   MacMillan, programme note to Symphony No. 3: 'Silence'.

Example 8.2   Bars 450–53 of the Symphony No. 3: 'Silence' showing allusion to Wagner's *Das Rheingold*

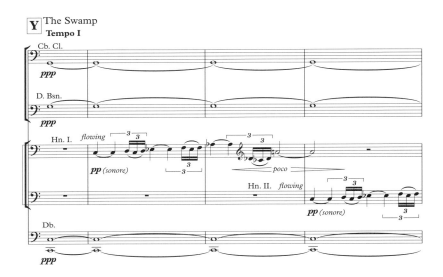

in turn revisits the opening material and that conceptual final bar of silence. In many ways Symphony No. 3 is another example of the arch form favoured by MacMillan and used so successfully in *The Confession of Isobel Gowdie* and *Veni, Veni, Emmanuel*, here the composer suggesting an almost-perfect arch, but subverting the descent to the opening with the interjection of contrasting material.

The Third Symphony is a hybrid work: part symphony, part tone-poem. For all its symphonic aspirations, it is the least recognisably symphonic of his four extant works in the genre, and although more succinct then its counterparts it does feel like an extension of MacMillan's extra-musical works of the early 1990s. The mix of the abstract and the programmatic is typical of the composer at this time: it looks back to his early works on emotive topics, but also looks forward to the more autonomous works of the next decade, where concerti with evocative titles such as *Ninian* and *The World's Ransoming* are replaced by generic titles like Oboe Concerto and Viola Concerto.

The work was a muted success with critics; some were positive and complementary (such as *The Sunday Times*) but others were left cold, none more so than the long-time MacMillan champion Ken Walton in *The Scotsman*. Walton recognised that the Third Symphony found MacMillan at a juncture in his career: no longer the angry young man of the late 1980s and early 1990s, but rather an establishment figure approaching middle age, with 'indications that the edge had gone out of MacMillan's writing'.[15] His review of the symphony, entitled 'A contrived silence', is blunt and to the point, stating that the work was suffering from a 'tendency towards creative navel gazing', and he provocatively refers to MacMillan's collaborator Michael Symmons Roberts as the 'overly precious Welsh poet'.[16] Tellingly, Walton mentions the continued repercussions following 'Scotland's Shame' and alludes to MacMillan's relationship with his homeland in its aftermath: 'MacMillan ... has in effect, gone from Scotland ... he now conducts most of his professional affairs ... south of the border or overseas.'[17] This continues a narrative that was present in the years after 'Scotland's Shame', of MacMillan's putative move to the north-west of England to be closer to Symmons Roberts and his work with the BBC Philharmonic. However, this move never happened, with the MacMillan family continuing to be based in Glasgow until the move to Ayrshire in 2015. When asked about this in 2018, MacMillan responded in no uncertain terms: 'I could have lived anywhere, I wasn't particularly joined-at-the-hip to Scotland, but my wife wanted to be in Scotland ... she had her own career in law ... we just became more settled.'[18] He did reflect Walton's accusations by stating that 'there were times after "Scotland's Shame" when we thought about going away as things had become unpleasant'.[19] The quote that lingers from 'A contrived silence' is the same issue that many creative artists have to deal with, the move from youth to middle age: 'If maturity has brought a softer, more ruminative edge, MacMillan has not quite found the gravitas required to replace the anger, at least not in this symphony.'[20]

The Sacrifice (2005–06)

By far the most substantial work in the 2000s to follow the Third Symphony was MacMillan's second foray into large-scale opera, *The Sacrifice*, which he composed in 2005–06 and which was premiered in September 2007. The

---

15   Ken Walton, 'A contrived silence', *The Scotsman* (28 July 2003).

16   Ibid.

17   Ibid.

18   Cooke, Interview with James MacMillan, 22 May 2018.

19   Ibid.

20   Walton, 'A contrived silence'.

work was a commission from Welsh National Opera (WNO) and was the most ambitious collaboration with Symmons Roberts to date: a three-hour, three-act opera that was almost ten years in gestation from initial commission to first performance. MacMillan himself conducted the orchestra and chorus of WNO in the premiere at the Wales Millennium Centre, Cardiff, in a production staged by leading opera director Katie Mitchell (who had directed MacMillan and Symmons Roberts's earlier operatic collaboration *Parthenogenesis* in 2000).

Although *Inés de Castro* had been something of a bruising experience for MacMillan, it did not prevent him returning to the medium ten years after his first experience. The working relationships were very different second time around, with the composer now free to choose his own librettist and an impressive creative team (which MacMillan referred to as a 'gang of four'), spearheaded by Mitchell and designer Vicki Mortimer.[21] The conceiving of the libretto was an fecund time, with composer and librettist working tirelessly on the right tone, mood and narrative for the work, 'retreating periodically to a little cottage on Skye' to focus their creativity.[22]

The Sacrifice is loosely based on a tale from the *Mabinogion*, the medieval Welsh anthology of stories, one of Wales's most revered literary documents that blends together Celtic myths with contemporary events and locations. *The Sacrifice* takes 'The Second Branch of the Mabinogi' as its source material with the original's depiction of two warring nations (England and Ireland) seemingly pacified by an unhappy marriage and a male issue, with tragedy and repercussions ensuing before an enigmatic conclusion (involving decapitation, seven years of feasting and birds that can awaken the dead). In Symmons Roberts's libretto, the Mabinogi is updated to an unspecified nation, ravaged by civil war, in which the General of one faction offers the hand of his daughter, Sian, in marriage to the leader of the other faction, Mal. Sian forsakes the love of Evan (a leading soldier of her group) for the good of her people and has two sons by her new husband. Seven years later, at the investiture of her eldest son Gwyn, Evan returns and breaks the accord by shooting the child dead. The General then realises the union has not worked and offers his own self-sacrifice, dressing as Evan to instigate his own death at the hands of Mal. The opera ends with Sian prostate over her father's dead body, comforted by her younger son Elis and the songs of her sister Megan. Although *The Sacrifice* has its roots in the *Mabinogion*, MacMillan and Symmons Roberts made extensive changes to the original narrative, mainly through the inclusion of the character Elis as a

---

[21]   James MacMillan, 'My Mabinogion opus', *The Scotsman* (16 September 2007).

[22]   Ibid.

second son: in the original there is only one son, whose death signals the end of reconciliation between the warring nations. By having two in *The Sacrifice* all hope is not lost, and the 'sacrifice' of the opera's title may not be in vain.

The Sacrifice was not the first time that MacMillan and Symmons Roberts had turned to the *Mabinogion* for inspiration for a large-scale work. Six years before the premiere of the opera came the 'tone-poem for orchestra with optional chorus', *The Birds of Rhiannon*, a major new work for the BBC Philharmonic at the 2001 Proms. This is one of MacMillan's most unusual orchestral works, with the choir only entering at the end of the piece for a short coda (lasting some 7 minutes of the work's 24-minute duration), incanting words, not from the *Mabinogion*, but Symmons Roberts's own reflections on the events portrayed in the medieval source. MacMillan's description of *The Birds of Rhiannon* as a 'dramatic concerto for orchestra with a mystical coda for choir' is apt, and goes some way to describing the unfamiliar nature of the work.[23] In many ways the tone-poem acted as a test-bed for *The Sacrifice*, not only in the exploration of inspiration and source material, but in the actual music itself, much of which is recycled in the later work. The birds of Rhiannon of the title are mythical creatures that can raise the dead and lull the living to sleep (they feature at the denouement of 'The Second Branch of the Mabinogi') and MacMillan alludes to their role in the drama by naming his on-stage wedding band in *The Sacrifice* 'The Birds (of Rhiannon)'.

The Sacrifice is much in the mould of the grand operatic statement of *Inés de Castro*, but rather than inspiration coming from the models of Verdi and Wagner (though they are there in places), it is the heightened emotional and expressive worlds of Strauss's *Elektra* and Berg's *Wozzeck* that are evident in MacMillan's work. Britten is never far away, both in the scale and ambition of *Peter Grimes* and the intensity of some of Britten's smaller works in the genre, as Symmons Roberts's revealed in 2007: 'On one particular afternoon ... we watched [Britten's] *The Turn of the Screw* back to back with Strauss's *Elektra* ... Piper's subtle, understated text was in astonishing contrast to Hofmannsthal's superheated expressionist outpouring.'[24] It was the blending of these two

---

23   James MacMillan, programme note to *The Birds of Rhiannon*, http://www.boosey. com/cr/music/James-MacMillan-The-Birds-of-Rhiannon/15179 (accessed 3 July 2018).
24   Michael Symmons Roberts, '*The Sacrifice* Collaboration', programme to *The Sacrifice*, WNO (2007), 22. Myfanwy Piper (1911–96) was a British art critic and librettist who collaborated with Britten on three operas. Hugo von Hofmannsthal (1874–1929) was an Austrian poet and librettist who wrote the text for many of Strauss's most successful operas including *Der Rosenkavalier* and *Die Frau ohne Schatten*.

different approaches that characterises Symmons Roberts's offering for *The Sacrifice*. Although MacMillan's two large-scale operas do share similar themes (infanticide, war, conflict and redemption), *The Sacrifice* is a much more positive and nuanced narrative than *Inés de Castro*, perhaps suggesting that the 'blood-boltered melodrama'[25] of his first opera that had so offended the critics had led the composer to tone down the bloodletting in his second.

Although the location of the drama in *The Sacrifice* is unspecified (the opening scene is subtitled 'Wasteland/derelict ballroom of a hotel') MacMillan gave some clues to his thoughts on the matter in 2007: 'Placing the opera geographically is a matter of ambiguity: it takes place in a society like ours, maybe in this country, or elsewhere in Europe, maybe now, maybe in the near future.'[26] He gave further insight in *The Scotsman*: 'I'd liken the atmosphere to Alfonso Cuarón's 2006 film *The Children of Men*, set in a recognisable future where society has been blown apart by terrorist bombs and civil disturbance.'[27] Although unspecified, the warring states, united by ties of blood, language and religion, 'elsewhere in Europe', brings to mind the Balkan wars which had only recently ceased when MacMillan first began conceiving the opera. He alluded to this: 'the fact that a society not dissimilar to our own had descended into apocalyptic destructiveness seemed very pertinent'.[28] The initial production of *The Sacrifice* emphasised this, with militaristic garb and grey hues redolent of the conflict in the former Yugoslavia.

MacMillan binds together *The Sacrifice* through several key themes that return throughout (much in the Wagnerian mould), the most striking being the 'love' theme which first occurs in the prelude to the opera and is woven into the material of the emotional duets between Sian and Evan (see Example 8.3).

This modal, rhapsodic and arioso theme is in sharp contrast to the 'white song' of Megan ('I've made a white song for the bride. Do you like it?') with its prominent repeated minor third and ambiguous resolution (see Example 8.4). This theme, first encountered in Act I Scene 2, is found throughout the opera performed by both Sian and Megan, with its apotheosis in a heart-wrenching final iteration as the General and Megan part company in Act III Scene 2.

Like *Inés de Castro*, *The Sacrifice* features many traditional operatic set-pieces including the aforementioned love duets, powerful monologues and an absorbing trio. It also utilises tropes of the genre, with a wedding, a funeral,

---

[25]   Whittall, 'Elegies and Affirmations: John Casken at 60', 46.

[26]   Simon Rees, 'Making words sing', programme to *The Sacrifice*, 15.

[27]   MacMillan, 'My Mabinogion opus'.

[28]   Ibid.

Example 8.3   Bars 22–24 and 91–92 of Act I of *The Sacrifice* showing the first instance of the 'love' theme and Sian's adaptation

Example 8.4   Bars 276–79 of Act I and 299–302 of Act III of *The Sacrifice* showing the first instance of the 'white song', first performed by Megan and then the General (vocal parts only)

a murder and mistaken identity, all taking place amidst a lush, post-romantic soundscape featuring some of MacMillan's most colourful and expressive orchestration. In keeping with the composer's new-found commitment to choral music, *The Sacrifice* features an extensive role for the operatic chorus, particularly in the two moments of high drama: the wedding of Sian and Mal, and the investiture of Gwyn. The choral writing is expansive and virtuosic in places, asking much more from the chorus than in many operas, particularly in Acts II and III where they are almost ever-present and a key part of the unfolding drama. MacMillan also includes a quirky on-stage wedding band (replete with electric guitar), whose eerie wedding song about the moon becoming a hunter is one of the opera's most memorable and beguiling moments, composed almost entirely of unrelated major and minor triads (one of the key harmonic devices in the piece).

Another similarity between MacMillan's two extended operas is the use of powerful female characters, often in roles where they act as an agent of redemption and amelioration. *Inés de Castro* ends with the ghost of Inés appearing to a young girl to warn her: 'They'll tell you that they have to kill … do not believe them … there is another way.' This idea of a 'principal female character appealing for a new future, transcending the enmities and hatreds of the past' is again present in *The Sacrifice*, where Sian extols to the warring nations: 'A great king has laid down his life between our battle lines. Enough. It's in our hands to break the feud. Enough sacrifice. Enough blood.'[29] In his article 'Crucifixion in the Concert Hall: Secular and Sacred in James MacMillan's *Passion of St John*', Hugh Pyper makes an interesting case that there is an issue with the redemption of men in MacMillan's operas, stating: 'Women can redeem and be redeemed, but men seem irredeemable.'[30] Indeed, despite the General's self-sacrifice, Evan's love for Sian and Mal's grief at his son's death there is little to commend the male characters in *The Sacrifice*: all have weaknesses, all are flawed. Ultimately, it is through the forgiveness of Sian – the mother that united the factions – that reconciliation and the promise of peace is possible.

As in *Inés de Castro*, *The Sacrifice* draws on parallels and allusions to the Passion story, though nowhere near as obvious as one might expect from a collaboration between Symmons Roberts and MacMillan. Yes, the self-sacrifice of the General echoes that of Christ, and Sian's sacrifice for the good of the wider community has strong Christian associations, but the opera does not draw on the complex religious threads that previous collaborations such as *Quickening* exhibited. Like the use of the *Stabat Mater* in the final Act of *Inés de Castro*, MacMillan introduces liturgical texts towards the end of *The Sacrifice*, with the chorus singing sections of the Requiem Mass as the drama unfurls around them. He emphasises the religious connotations by including the Agnus Dei at one of the most dramatic moments of the opera, as Mal is made aware that the man he has murdered was in fact the General and not Evan. Here, Mal's impassioned outburst (using the same material that the chorus had recently used for their Requiem setting) is accompanied by free-time chanting, the only point

---

[29]   Michael Fuller, 'Liturgy, Scripture and Resonance in the Operas of James MacMillan', *New Blackfriars*, vol. 96, no. 1964 (2015), 388.

[30]   Hugh S. Pyper, 'Crucifixion in the Concert Hall: Secular and Sacred in James MacMillan's *Passion of St John*', *Literature and Theology*, vol. 23, no. 3 (2009), 347.

where this ritualistic and striking sonority had been called upon. The inclusion of the Agnus Dei is hugely symbolic, as this final plea for mercy suggests that only through God can actual redemption be achieved.

Dominic Wells makes a persuasive argument for the influence of Wagner's *Tristan und Isolde* on *The Sacrifice*, or to be more specific, the original Celtic myth transfigured through Wagner's *Gesamtkunstwerk*.[31] Certainly there are many parallels between the Tristan myth and 'The Second Branch of the Mabinogi', with hostile Celtic states, a forlorn sea journey, forbidden love and sacrifice all featuring. Much of MacMillan's interest in the Tristan myth springs from a 2004 book by the British philosopher Roger Scruton, entitled *Death-Devoted Heart: Sex and the Sacred in Wagner's 'Tristan und Isolde'*.[32] MacMillan has gone on record many times to affirm his interest and appreciation of Scruton's book and the ideas within, none more so than the central theory that *Tristan und Isolde* is 'a search for the sacred in modernism' and that there is a Eucharistic association to the opera that emphasises this idea.[33] Although *The Sacrifice* may be the first MacMillan work to be influenced by Scruton's reading of *Tristan und Isolde*, it was not the first work to feature a quotation or allusion to the opera: as early as the Piano Sonata of 1985, MacMillan was incorporating references to *Tristan*, and this carried on through the Symphony No. 2 (1999), a reimagining of the Piano Sonata, to the works of the 2000s.

Unfortunately, like *Inés de Castro*, *The Sacrifice* was met with a frosty reception from the critics, though perhaps with not quite the savage glee that was meted out to MacMillan's first opera. Many of the reviews centred on issues with Symmons Roberts's libretto ('over-wordy ... each potentially dramatic moment ... rendered null by inflated comment and soliloquy' said *The Evening Standard*) or Mortimer's set design ('awful greyness ... amplified by the extreme banality of fluctuating electricity' moaned *The Guardian*), though MacMillan's music came off little better in some cases ('a patchwork quilt of Tippett and Britten, Strauss and Wagner, Mahler and occasionally himself' grumbled *The*

---

31   See Dominic Wells, 'Sacrificial passions: The influence of Wagner and Scruton in James MacMillan's *The Sacrifice* and *St John Passion*', in Robert Sholl and Sandor van Mass, eds., *Contemporary Music and Spirituality* (London: Routledge, 2016), 37–53.

32   Scruton, Roger, *Death-Devoted Heart: Sex and the Sacred in Wagner's 'Tristan und Isolde'* (Oxford: OUP, 2004).

33   Hallam, 'Conversation with James MacMillan', 22. In the same interview, MacMillan refers to Scruton as 'a kind of *agent provocateur*...and he likes to stereotype, but actually he's a very fine philosopher who reflects a lot on music.' Scruton's traditionalist and conservative ideas have no doubt influenced MacMillan in the new millennium.

Observer).[34] Not all reviews were quite so critical – *The Independent* gave the opera five stars, stating that the 'first performance, under the composer, was beyond praise' and *The Telegraph* opened its review with: 'Here is something rare, a new opera with instant appeal.'[35]

The critical response to his two operas have had a marked effect on James MacMillan, with *The Sacrifice* being his last large-scale work in the genre. He has mentioned his incompatibility with the medium in a number of interviews, stating in 2017: 'I think ... that I am not an opera composer of this age. I can see what the opera world wants, and I don't want that.'[36] It is an odd irony that MacMillan has had much success in breathing new life into older models and forms such as the tone-poem and oratorio, but his operatic output is often lambasted for being too traditional and too regressive. He returned to opera again, but in a much reduced form, in the one-act *Clemency* in 2010 (see chapter nine), a work that is a world away from its much grander predecessors.

St John Passion (2007)

For a composer who stated in 2000 'I seem to be drawn again and again to the Passion ... I do seem to be going round and round the same three days of history', to take until nearly his fiftieth year to attempt a full-scale Passion setting might seem a little incongruous, certainly when the vast majority of the mature music by that composer is somehow related to those three days and the events that followed.[37] However, it was not until 2007 that James MacMillan undertook his Passion setting, a 90-minute choral–orchestral rendering of 'The Passion of Our Lord Jesus Christ according to John' that is as full of drama, colour, anger and faith as any of the celebrated settings by his forebears. The *St John Passion* was first performed by the London Symphony Orchestra and Chorus, conducted by its dedicatee, Sir Colin Davis, at the Barbican in London, in April 2008.

---

34   Fiona Maddocks, 'Rich Melodies', *The Evening Standard* (15 November 2007). Rian Evans, 'The Sacrifice', *The Guardian* (24 September 2007). Anthony Holden, 'An uneasy marriage', *The Observer* (30 September 2007).

35   Stephen Walsh, 'The Sacrifice', *The Independent* (1 October 2007). Rupert Christiansen, 'The Sacrifice: Just a little too slick', *The Telegraph* (24 September 2007).

36   Cooke, Interview with James MacMillan, 16 November 2017.

37   MacMillan, 'God, Theology and Music', 19.

MacMillan had been commissioned to write a work for Colin Davis's eightieth birthday as early as 2005, but various ideas and suggestions had not taken shape, and it was not until Davis came on board with MacMillan's long-term desire to write a Passion that the composition began in earnest. MacMillan kept a short diary of the writing processes behind the work that was eventually published in *The Guardian* under the title 'Conceived in silence', in which he describes some of the decision-making behind the key events and texts of the Passion.[38] Although ostensibly a setting of the traditional St John Gospel in the Revised Standard Edition of the bible, MacMillan inserts and incorporates other texts, relating to the drama portrayed, in much the same fashion that had been so successful in *Seven Last Words from the Cross*. As he revealed in 2008: 'I knew from the outset that there would be extra texts interpolated into my piece, just as Bach uses chorales in his Passions.'[39] Instead of using Lutheran hymn-tunes, MacMillan includes Latin motets at the end of most movements, with the intention that 'these motets will move action from the vernacular into something that perhaps subliminally evokes the detachment of Bach's chorales'.[40] Although MacMillan may have been striving for 'detachment', some of the most expressive and heartfelt music can be found in these motets, not least the inclusion of the Papal hymn *Tu es Petrus* in a strident setting at the end of the third movement when Peter has denied Christ: a sudden reaffirmation of the disciple where other settings have him break down in tears.

Bach is never too far away in MacMillan's *St John Passion*, which is understandable when setting a text so associated with another composer, as MacMillan stated: 'he hovers over the heads of living composers like a terrifying ghost from history'.[41] However, MacMillan's setting is not a homage to the great master: some things he takes, some things he leaves behind in a typical 'magpie' fashion. One of the most substantial changes to the Bachian model is MacMillan's use of his assembled vocal forces: the *St John Passion* is scored for large symphonic chorus, small choir (8–24 singers) and solo baritone, with the last of these providing the voice of Jesus. It is the use of the small choir as a 'narrator chorus' that provides the biggest departure, with Bach's virtuosic solo tenor Evangelist replaced by this homogenous group of singers, providing much of the detail for the narrative. This was not without its challenges for the composer who confessed to 'wondering if I need more soloists' in the movement

---

38 James MacMillan, 'Conceived in silence', *The Guardian* (25 April 2008).

39 Ibid.

40 Ibid.

41 MacMillan, 'James MacMillan in Scotland'.

where Jesus is brought before Pontius Pilate, with the solution arriving in the form of more 'character' roles for the large chorus.[42] This carries on throughout the Passion, with the choir representing Peter, the Virgin Mary and many others including the 'turba' (the crowd). This simple decision gives the work a more human touch, with the otherworldly and rarefied voices of soloists replaced by those evoking the common people.

One of the most controversial interpolations in the *St John Passion* was MacMillan's decision to include the *Reproaches* (also known as the *Improperia*) as the eighth movement of the work. This set of Good Friday prayers, traditionally recited during the veneration of the cross (see chapters four and five) has had a chequered history, particularly as it hints at the perceived anti-Semitism of the Catholic Church. The *Reproaches* are very different in tone and direction to the rest of the text (they do not form any part of St John's Gospel) and 'represent Christ addressing a series of questions to his hearers which contrast the self-giving of his ministry with their ingratitude'.[43] That MacMillan should include this text in his Passion is no real surprise: like the St John Gospel, the *Reproaches* form an important part of the Catholic Good Friday tradition, and the inclusion reflects the composer's religious heritage rather than any latent anti-Semitism. MacMillan emphasised this in 2011: 'No sane Catholic today ... imagines that they are accusing the Jews of deicide. Neither would any sane secularist believe them to be an occasion for heightening anti-Semitism. The *Reproaches* are a liturgical tool to remind Catholics ... of their own sinfulness.'[44] It appeared that not everyone shared MacMillan's view of the text – at the US premiere performances of the *St John Passion* in Boston, a man rushed on the stage to confront the composer – 'by the look in his eyes he could have done me real damage'[45] – and the following night's CD signing was accompanied by an increased security presence.

The role of the solo baritone as Christ in MacMillan's Passion is another striking decision. This character has a very different sound-world to the other vocal parts, as MacMillan states: 'His music has an eastern, Semitic feel – lots of

---

[42]   MacMillan, 'Conceived in silence'. MacMillan refers to the music for Pilate as 'a particular colour ... a desiccated, dry clicking sound ... with low bassoons and parping trombones'.

[43]   Pyper, 'Crucifixion in the Concert Hall: Secular and Sacred in James MacMillan's *Passion of St John*', 349.

[44]   MacMillan, 'James MacMillan in Scotland'.

[45]   Ibid.

melismas and *glissandi*.[46] This sense of Jesus as an 'other', somewhat 'apart from the convulsions unfolding around him' is a marked decision by the composer and one that is compounded by this being the only solo role in the work (see Example 8.5).[47] If MacMillan's choice to reduce the solo parts in the *St John Passion* was to lead to a more communal, earthly setting, his decision to have Christ so noticeably soloistic and ethereal seems to contradict this, as Pyper notes: 'MacMillan's Christ is given florid melismata to sing out of a sort of chora of percussion and muttering winds which increases his otherness.'[48]

One of the most poignant sections of the Passion is the seventh movement, 'Jesus and his Mother', which finds MacMillan interpolating the *Stabat Mater* into the Gospel text to provide the 'detachment' to the pained narrative. However, it is the inclusion of a second text that gives the movement its real humanity and soul, with MacMillan adapting the Christmas carol *Lully, lulla, my dear darling* to heart-wrenching effect. He sets this plaintive text in a simple, unadorned fashion for the sopranos and basses, in great contrast to the highly melismatic Latin material exhibited in the inner choral parts. The final coalescence of the choir on the line 'your sacred head is wounded' is one of the most moving moments in the *St John Passion*.

One of the main criticisms levelled at the *St John Passion* is that the work is overly masculine, with very little material for the female voices and for femininity in in general. Removing the solo soprano that represented Mary in Bach's Passion reinforces this, and although the seventh movement of MacMillan's gives focus to the female perspective, the Latin text leads to this

Example 8.5   Bars 26–29 of 'The arrest of Jesus' from the *St John Passion* showing Christ's ornamented vocal lines (baritone part only)

46   MacMillan, 'Conceived in silence'.

47   MacMillan, James, 'Interview about his *St John Passion*', http://www.boosey.com/cr/news/James-MacMillan-interview-about-his-St-John-Passion/11805 (accessed 20 June 2018).

48   Pyper, 'Crucifixion in the Concert Hall: Secular and Sacred in James MacMillan's *Passion of St John*', 349.

section being 'more of an impersonal lament than an expression of a mother's grief'.[49] Like much of MacMillan's work, the *St John Passion* features a conflict that needs resolving, however the conflict in this work is 'one man against many men, a clash of masculinities', understandable for a story that is dominated by male characters, but noticeable nonetheless.[50]

Like *The Sacrifice*, the *St John Passion* is written firmly under the spell of Wagner's *Tristan und Isolde* and Scruton's book on the opera, with the same 'search for the sacred in modernism' permeating MacMillan's work. He makes the link to Wagner's music drama even more evident in his Passion by having a direct quotation from *Tristan* in the final movement of the *St John Passion*, with the cor anglais and divided cellos suddenly presenting the opening theme of Wagner's work in an unadulterated fashion (see Example 8.6).

Dominic Wells proposes that by 'quoting *Tristan* at the end of his *St John Passion*, MacMillan suggests that the ultimate "Liebestod" is the crucifixion: Christ's agapé for the world through his own self-sacrifice.'[51] Certainly this quotation is of huge personal and theological significance to MacMillan, though conversely it does form another thread in a patchwork quilt of quotations in the Passion which includes sections of Bach, Victoria, more Wagner and even an allusion to Britten's *War Requiem*.

Perhaps the piece that the *St John Passion* is influenced by the most is actually a work of MacMillan's himself, as he recalled: 'I just felt it came off the back of *The Sacrifice* and is absolutely saturated with opera ... it was all that was in my head at that stage and some of the music has crossed from one to another.'[52] MacMillan finished the Passion in Cardiff in September 2007 during rehearsals for the opera, using the mornings and breaks from performing to put the finishing touches to the new work. It was understandable for such a major and substantial piece as *The Sacrifice* to bleed into subsequent work, particularly when composition and performances coincided in such a marked way. However, the link between the two pieces goes deeper than just a compositional timeline;

[49]   Stein, 'London, Barbican: MacMillan's "St John Passion"', 51.

[50]   Pyper, 'Crucifixion in the Concert Hall: Secular and Sacred in James MacMillan's *Passion of St John*', 347.

[51]   Wells, 'Sacrificial passions: The influence of Wagner and Scruton in James MacMillan's *The Sacrifice* and *St John Passion*', 47. The 'Liebestod' is a reference to Isolde's final music in *Tristan und Isolde* and literally translates as 'love death', meaning the consummation of the love of two people only through their death.

[52]   Cooke, Interview with James MacMillan, 22 May 2018.

Example 8.6   Bars 23–26 of 'Sanctus Immortalis, miserere nobis' from the *St John Passion* showing quotation from Wagner's *Tristan und Isolde* (cor anglais part only)

they are joined together by profound personal and theological underpinnings that go to the very heart of MacMillan the composer in the 2000s and these febrile works composed under the influence of Wagner and Scruton's ideas are inextricably linked.

The bond between the pieces is both philosophical and musical, with the former being represented by the ultimate sacrifice: Jesus's crucifixion. The latter is perhaps more subtle, a 'cross-fertilisation of two worlds', with the liturgical impulse behind the *St John Passion* influencing the opera and the theatrical nature of *The Sacrifice* being evident in the oratorio: a characteristic MacMillan trait of mixing the sacred and the profane.[53]

The moment where the sacred and the secular are brought together in the most meaningful fashion in the *St John Passion* is in the final movement, 'Sanctus Immortalis, miserere nobis' (Holy immortal One, have mercy on us), a line taken from 'The Reproaches' movement, where MacMillan brings back a familiar theme to great effect. *The Tryst* is used for the first time since the Cello Sonata No. 1 of 1999 and over twenty years since its first appropriation in the *St Anne's Mass* in 1985. This final movement of the Passion again follows on from the model of *Seven Last Words from the Cross* by leaving the closing material of the work to instruments alone, a 'Song without Words'. As MacMillan describes it: 'no text could suffice here ... it is left to music alone to explore the deeper tragedy which has just unfolded'.[54] Whereas the final movement of *Seven Last Words* finds the string orchestra finishing the narrative set forth by declamatory choral statements, the final movement of the *St John Passion* is purely instrumental: ten minutes of orchestral drama,

---

53   MacMillan, as quoted in Tavener, liner notes to *Tenebrae: New Choral Music by James MacMillan*, 10.

54   MacMillan, 'Interview about his *St John Passion*'.

Example 8.7   Bars 57–66 of 'Sanctus Immortalis, miserere nobis' from the *St John Passion* showing *The Tryst* theme (horn parts only)

acting as a microcosm for the work as a whole. *The Tryst* material rises from the orchestral texture like a 'long, noble optimistic theme', beginning in the horns and infusing the whole palette, giving hope to this final offering (see Example 8.7).[55]

That MacMillan should choose to include *The Tryst*, which he described as having 'commitment, sanctity, intimacy, faith ... love, but it is also saturated with a sadness as if all these things are about to expire' in the *St John Passion* is perhaps no surprise, he had already done a very similar procedure in adapting this to form a 'love song for the church' in the Sanctus of the *St Anne's Mass*.[56] Again, music of a vernacular or traditional nature is being used to ameliorate previous transgressions. The words that MacMillan used to describe the similar technique in *Seven Last Words* rings true: 'the liturgical detachment breaks down and gives way to a more personal reflection'.[57] For MacMillan, nothing is more personal and meaningful than the inclusion of *The Tryst*.

MacMillan stated in 2008 that the *St John Passion* was 'a significant piece, not least because it's one that I've been hoping to write for many years', and the work has gone on to be one of his most discussed works from the 2000s onwards.[58] It also represented the beginning of a project to set all four Passion

55   Stein, 'London, Barbican: MacMillan's "St John Passion"', 51.

56   MacMillan, liner notes to *James MacMillan: Veni, Veni, Emmanuel; Tryst*, 3.

57   MacMillan, programme note to *Seven Last Words from the Cross*.

58   MacMillan, 'Conceived in silence'.

texts, with MacMillan musing: 'I want to take the rest of my life to do the other three ... I'm already talking to people about the St Mark ... then maybe I'll think about the St Matthew'.[59] MacMillan followed the *St John Passion* in 2013 with his setting of the *St Luke Passion* (see chapter nine), a smaller scale but no less dramatic work.

---

[59]   Ken Walton, 'Interview: James MacMillan, composer', *The Scotsman* (2 August 2012).

9 | *Serenity* – Violin Concerto, *Clemency* and the *St Luke Passion*

Amidst the outpouring of choral pieces and grand Wagnerian statements from James MacMillan in the 2000s there was a new, unexpected strand to the composer's work that began to take shape in the latter part of the decade and has become an important facet of his oeuvre ever since: the move to a greater form of abstraction in his orchestral and chamber works. For a composer whose reputation was built on tone-poems and concerti with evocative, programmatic names (none more so than his calling card *The Confession of Isobel Gowdie*), the move to more generic, autonomous titles was an unusual one, but one that MacMillan was aware of nonetheless, as he stated in 2007:

> More recently, I've noticed that I've been leaving the extra-musical starting points behind. I don't know if this is a new direction or not. This might come as a surprise to the people who see me as someone who has this other aspect, but I've always written abstractly. Perhaps I'm just moving into another phase now, where the theology and the pre-musical are much more subliminal, taken for granted.[1]

MacMillan may have 'always written abstractly', but his body of work in the 1980s and 1990s has few purely abstract pieces, the Piano Sonata (1985), the *Sinfonietta* (1991) and the Cello Sonata No. 1 (1999) being examples from a small pool. It is telling that even those pieces that traditionally had generic titles such as the string quartet and the symphony are given extra-musical names by MacMillan – the first two quartets are titled *Visions of a November Spring* and *Why is this night different?* and the symphony contains the poetic addendum 'Vigil' – and his early concerti have some of the most programmatic titles of all the composer's works.[2] However, 2007 does appear to have been something of

---

[1]   Hallam, 'Conversation with James MacMillan', 17.

[2]   It is worth noting that although the Cello Concerto from 1996 has an abstract title, as chapter five shows it is anything but abstract and MacMillan goes to great lengths to highlight the extra-musical programme behind the work.

turning-point for MacMillan, for although the year was dominated by the *St John Passion* and works from *The Strathclyde Motets*, two substantial chamber works were composed, neither of which had any overt pre-compositional stimuli: the String Quartet No. 3 and the Horn Quintet. These two pieces mark the beginning of a new focus on autonomous music (MacMillan referred to the String Quartet No. 3 as 'just the notes and nothing but the notes'[3]) that saw concerti for oboe (2010), viola (2013) trombone (2016) and saxophone (2017) and arguably culminated in the epic Symphony No. 4 in 2015. Perhaps the most overt manifestation of this new abstraction was the Percussion Concerto No. 2 of 2014, a title as far removed from its predecessor *Veni, Veni, Emmanuel* as possible, the composer firmly letting the musical world know of these new aesthetic developments.

MacMillan is coy as to the reasons behind his new-found adoption of the abstract in music; as with many of his decisions in the 2000s it has its roots in the reaction to 'Scotland's Shame' and his political conversion that saw him move from the left to the right of the spectrum in the wake of the criticism of his Edinburgh Festival speech. In 2015 he railed against the politicisation of *Isobel Gowdie* by certain classes, stating that the work was

> something abstract, a piece of pure music that people engaged with without knowing anything about it ... that militates against those who say music and the arts have to be political ... if people heard it without reading the programme note, would they say 'here's a political piece of music'? I don't think so.[4]

The assumption that any of his works that touched on national, historical or ethnic themes, as opposed to his overtly religious pieces, were open to interpretation and criticism from the left-leaning media has obviously hurt MacMillan, and it is easy to view his move to abstraction as a retreat to the safety of the purely musical. He has often referred to the abstraction of music as 'its most precious thing'. If pre-musical ideas are there, he is much less likely to be open about them to those who may criticise and demean his art.[5] However, despite the political connotations of MacMillan's decision, he is following the trend of many composers who move from the poetry and directness of

---

[3]   Hallam, 'Conversation with James MacMillan', 17.

[4]   Cooke, Interview with James MacMillan, 30 November 2015.

[5]   Ibid. In the same interview MacMillan referred to the Fourth Symphony having an unacknowledged extra-musical programme that 'some writers have twigged about ... not the mainstream writers though.'

programmatic titles to the more arcane and 'respected' nature of the abstract in their later years, a symptom of age, status and intellectualism, and in this case MacMillan is no different to earlier models such as Ralph Vaughan Williams and Peter Maxwell Davies.[6]

Although abstract pieces have increased in MacMillan's output since 2007, programmatic works are still being composed, including pieces that might broadly be classed as tone-poems: *Woman of the Apocalypse* (2012) and *The Death of Oscar* (2012) being two prominent recent examples.[7]

Violin Concerto (2009)

Perhaps the most emblematic work of MacMillan's renewed foray into abstraction is the Violin Concerto of 2009, a powerful three-movement work written for and dedicated to the celebrated Russian virtuoso Vadim Repin, who gave the first performance with the London Symphony Orchestra under compatriot Valery Gergiev at the Barbican, London in May 2010. Although the first work of MacMillan's to have the title of violin concerto, it was not the first work for violin and orchestra from the composer – in the previous seven years he had written two shorter works for this combination with vastly different aesthetic and technical considerations: *A Deep but Dazzling Darkness* (2002) and *From Ayrshire* (2005). These two works, representing two differing sides of the composer's persona, are both test-beds for the larger work and both feed into the concerto in one form or another.

In many ways these two concertante works are something of a red herring in MacMillan's output in the 2000s: neither seem to fit the narratives that MacMillan was carefully constructing and both are amongst his most obscure orchestral works. *A Deep but Dazzling Darkness* was commissioned for the opening of the LSO's new St Luke's Centre in London and was premiered in

---

6   Peter Maxwell Davies is an interesting case to substantiate this claim: his early successes centre on works with pre-musical titles such as *Worldes Bliss* (1966–69) and *St Thomas Wake* (1969), though towards the end of his career (when he had been both knighted and appointed Master of the Queen's Music) he had embarked on a set of symphonies, concerti and string quartets with little programmatic content.

7   *Woman of the Apocalypse* takes its inspiration from visual art works on the topic from throughout history and *The Death of Oscar* is a response to the Celtic warrior and poet Ossian and the saga of his son, Oscar's death. Both are firmly in the tone-poem mould of *The Confession of Isobel Gowdie* that was central to establishing MacMillan's career.

a private performance conducted by the composer with Gordan Nikolitch as the soloist. The piece is one of MacMillan's most angular, dissonant and overtly modernist works, eschewing the modality and gentle polystylism of the *Triduum* and *Quickening* for a fierce, kaleidoscopic showpiece that at times feels like it is by a very different composer to MacMillan in 2002. Although springing from a characteristic MacMillan source of inspiration, a poem about divinity from Henry Vaughan entitled *The Night* ('There is a God, some say, A deep but dazzling darkness'), and incorporating a pre-existing traditional melody (in this case *L'homme armé*), *A Deep but Dazzling Darkness* asks very different questions of the listener and the piece as a whole has the feel of experimentation rather than further aesthetic consolidation. The opening of the piece sets the agenda immediately with a trio of low, scurrying instruments accompanying a disjunct soloist, against a pre-recorded sonic tapestry of bewildering noises and dramatic *glissandi*. The inclusion of a 'taped' element is unusual in MacMillan's output, and seems a somewhat anachronistic gesture from the composer as it had been twenty-five years since he had first utilised the medium in the now withdrawn *Litanies of Iron and Stone*, and had used it only fleetingly in the intervening years (there is an electronic element to the music theatre work *Parthenogenesis* from 2000). The pre-recorded material leads to the most striking moment in *A Deep but Dazzling Darkness* when screaming male voices suddenly puncture the mysterious sound-world with dramatic and startling effect, a gestural moment not out of keeping with mature MacMillan, but all the more noticeable for its electronic content. The inclusion late in the work of both a jig and a waltz are antecedents of similar sections in the Violin Concerto, and these combined with an out-of-tune piano and copious metric modulations gives the whole piece the feel of a homage to Peter Maxwell Davies, himself no stranger to *L'homme armé*.

From Ayrshire is much more recognisably by James MacMillan, particularly the composer of stirring, folk-influenced modality such as the opening of *The Confession of Isobel Gowdie* or the end of *Seven Last Words from the Cross*. The piece was written for Nicola Benedetti, the Scottish violin prodigy who had recently sprung to fame by winning the 2004 BBC Young Musician of the Year with an astonishing performance of Szymanowski's First Violin Concerto.[8] Benedetti was born and raised in Ayrshire, like MacMillan, so a collaboration

---

8   The BBC Young Musician of the Year is a biennial competition to find an exceptional musical talent, that has been running since 1978. Past winners have included Nicholas Daniel (oboe, 1980, who gave the premiere of MacMillan's Oboe Concerto in 2010), Natalie Clein (cello, 1994) and Jennifer Pike (violin, 2002).

between the two seemed a logical decision and they have worked together sporadically from 2005 onwards. *From Ayrshire* is MacMillan at his lightest and most accessible, still retaining many of the thumbprints of his mature style, but all delivered in a softer, less declamatory fashion than other orchestral works from the period. Although commissioned and released on CD by Universal Classics and Jazz (a record label catering for the 'lighter', more popular end of the classical market), MacMillan's piece does not pander too much to this new audience, and the work has some surprising thorny edges and unexpected diversions. It is perhaps a sign of the high esteem in which Benedetti was held by her record company that the work was commissioned, particularly on a disc featuring the tried-and-tested repertoire of Mozart, Schubert and Mendelssohn – one can only imagine some of the disgruntled record company executives when faced with the oblique finales to both of the movements of *From Ayrshire*. To cement the links with the county of their birth, MacMillan includes a quotation from south-west Scotland's most famous son, Robert Burns, and his song *Ca' the Yowes* which 'hovers like a subliminal message, melodically and harmonically' in the first movement.[9] Much of the material in *From Ayrshire* finds its way into the Violin Concerto, not least another quick traditional dance (this time a reel) and the interplay between more melancholic and forceful music.

Although dedicated to Repin, the Violin Concerto has a second dedication, 'in memoriam Ellen MacMillan (1935–2008)', a reference to the composer's mother who had passed away shortly before completion of the work. This dedication is key to understanding the concerto and many of the musical and conceptual decisions that MacMillan makes, for although an abstract work in one sense, it still takes much influence from external events and people. The work is in the traditional three-movement, fast-slow-fast form, with the movements bearing the titles 'Dance', 'Song' and 'Song and Dance', and these simple descriptions give the sections their individual character and colour. The first movement begins with a 'short, punchy refrain motive',[10] a typical MacMillan opening gesture that sets the mood of the work and begins the narrative of the energetic opening. Robert Stein refers to the movement titles as 'MacMillan's unpretentious directness of style ... signalling

9   James MacMillan, programme note to *From Ayrshire*, https://www.boosey.com/cr/music/James-MacMillan-From-Ayrshire/48593 (accessed 22 July 2018).

10   James MacMillan, programme note to Violin Concerto, http://www.boosey.com/cr/music/James-MacMillan-Violin-Concerto/52082 (accessed 10 July 2018).

singing and dancing, the roots of Scottish folk music as the touchstones of the piece',[11] and although the titles are disarmingly simple they shape the music in as fundamental a way as do 'The Mockery' or 'Dearest Wood and Dearest Iron' in the Cello Concerto.

MacMillan has referred to the Violin Concerto as containing 'filial relationships ... a maternal relationship ... but there is also an oblique reference about going "beyond the veil" ... into a new life and a new state'.[12] His reference to going 'beyond the veil' is interesting, for MacMillan associates the work with a 'dream world', both literal and musical, and the notion of not everything being what it seems becoming apparent in the third movement, with some of the surreal devices employed by the composer suggesting a hidden and misty world of nocturnal imagination.

The second movement of the concerto, 'Song', finds MacMillan at his most emotive and the work in its purest memorial mood, the wild Celtic dance of the first now evolving into a 'hazy, remembered amalgam of Irish tunes', with plangent oboe and cor anglais announcing one of the composer's most expansive slow movements.[13] MacMillan marks the solo violin in this Irish melody as 'semplice, child-like, folksy, dancing', using many of the descriptive terms he had embraced in his earlier work, but he adds further words to his lexicon: pleading, keening (a firm MacMillan favourite), fragile, intense, playful, capricious – if the concerto is a memorial then this most heartfelt movement finds MacMillan communicating the whole gamut of expressions in remembering his recently deceased mother.[14] The entire movement has an intimate feel, with MacMillan reducing the orchestration throughout, often relying on divided strings, piano and carefully chosen woodwind to enhance the whimsical nature of the soloist. The movement has a poignant ending with the Irish tune returning (see Example 9.1) in a bravura rendition for the soloist

---

[11] Robert Stein, 'London, Barbican: James MacMillan's Violin Concerto', *Tempo*, vol. 65, no. 255 (October 2011), 58–59.

[12] James MacMillan, 'James MacMillan – Violin Concerto', https://www.bbc.co.uk/programmes/p03l64c5 (accessed 22 July 2018).

[13] MacMillan, Programme note to Violin Concerto (2009).

[14] The work's memorial quality is enhanced by an unstated allusion to the most celebrated memorial work for violin and orchestra, Alban Berg's Violin Concerto of 1935, dedicated 'to the memory of an angel', the deceased eighteen-year-old Manon Gropius. The syncopated horns and cellos in bars 42–46 suggesting a similar passage in the opening of Berg's work, this heightened by MacMillan's performance direction for the violin of 'intense and sad'.

Example 9.1   Bars 187–89 of 'Song' from the Violin Concerto showing Celtic influences (solo violin, piano and bodhrán only)

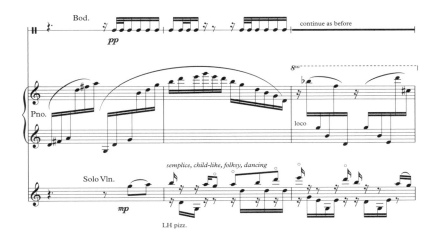

(replete with harmonics and left-hand *pizzicato*, suggesting a fiddle virtuoso at play) accompanied by flute, piccolo (possibly suggesting the tin-whistle), piano and bodhrán: a stylised but sincere portrayal of Celtic music-making in its purest sense.

The third movement of the concerto, 'Song and Dance', is the most memorable, but most bemusing, as the characteristic MacMillan concepts of the first two are hijacked and subverted in the finale. Alongside staccato bass drum and timpani, the movement begins with the male members of the orchestra (excluding some instruments) instructed to exclaim (in German): 'Eins, zwei, drei, vier: Meine Mutter tanz mit mir' (one, two, three, four, my mother dances with me). This extremely unusual departure gives the work what MacMillan refers to as 'a new feeling of burlesque',[15] with the sense of German exclamation enhanced by comedic *glissando* horns, and a lurch into a waltz section complete with a prominent 'wah-wah' mute on the trumpet. MacMillan had been no stranger to the 'burlesque', with the first movement of the Cello Concerto inhabiting a similar concept and sound-world, the earlier work no doubt influencing the later concerto. The spoken

---

[15]   MacMillan, programme note to Violin Concerto.

German returns towards the end of the movement, now in the female voices with the haunting text: 'Fünf, sechs, Sieben? Bist Du hinter das blaue Glas gegangen?' (Five, six, seven? Have you passed on to the blue heaven?). The link to MacMillan's suggestion of 'beyond the veil' now apparent, enhanced by the female voices and sudden cessation of musical activity, leading to a 'tragic outburst' of Mahlerian proportions before ushering in the violin's only cadenza in the concerto.[16]

MacMillan was candid as to the inclusion of these snippets of text in 2016: 'Why is it in German? – I have no idea. Why those texts the way they are? – I have no idea. It's the way I heard them.'[17] The inclusion of the spoken German, delivered in a martial fashion and puncturing the orchestral texture, is peculiar – there is something disturbing about the concept: an unexpected voice, in an unfamiliar language calling from beyond the veil, the shattering of a constructed reverie by otherworldly utterances. Paul Conway refers to this finale as full of 'self-parody'; this is a thought-provoking concept as MacMillan has not gone into any detail about the subject and it is interesting to surmise what the composer is parodying.[18] Certainly parody is an element of MacMillan's compositional aesthetic and the inclusion of a quotation from *The Confession of Isobel Gowdie* in *Britannia* suggests that self-parody had been attempted before, but nothing as obvious is present in the Violin Concerto. Perhaps the title of the movement, 'Song and Dance', is not, as it seems, related to traditional music, but instead refers ironically to another meaning of the term: to a big fuss, or a long-winded story which is neither relevant nor true.

Like MacMillan's large-scale operas, the Violin Concerto looks to romantic models for inspiration, as Stein proffers: MacMillan 'seems to be yearning to be a nineteenth-century composer, collecting folk-songs in a notebook and giving the soloist ... plenty of authentic opportunities to show off'.[19] Certainly, formally, the concerto is much more traditional than his earlier concertante works, with the move to abstraction suggesting a change to more recognisable forms and models associated with the genre, as with the later concerti that have appeared in the years following the Violin Concerto.

---

[16]   Ibid.

[17]   MacMillan, 'James MacMillan – Violin Concerto'.

[18]   Paul Conway, 'James MacMillan premieres in Edinburgh, Glasgow and London', *Tempo*, no. 269 (October 2014), 72.

[19]   Stein, 'London, Barbican: James MacMillan's Violin Concerto', 59.

Clemency (2009–10)

Few people would have expected James MacMillan to return to the operatic world so soon after the cool reception and criticism of *The Sacrifice*, but only four years after the premiere of his *Mabinogion*-inspired opus came the one-act, 50-minute chamber opera *Clemency*, a co-commission from the Covent Garden Royal Opera House, Scottish Opera, the Britten Sinfonia and Boston Lyric Opera in the USA, and first performed at the Linbury Studio Theatre, London, by the Britten Sinfonia, conducted by Clark Rundell. *Clemency* found MacMillan returning to his regular operatic collaborators: librettist Michael Symmons Roberts and director Katie Mitchell for a concise, powerful adaptation of chapter 18 of the Book of Genesis for five singers and string ensemble. This small-scale, intimate portrayal of one of the most puzzling episodes of Genesis is a world away from the excesses of *The Sacrifice*, a pared-down, concentrated meditation on the biblical text and its ramifications in twenty-first century society.

Clemency was not MacMillan's first foray into chamber opera: the earlier works *Búsqueda* and *Visitatio Sepulchri* and the quickly forgotten *Tourist Variations* were all very different attempts at the genre, with the last named being the only recognisably operatic offering. However, a work from 2000 had seen MacMillan attempt a work of similar proportions again, this time with the 'dramatic scena' for soprano, baritone, actress and ensemble, *Parthenogenesis*, which saw its premiere in Cambridge in September of that year.[20] This work was the first operatic collaboration with Symmons Roberts and Mitchell, and also found the future Archbishop of Canterbury, Rowan Williams, involved in the project as a theologian. *Parthenogenesis* takes its title from the phenomenon of reproduction occuring in nature without fertilisation; this scenario is transported to war-time Hanover, where a young woman is knocked to the ground during an Allied bombing raid, subsequently finding herself pregnant and giving birth nine months after the highly traumatic event. Although this modern 'virgin birth' may be highly dubious, it struck a chord with the creative team behind the opera, having obvious parallels with the Immaculate Conception and more contemporary issues such as genetic cloning.

Although *Parthenogenesis* is ostensibly a work relating to contemporary events and ideas, it undeniably has strong links with the sacred, more specifically

---

[20] MacMillan has variously described *Parthenogenesis* as both 'music theatre' and 'dramatic scena', though the score has the latter on its title page. It is one of the few major works by MacMillan still to be professionally recorded and released on a record label.

with the Annunciation, as MacMillan stated: 'There is a dark annunciation at the heart of this work. The father of the child is not God but human evil in the shape of a bomb ... to cast human evil as the progenitor in our story throws a negative mirror on the Annunciation.'[21] The mix of sacred and secular, and ancient and modern, is characteristically MacMillan, and very typical of his collaborations with Symmons Roberts (such as the preceding works *Raising Sparks* and *Quickening*), as is the engagement with human suffering and the religious amelioration that so defined *Búsqueda*. The form, scope and tone of the work all feed directly into *Clemency*, nowhere more so than the concept of bringing a biblical event into modern society, and judging it with our contemporary views and morality.

Clemency is structured in five scenes with accompanying prologue, and is a retelling of the story of Abraham and Sarah, an elderly couple who are visited by three travellers to whom they offer hospitality. The travellers inform Sarah that in a year hence she will bear a son (who will become Isaac) and that this is the 'word of God', news which both Abraham and Sarah greet with some incredulity. The couple soon realise that their guests are in fact angels, who are en route to neighbouring towns – 'twin towns by the lake', a thinly veiled reference to Sodom and Gomorrah – to enact retribution on the citizens for their evil ways and deeds. When Abraham realises the intentions of the travellers, he pleads with them to spare the lives of some of the people (the clemency of the work's title) if they encounter 'fifty acts of selflessness', which he barters down to forty-five, forty and finally five, to which the angels consent. As the trio leave the couple, there is an ambiguity that shrouds their visit, as both joy and fear have been left in their wake, and the opera ends with Sarah ruefully speculating on what the future will hold for her and her unborn child.

Although MacMillan states that *Clemency* is 'set in the present day and could be located in the Middle East or Eastern Europe',[22] the work has a decidedly Middle Eastern flavour to it, nowhere more so than in Abraham's long prologue, full of the staple MacMillan ornaments and embellishments, but combined with an invented quasi-Aramaic language to give a sound-scape from much further east than the composer's usual turns and trills (see Example 9.2).

This made-up language is an odd departure for MacMillan, although he is partial to including obscure or dead languages in his work. He referred to it as 'a quasi-onomatopoeic, sonic deconstruction but with also a kind of strange

---

21   James MacMillan, 'Parthenogenesis', in Jeremy Begbie, ed., *Sounding the Depths: Theology through the Arts* (London: SCM Press, 2002), 37.

22   James MacMillan, liner notes to *Clemency*, BIS-2129 CD (2014), 5.

Example 9.2   Bar 1 (excerpt) of 'Prologue' from *Clemency* showing Middle Eastern influences on Abraham's solo

Aramaic influence thrown in'.[23] The language is featured most intensely in the 'Who are these angels?' section of Scene 2, where Abraham and Sarah question the nature of the travellers, who have entered a 'strange moment of trance or reverie'. The three travellers (who MacMillan calls 'The Triplets' in the score) are the key narrative device in *Clemency* and it is their ambiguity that gives the work its drama. This was emphasised in the initial production of the opera by having the trio arrive in unremarkable khaki overalls before changing into the uniform of Hollywood assassins: black suits with accompanying gun holsters. The Triplets sing much of their material as a homogenous group, a device that MacMillan used to great effect with a similar trio of angels in *Visitatio Sepulchri* (see Example 4.1), the 'Birds (of Rhiannon)' in *The Sacrifice* and the Hilliard Ensemble in *Quickening*. Their move from everyday travellers to bringers of unexpected news and then to eventual vengeful angels is the dramatic arch of *Clemency*, and their ultimate ambiguity is what gives the opera its central theme.

Although *Parthenogenesis* may be the most obvious model for *Clemency*, the earlier 'liturgical drama' of *Visitatio Sepulchri* has had a strong influence too. The earlier piece is 'entirely anti-dramatic' in its conception, but the nature of the work – a stylised religious drama, timeless and unmoving – has undoubtedly had some bearing on *Clemency*, and the production's set, inspired by Rublev's icon of *The Hospitality of Abraham*, encouraged parallels with the 'minimal theatricality' of *Visitatio*.[24] However, whereas the earlier piece has always sat uncomfortably in MacMillan's output (questions still remain as to whether it is opera, music theatre or choral work), *Clemency* is most definitely a one-act opera, religiously inspired, but operatic in design.

Like many of MacMillan's larger works, there is a smaller piece that has been cannibalised and used in the newer work; in the case of *Clemency* it is

23   MacMillan, as quoted in Tavener, liner notes to *Who Are These Angels: New Choral Music by James MacMillan*, 6.

24   MacMillan, programme note to *Visitatio Sepulchri*.

Who are these Angels? from 2009. This unusual piece for male vocal ensemble (two tenors, baritone and two basses, though an SATBB choral version also exists) and string quartet forms the basis for the aforementioned 'trance' section of Scene 2, providing a framework for this expressive and mystical moment in the opera.[25] In the shorter work, MacMillan divides his vocal forces into a duet and a trio, mirroring Abraham, Sarah and The Triplets in *Clemency*, but rather than give the trio the invented language of Symmons Roberts, in *Who are these Angels?* they sing text attributed to St Augustine in a similar and equally numinous fashion. Much of the material remains unchanged, including the succinct vocal phrases of the duet (which sings the same 'Who are these angels?' refrain as in *Clemency*) and the powerful, Tippettesque string writing that underpins the whole section. One of the most striking moments of *Who are these Angels?*, the quiet, slowly-descending string *glissandi* which MacMillan marks 'like cooing doves or whale-song' and which finishes the work is transplanted in whole into *Clemency*, where it loses little of its angelic effect (see Example 9.3).

If the string writing in *Clemency* is redolent of Michael Tippett, then the work as a whole is indebted to another major British composer of a previous era: Benjamin Britten. MacMillan has been a long-term advocate of Britten's music and has conducted various works by the composer across the globe, and continues to do so. The influence of Britten can be seen across MacMillan's output from *Into the Ferment*, to *Quickening*, *The Sacrifice* and beyond. Like many British composers who came to prominence in the generation after Britten's death, Britten is an inescapable figure who still represents to many the model of what a British composer should be and how they should interact with society. Perhaps the greatest legacy of Britten's influence on MacMillan is the creation of The Cumnock Tryst music festival in 2014 (see chapter ten) whereby MacMillan has sought to set up his own Aldeburgh in his hometown and locality. The works that have arguably had the greatest influence on *Clemency* are Britten's three 'Church Parables' which he wrote between 1964 and 1968, representing some of his most inventive and concise composition in

---

[25] In a 2011 interview, MacMillan stated that the Latin sections of *Who are these Angels?* were written 'as a separate motet when I was seventeen and still at school. I tried to sing it with two friends in a local church and then it lay in a cupboard along with a lot of other material ... I didn't think it was ready as it stood ... I wanted to expand it in some ways.' MacMillan, as quoted in Tavener, liner notes to *Who Are These Angels: New Choral Music* by James MacMillan, 5.

Example 9.3   Bars 394–98 of Scene 2 of *Clemency* showing string *glissandi* that ends the 'Who are these angels?' section

* Soft, little glissandi – very high (harmonics?) to begin with, like cooing doves or whale-song, descending gradually to the lowest registers; very free, *ad lib*

the operatic medium.[26] There is a single-mindedness to Britten's parables that is missing (for good or bad) in MacMillan's offering, though the concept of a religiously inspired work for reduced forces in an operatic vein is at the core of both the parables and *Clemency*, and it is hard to imagine the later work existing without Britten's trio of late works.

Like *Raising Sparks*, *Parthenogenesis* and *Quickening*, *Clemency* is another work to feature conception and creation as a key part of the story (it shares the notion of a miraculous birth with *Parthenogenesis*), a characteristic trope in Symmons Roberts's work and a clear allusion to the collective faith of librettist and composer. However, the links between the two chamber operas are deeper than shared concepts, with both dwelling on the dissonance between the ancient and the modern, as Michael Fuller explains: 'If *Parthenogenesis* represents a reflection on a contemporary story in the light of a biblical antecedent, *Clemency* may be seen as the opposite: a reflection on a biblical

---

26   The three Church Parables are: *Curlew River* (1964), *The Burning Fiery Furnace* (1966) and *The Prodigal Son* (1968).

story in the light of present-day realities.'[27] The 'present-day realities' in this case related to the ongoing War on Terror that was waged by the USA and its allies in the aftermath of 11 September 2001: the Middle Eastern setting, the would-be assassins and the search for clemency in the face of vengeance all become of great pertinence when faced with global atrocities.

Unusually for a MacMillan operatic work, *Clemency* was greeted with good reviews from the critics, with very little negativity or disapproval. *The Independent* praised a 'terrifically intense, focused and inspired musical work on a thought-provoking parable', whilst *The Sunday Times* noticed the 'inventive string writing' and the 'concisely achieved' drama.[28] Fiona Maddocks, writing in *The Observer*, was perhaps the most effusive, referring to the work as the 'best MacMillan score I have heard' and adding that the piece 'ends too soon – scarcely a typical response to new opera'.[29] There were occasional criticisms of Symmons Roberts's libretto and Mitchell's production, but the overall response was far more positive than the reaction to any of MacMillan's other operatic offerings. This positivity has not gone unnoticed by the composer who stated in 2017: 'What I have enjoyed recently is small things, such as *Clemency*: one act, a handful of singers and just strings. That suited me more [than large-scale opera].'[30] It is safe to presume that any further operatic experiments by MacMillan will be similar in scope and design to his greatest success on the stage to date.

St Luke Passion (2012–13)

'I want to take the rest of my life to do the other three', said James MacMillan in 2012, referring to his ongoing settings of the four gospels, which had begun with the mammoth *St John Passion* in 2007 and continued with his second offering, the *St Luke Passion*, in 2013.[31] The triumph of his first Passion and the continued success of *Seven Last Words from the Cross* suggested that a second gospel setting was always on the cards, and a joint commission from the Concertgebouw and the City of Birmingham Symphony Orchestra (amongst

---

27   Fuller, 'Liturgy, Scripture and Resonance in the Operas of James MacMillan', 389.

28   Jessica Duchen, 'Clemency', *The Independent* (11 May 2011). Paul Driver, 'Mercy Mission', *The Sunday Times* (15 May 2011).

29   Fiona Maddocks, 'Clemency', *The Observer* (15 May 2011).

30   Cooke, Interview with James MacMillan, 16 November 2017.

31   Walton, 'Interview: James MacMillan, composer'.

various others) led to the *St Luke Passion*, which was composed in 2012–13. The work was first performed at the Concertgebouw, Amsterdam in March 2014 by the Netherlands Radio Philharmonic and Choir and the Netherlands National Youth Choir, conducted by Markus Stenz.

Plate 5   James MacMillan (Photo: Philip Gatward, 2012)

From the outset, the *St Luke Passion* is a very different beast to its predecessor: whereas the *St John Passion* was operatic, Wagnerian and grand in all dimensions, the *St Luke Passion* is smaller, more economical and does not aim as high. As MacMillan had said, each subsequent Passion would get 'smaller and smaller', with each setting becoming increasingly intimate, introverted and meditative: the *St Luke Passion* certainly exhibits these traits.[32] The *St Luke Passion* is scored for a chamber orchestra (with reduced woodwind and brass), organ and only timpani for percussive support, a world away from the battery of drums and bells that give the *St John Passion* its dramatic orchestral palette. The reasoning behind this reduction seems to be both conceptual and commercial, with the pared-back approach fitting MacMillan's desire for intimacy, but he also wanted the work to appeal to as broad a church as possible – many choirs are not able to afford larger orchestras featuring lower brass and an arsenal of percussion. In fact, the desire to appeal to the amateur choral world was one of the key rationales behind the composition of the *St Luke Passion*, and as MacMillan has indicated, this is reflected in the actual music produced, with the composer 'providing pitch cues and harmonic support, using simple modalities, avoiding angular leaps and keeping sections in repeating metrical schemes'.[33] As will be shown shortly, this change in aesthetic has had a direct impact on the nature of the work created.

One of the most striking differences between the two Passion settings is the depiction of Christ: whereas in the *St John* setting, MacMillan has a recognisable human figure of the solo baritone, the *St Luke* setting has a very different entity, a children's choir, providing the words of Christ, an ethereal and otherworldly sound far removed from the traditional protagonist as handed down by Bach. MacMillan explained this decision in 2014: 'I wanted to examine his [Christ's] otherness, sanctity and mystery ... employing a children's choir grants a measure of innocence to Christ as the sacrificial lamb.'[34] The three voices representing an integral character (or characters) carries on MacMillan's use of this technique in *Visitatio Sepulchri*, *The Sacrifice* and *Clemency*, and the choir's role as either three voices or a unison voice has a clear symbolism, as the composer explains, 'reflecting the oneness or Trinitarian implications of God'.[35] Combined with

---

32   Ibid.

33   James MacMillan, 'Interview about *St Luke Passion*', http://www.boosey.com/ cr/news/James-MacMillan-interview-about-St-Luke-Passion/100345&LangID=1 (accessed 10 July 2018).

34   Ibid.

35   Ibid.

the opening reference to the Annunciation in the Prelude, there is a definite stressing of Christ's infancy in the *St Luke Passion* (the gospel which deals most with Christ's birth), which is very different to the end-orientated narratives that usually exist in Passion settings, including MacMillan's earlier *St John Passion*. The 'measure of innocence' that MacMillan was striving for with the children's choir is a further link with Britten, who utilised young voices throughout his oeuvre, perhaps most pertinently in his Westminster Cathedral Choir commission, *Missa Brevis*, from 1959. Although cut from very different cloth, the influence of Britten's work can be felt in the *St Luke Passion*, with the children's sections having the same translucent effect, appearing angelic and terrestrial in equal measure.

The *St Luke Passion* is a setting of chapters 22 and 23 of the St Luke Gospel in the Revised Standard Edition of the bible, with MacMillan bookending the chapters with a Prelude and Postlude. The Prelude features various snippets of Luke (including a section of the Magnificat) to provide an introductory narrative, and MacMillan delivers them in a respectful manner as the drama begins in earnest. The inclusion of a Postlude is more unusual, as the focus shifts from the crucifixion to the resurrection and the ascension: an air of positivity and hope in the bleakest of stories. The *St Luke* setting differs from its predecessor in that it is entirely in English (the *St John* setting interpolated English and Latin throughout), a decision made early in the compositional process by MacMillan in order for the audience to engage with the story in its fullest, and further cementing the composer's desire for the work to have the broadest appeal. MacMillan's decision to set the two chapters of Luke in their entirety is a bold one, and leads to him using much text that other composers may have chosen to omit for reasons of furthering the narrative, leading one critic to state 'pared-back it certainly is, but there is no stinting on the theological detail'.[36] Although the text of St Luke's Gospel may lack some of the drama of St John's, there were no protests or commotion at this work's premiere (see chapter eight).

One of the most noticeable features of the *St Luke Passion* is MacMillan's decision to limit the amount of vocal ornamentation and elaboration, a cornerstone of his mature musical voice. The setting of chapter 22 is largely

---

[36]   Robert Stein, 'James MacMillan *St Luke Passion*, Barbican Centre, London', *Tempo*, vol. 69, no. 274 (October 2015), 65. Stein goes further with his criticisms of the text: 'there are indications in this Passion that biblical exegesis has the upper hand ... plenty of text – too much even – for a 75-minute setting ... it is as if the story itself is prioritised rather than the drama of communicating it'.

free of these thumbprints (though they do begin to return towards the end of the movement) leading to a much more earnest and simple form of delivery, no doubt a further example of his desire for the work to appeal to amateurs. As the piece moves closer to the crucifixion, the ornamentation returns more and more, with the beautiful 'Daughters of Jerusalem' section for the children's choir exhibiting fully MacMillan's array of turns, trills and grace notes (see Example 9.4). The more elaborate delivery continues until Jesus's final words, and the rather perfunctory setting of 'And having said this he breathed his last' from the bass voices.

Perhaps the most perceptible outcome of MacMillan's desire for amateurs to be able to perform the *St Luke Passion* is that the musical language for the piece feels somewhat removed from the composer's similar works in the genre. In eschewing the ornamentation, the quickly changing rhythmic emphasis and the chromatic fluidity of his normal style, the music becomes much more traditional in essence, with easily audible key areas, obvious voice leading, and a preference for strong beats and metric stability. Although MacMillan tries his best to make the work as colourful and dramatic as possible, the more prosaic text and reduced orchestration further enhance the work's traditional British oratorio style.[37] This is most pronounced in chapter 22; however, as the narrative quickens and the more recognisable MacMillan mannerisms return in chapter 23, the piece more resembles the composer's mature works, and the Postlude, with a wordless chorus accompanying an orchestral epilogue, is pure MacMillan.

Like *Clemency*, the *St Luke Passion* finds MacMillan retrospectively including previous material and quoting from an earlier work: however, rather than the quotation of a relatively obscure motet in the opera, MacMillan chooses to make several quotations from one of his most famous works of the Passion, the *Seven Last Words from the Cross*. These borrowings occur in chapter 23, where MacMillan sets the same sections of Luke that he did so memorably in the 1993 work, making a clear and audible link with the earlier piece. The first quotation is for the text 'Father forgive them; for they know not what they do'. After a turbulent section for woodwind, organ and timpani, the melancholy string refrain first heard in *Tuireadh* in 1991 and which also begins

---

[37]   Although it is perhaps a little too harsh, sections of the *St Luke Passion* feel somewhat reminiscent of such Passiontide choral 'favourites' as John Stainer's *The Crucifixion* (1887) and John Henry Maunder's *Olivet to Calvary* (1904). But don't tell MacMillan I said so.

Seven Last Words slowly comes into focus in the subdued key of G♭ major (see Example 9.5, and Example 3.4 for the earlier appearances).

The quotations continue with the text 'Truly, I say unto you, today you will be with me in Paradise', where MacMillan invokes the soprano duet from the

Example 9.4   Bars 238–41 of chapter 23 of the *St Luke Passion* showing the use of ornamentation (children's choir only)

Example 9.5   Bars 304–07 of chapter 23 of the *St Luke Passion* showing the inclusion of a quotation from 'Father, forgive them for they know not what they do' from *Seven Last Words from the Cross*

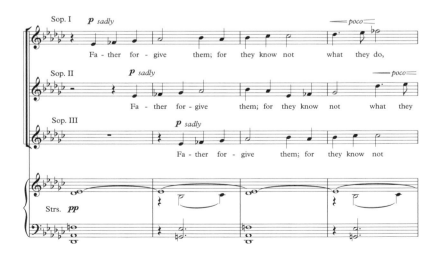

end of the third movement of *Seven Last Words*, now for the children's choir, with a much fuller accompaniment than the stratospheric two-part violin texture in the corresponding section of the earlier work.[38] The third quotation is for the most powerful section of text in the whole work, Jesus's final words before the crucifixion: 'Father, into thy hands I commend my spirit.' MacMillan uses the same melodic material from the final movement of *Seven Last Words*, though replacing the desolate full chorus cries of the earlier work with an equally captivating setting for the children's choir, now accompanied by strident organ chords (see Example 9.6).

MacMillan's decision to include material from the earlier work is obviously of great personal and theological significance, and links the full account of Jesus's Passion from Luke with the emotive final utterances that make up the *Seven Last Words*. It also binds together MacMillan's Passiontide offerings in a neat and engaging fashion, suggesting a larger compositional and theological

Example 9.6   Bars 1–16 of 'Father, into Thy hands I commend my Spirit' from *Seven Last Words from the Cross* (first soprano part only) and bars 381–90 of chapter 23 of the *St Luke Passion* (children's choir only) showing the quotation of material

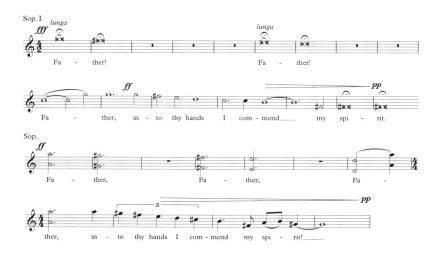

concern at work. It may also be viewed as a shrewd piece of self-referencing from the master of self-quotation: with the increasing success of *Seven Last Words* in the UK and the USA it is no surprise to find MacMillan paying homage to one of his most successful creations and putting this work in the mind of choirs, congregations and audiences.

MacMillan continues the quotations at the very end of the chapter, by including the Bach chorale 'O Haupt voll Blut und Wunden' (known in English by the incipit 'O Sacred Head, sore wounded'), used so memorably in the *St Matthew Passion*. The orchestral epilogue that ends the chapter weaves this chorale into an expressive finale, before characteristic repeated brass chords finish the movement in dramatic fashion.

The Postlude that finishes the *St Luke Passion* is the greatest deviation from the gospel and the only place in the Passion where MacMillan sets text from outside Luke, here setting a short section on the ascension from the Book of Acts (though likely to have been written by Luke as well). The drama shifts quickly from the crucifixion to the resurrection, with Jesus gently intoning 'Why are you troubled, and why do questionings rise in your hearts?', with a melodic contour alluding to the opening of *Seven Last Words*. Following this, the main choir enters with chanted dialogue in free time, reminiscent of the cantor sections of the *Mass*, quietly and impassively describing the events of the ascension with minimal orchestral accompaniment. The Postlude finishes with a wordless choir supplementing the orchestra: expressive vocal sounds to accompany the short waves of crescendos that MacMillan requires. Like the precursors to the *St Luke Passion*, the orchestra has the final commentary on the drama, but the inclusion of the wordless choir gives the ending a different quality to the earlier works: perhaps reflecting on the more optimistic ending to the piece, perhaps suggesting the commending of the spirit, proposed by Jesus's words at the end of the preceding chapter – certainly the changing vocal sounds of the choir are reminiscent of breathing. MacMillan finishes the work in a poignant fashion with the orchestration thinning to leave a sustained B major chord (the main key area of the whole Passion) before the children's choir returns to join the humming, finally ending the piece unaccompanied and fading into the distance.

MacMillan's declaration in 2012 that 'I'm already talking to people about the St Mark [Passion], which would be about ten years from now ... then maybe I'll think about doing the St Matthew ten years after that', suggests a composer with a long-term plan for these impressive gospel settings, and few would be surprised to see these works appear in due course.[39] In the same

---

39   Walton, 'Interview: James MacMillan, composer'.

interview, MacMillan explained the compositional reduction that had already taken place from the *St John Passion* to the *St Luke Passion* and beyond: 'the St Mark will be for choir and organ ... the St Matthew will just be for unaccompanied singers.'[40] It will be intriguing to see how the future James MacMillan attempts these hugely significant works with such reduced forces, particularly the setting of the St Matthew Gospel for unaccompanied choir. Whether the amateur singers of the *St Luke Passion* will be able to perform it remains to be seen.

---

40   Ibid.

10 | *Tu es Petrus* – Bellahouston Park and the Return to Cumnock

If 'Scotland's Shame' was the major political, theological and personal moment of crisis in James MacMillan's creative life, then the Papal visit of Pope Benedict XVI to the United Kingdom in September 2010 was a definite second crisis, again leading to much soul-searching, introspection and questioning of the composer's relationship with his homeland and the church, and of the very essence of himself as an artist in contemporary society. For although the visit of Benedict ultimately passed with little controversy (there was much grumbling in the left-leaning press in the run-up to the event, particularly the funding of the visit), MacMillan's involvement and the preceding ill-feelings that were engendered have left another indelible mark on the composer which continues to be felt to this day.

The state visit was the first by a pope since Pope John Paul II's visit to the UK in May 1982 and was a hugely significant moment, not just for Britain's Catholic community, but for all religious faiths and denominations, leading to much publicity and scrutiny throughout the media and wider society. Benedict held meetings with all the major political leaders, the Queen and the Archbishop of Canterbury during a four-day visit that saw open-air masses in Glasgow and Birmingham and a mass in Westminster Cathedral, the centre of Catholicism in England. The visit also saw the beatification of Cardinal John Henry Newman, one of the leading Catholic theologians of the nineteenth century and a key figure in the resurgence of the Catholic Church during that period. As the country's most prominent Catholic composer, it was no surprise that MacMillan was involved in various musical events during Benedict's visit, and he provided two new works: the anthem *Tu es Petrus*, for brass, organ, percussion and choir and the congregational *Mass of Blessed John Henry Newman* that was first performed in the open-air mass at Bellahouston Park, Glasgow that welcomed the Pope to Scotland. It was the latter of these two works that caused the greatest controversy for both composer and religious community.

As with events in 1999, MacMillan's exploits made the news in certain quarters in Scotland, this time regarding the suitability of his new setting for the Papal mass. Having been commissioned by the Archbishop of Glasgow, Mario Conti, MacMillan's mass soon became mired in issues regarding appropriateness, performability and aesthetic quality amongst certain members of the Scottish Church, who were no doubt concerned about how the piece would fare under the world's spotlight. This moment of intense questioning of MacMillan's music and its suitability for this most prestigious occasion obviously hurt the composer deeply, and he wrote about the events in no uncertain terms on his blog. Here MacMillan highlighted the criticisms of the *Mass of Blessed John Henry Newman* by the church as 'not pastoral enough', 'unsingable' and 'not fit for purpose', and described the agenda of the church's National Music Advisory Board to 'pursue the 1970s Americanised solution to the post-Conciliar vernacular liturgy, to the exclusion of more 'traditional' possibilities'.[1] He mentioned the advisory board's 'hostility to Gregorian chant' and their preference for 'cod-Celtic-ness that owes more to the soundtracks of *The Lord of the Rings* and *Braveheart*, than anything remotely authentic'.[2] The advisory board did eventually back down, after MacMillan contacted the bishops individually to canvas for their support, but the affair did little to bridge the divide between MacMillan and certain factions in the church, and he has since waged a constant war on the music often found in Scottish Catholic churches which he refers to as 'musically illiterate, almost as if it were written by semi-trained teenagers ... The style is stodgy and sentimental, tonally and rhythmically stunted and melodically inane.'[3]

The *Mass of Blessed John Henry Newman* is much in the mould of MacMillan's previous congregational mass settings (see chapter seven) with the same mix of traditional, progressive and vernacular that have made those works so successful. It is hard to find much about the work that would have angered the church – apparently their concern was that not enough parishes would have a competent enough organist to perform the piece – with MacMillan taking care to shape easy, flowing melodies with repeated material and rhythmic and metric constancy. The piece is not without its challenges for congregations, particularly the Gloria, which has several modulations and quickly changing textures underpinning the conjunct melody, but the rest of the work asks for little more skill than the *St Anne's Mass*. Perhaps some of the consternation

---

[1]   jamesmacmillaninscotland.wordpress.com/.

[2]   Ibid. It is something of an irony that MacMillan stressed the 'cod-Celtic-ness' that the committee found appealing, as this has undoubtedly been one of the major selling points of MacMillan's own congregational *St Anne's Mass* from 1985.

[3]   'The Holy Warrior with a baton'.

resulted from the inclusion of another quote from Wagner's *Tristan und Isolde* that creeps into the Kyrie, continuing MacMillan's fascination with the German composer's ideas, as expounded by philosopher Roger Scruton. Whereas quotes from *Tristan* seemed entirely appropriate in the dramatic and colourful orchestral sound-scapes of *The Sacrifice* and the *St John Passion*, the inclusion in the *Mass* seems a little too high-brow, giving the short Kyrie a veneer of intellectualism whilst much of the work is earnest and thoughtful. Like the previous two congregational settings, material from the *Mass of Blessed John Henry Newman* has found its way into later works, particularly the more florid mass setting *Missa Dunelmi* (2011) and the concertante work for trumpet and strings, *Seraph*, that followed soon after the *Mass*.

MacMillan was subdued in appraising the situation he found himself in, referring to it as a 'sad business' and recognising that 'not all parishes in Scotland could introduce the setting', despite road-testing the piece on his own parish choir in Maryhill.[4] He still bears the scars today: in a 2015 interview he referred to the affair as 'nearly driving me mad in the end, trying to deal with church authorities' and declared that he would never write another congregational setting: 'there is too much congregational music out there and they [parishes] should get back to chant'.[5] Nevertheless, the visit of Pope Benedict raised MacMillan's profile even further, both inside and outside of the Catholic Church, and cemented his role as a composer of major national and civic events. His position within the church has steadily increased since the Papal visit, with Benedict recognising MacMillan's contribution in 2012 with an invitation to a special mass at the Vatican in celebration of the fiftieth anniversary of the Second Vatican Council, MacMillan being presented with a symbolic copy of the Catholic Church's 'Message to Artists'.[6] 2018 saw MacMillan's *Stabat Mater* as the first piece to be live-streamed from the Vatican's Sistine Chapel in a performance from The Sixteen and the Britten Sinfonia, one of relatively few performances from St Peter's featuring visiting performers.[7]

---

4   jamesmacmillaninscotland.wordpress.com/.

5   Cooke, Interview with James MacMillan, 30 November 2015.

6   For more information see 'James MacMillan honoured in Papal ceremony', https:// scmo.org/news-releases/perma/1349777184/article/james-macmillan-honoured-in-pa. html (accessed 11 August 2018).

7   As mentioned in chapter six, MacMillan was also dubbed 'Catholic of the Year' in 2015 by *The Catholic Herald* newspaper, the first time that the accolade had been awarded. MacMillan was praised for being 'intellectually ambitious' and for 'working so

The honours that MacMillan were accumulating were not solely received from the church, the composer achieving one of the highest accolades with a knighthood in the Queen's Birthday Honours of 2015. The knighthood was received for services to music and MacMillan was presented with the award by Prince William at Windsor Castle in December of that year.[8] It was a high-profile honour in the world of contemporary classical music, with MacMillan being the first composer to be knighted since John Tavener in 2000, something that he noted: 'I see it obviously as a personal honour but also as an honour for music, and modern music in particular.'[9]

For MacMillan, the legacy of Benedict's visit to the UK in 2010 did not end with the performance at Bellahouston; the wrangling over the future of Catholic music in Scotland continued for the next couple of years, and as late as 2014 MacMillan was still at odds with the National Music Advisory Board (and in particular its chairman Monsignor Gerry Fitzpatrick) over its unwillingness to enter into discussion regarding musical reform. One of the by-products of this dissension was the forming of Musica Sacra Scotland, an initiative aimed at increasing awareness and use of Gregorian chant in modern-day church worship. The first of its 'National Music Days' was held at Glasgow University in 2013 and featured addresses from the current and previous Archbishops of Glasgow as well as workshops, performances and a closing service. Musica Sacra continued until 2017, though MacMillan's commitment to chant and the heritage of Catholic music has continued unabated: in 2011 he was instrumental in setting up The Blessed John Henry Newman Institute for Liturgical Music at the Birmingham Oratory and has been involved in similar projects on both sides of the Atlantic.

The Papal visit may have caused MacMillan personal trauma, but it has not stopped the flow of new works and commissions in the years that followed it: the 2010s has been one of the composer's most fecund decades so far, with

---

hard to bridge the gap between the Church's liturgy as it is and as it should be'. ('The Holy Warrior with a baton').

[8]   Interestingly, in an article in September 2015 MacMillan was 'still deciding whether to be knighted at Holyrood Palace or Buckingham Palace'. Phil Miller, 'Composer James MacMillan on his music festival, growing up in Ayrshire ... and why he's given up on social media', *The Sunday Herald* (27 September 2015).

[9]   Ibid. Karl Jenkins (of *Adiemus* and *The Armed Man* fame) was also awarded a knighthood in the same Queen's Birthday Honours and actually received his two months earlier than MacMillan in a ceremony at Buckingham Palace.

many new orchestral, operatic, chamber and instrumental works and countless choral pieces following hot on the heels of *The Strathclyde Motets*. The most substantial works of the 2010s have included the Symphony No. 4 (2015), the tone poems *Woman of the Apocalypse* and *The Death of Oscar* (both 2012), the *St Luke Passion* (2013), five concerti, the chamber opera *Clemency* (2010) and the hour-long successor to *Seven Last Words from the Cross*, the *Stabat Mater* of 2015. Of the works composed in this new decade, the vast majority (in number if not scope) have been for choirs, with over fifty having been composed and published, ranging from small communion motets and folk arrangements to grand cantatas and oratorios, such as the Coventry Cathedral anniversary setting of the *Gloria* (2012) or *A European Requiem*, an unfortunately titled work of 2015.[10]

The decade has also seen some of the most diverse compositions from MacMillan, including *I Awoke Today* and *Hirta*, showing the range of the composer's interests and creative energies. *I Awoke Today* was written as the conclusion to *Passion*, a 2016 project in Manchester in which homeless people joined The Sixteen to perform an abridged version of Bach's *St Matthew Passion* in a semi-derelict market hall. MacMillan's contribution moves the action from the crucifixion to the resurrection (as did the *St Luke Passion*), setting a text written by the homeless cast members in a somewhat popular style, mixing Bach with more popular idioms. *Hirta* is an arrangement of a folksong from the islands of St Kilda, one of the most isolated communities in the United Kingdom until the relocation of the final residents in 1930. How the folksongs came to MacMillan's attention is interesting: an elderly care home resident, Trevor Morrison, had been taught the songs as a child by a former St Kilda inhabitant and was recorded playing them in 2006. Fast-forward ten years, and MacMillan was one of five Scottish composers asked to 'reimagine' the songs

---

[10]   *A European Requiem* was a commission for the Oregon Bach Festival, the title stemming from MacMillan's desire to write a 'concert requiem', a 'particularly European form that composers have turned to when they identify with a sense of loss, often as much within themselves, as prompted by a specific death' (James MacMillan, programme note to *A European Requiem*, http://www.boosey.com/cr/music/James-MacMillan-A-European-Requiem/100418, accessed 11 August 2018). The work's title has not benefitted from what is commonly known as 'Brexit', the United Kingdom's decision to leave the European Union in the referendum of June 2016. MacMillan has had to spend the past three years explaining that his new requiem has nothing to do with politics, nor with this particular phenomenon.

for piano and strings for a 2016 album release, *The Lost Songs of St Kilda*.[11] In one of the more unusual promotional appearances in his career, MacMillan was sailed to St Kilda (a six-hour journey) by Classic FM in September 2016 to perform some of the songs on the island to a bemused audience of Scottish National Trust staff and sheep researchers.

Much of James MacMillan's creativity in the 2010s has been directed towards the creation of a music festival in his hometown of Cumnock, The Cumnock Tryst, which was founded in 2014 by MacMillan and his wife, Lynne.[12] This new venture has become one of the main focal points of MacMillan's time and energy and necessitated a move away from Glasgow in 2015, to the north Ayrshire countryside near the coastal town of Largs (the first time MacMillan had lived in the county of his birth since 1986). The move from Glasgow and the relinquishing of his position at St Columba's was a bittersweet affair, as Scotland's second city had been home since 1988 and much intertwined with the composer's early successes and formation as a serious artist. He admitted in 2015 that the move was 'a wrench' and that 'I love Glasgow and brought up our children there', but the call of a quieter life free from 'car alarms, house alarms, workmen playing their transistor radios outside' was too great, and the desire to place himself within the community that had given him so much was ever-present.[13]

The Cumnock Tryst (with its appealing tag-line of 'A meeting place for music') has quickly become a major Scottish music festival following the similar eclectic mix of classical, folk and traditional music with other artistic events that has made Peter Maxwell Davies's St Magnus Festival so successful. Like the St Magnus Festival, The Cumnock Tryst has featured performances and premieres of its founder's music including the first performances of such diverse works as *Domus infelix est* (2014), *Knockroon Waltz* (2015), *Bennett!*

---

[11]   For more information visit https://lostsongsofstkilda.com (accessed 3 February 2019).

[12]   The 'tryst' from the festival's title is taken from MacMillan's own *The Tryst*, which has gone from being hidden in various orchestral works to being centre-stage in its own music festival. A strange, but no doubt pleasing journey for the composer's most enduring melody. The festival's patron is Nicola Benedetti, who also performed in the inaugural Cumnock Tryst.

[13]   Miller, 'Composer James MacMillan on his music festival, growing up in Ayrshire ... and why he's given up on social media'.

(2016) and *All the Hills and Vales Along* (2018).[14] It has also featured more well-known pieces from MacMillan's output including the *Miserere* (performed by The Sixteen in 2014) and *Seven Last Words from the Cross* (performed by the choir of Westminster Cathedral and the Scottish Ensemble in 2017) and continues to go from strength to strength with each passing year. MacMillan has made community engagement and education key tenets of the festival, as well as an annual Festival Service, and has undertaken education projects with local schools, community groups and amateur musicians, bringing to mind his own work with the SCO and *Into the Ferment* early in his return to Scotland. As the festival progresses, more events and more days are being added, with brass music (a nod in the direction of Cumnock's mining past), more folk music and a tie-in with a local literary festival all rubbing shoulders with artists of the calibre of The King's Singers and The Sixteen.

MacMillan's reasons for the foundation of The Cumnock Tryst are no doubt altruistic, the 'local boy made good' wanting to give something back to the community that nurtured him and sent him on his way to respect and success. Certainly MacMillan holds Cumnock dear to his heart, and the formative experiences (both good and bad) living in the town have shaped his life and work inextricably. As MacMillan explains on the website for the festival: 'Because of these seminal experiences [concerts in Cumnock] I have followed a life in music ... now I want to bring something of that back.'[15] Despite his obvious desire to bring high-quality music-making and a continued sense of regeneration to his hometown, there is a feeling of MacMillan following a well-trodden path set down by other British composer luminaries; somehow the recognition of bringing your art to your area of birth gives ultimate legitimacy and respect. MacMillan and The Cumnock Tryst are in very good company, and if it has half the impact that Aldeburgh or St Magnus had for their respective founders, he will remain a happy composer, with the continued success of the festival one of his paramount concerns.

Not all of the 2010s has been taken up with the founding and directing of his music festival; there have been many other milestones in MacMillan's

---

[14] This is indeed a diverse selection of MacMillan's compositions, with two of the works being short pieces for solo instrument (including the highly unusual contra-bass clarinet). MacMillan has yet to use his festival to premiere a substantial work for ensemble or orchestra.

[15] James MacMillan, 'About the Festival', https://www.thecumnocktryst.com/about-the-festival (accessed 11 August 2018).

career reflecting his increasing success and prominence in the contemporary musical world. MacMillan's work as both composer and conductor has taken him to all corners of the globe, with prominent trips to South America and China in recent years, as well as multiple residencies in the United States and stints as featured composer in festivals in Europe and beyond. One of the most eye-catching projects that he has been involved with was the BBC SSO trip to India in March 2014, a two-week tour featuring concerts in Chennai, Delhi and Mumbai, all conducted by MacMillan. The tour was scheduled to coincide with Glasgow hosting the 2014 Commonwealth Games and featured a strong British Council presence amongst the various outreach, community and education projects that accompanied the tour.[16] The orchestra were accompanied by Nicola Benedetti and educator Paul Rissmann, with MacMillan conducting a mixed programme including Mendelssohn, Mozart and Tchaikovsky, and additional Scottish reels for cross-cultural encores.

There has been a strong recognition of MacMillan's work in his homeland in recent years, which will no doubt increase in his sixtieth year in 2019. In March 2017, Glasgow rewarded MacMillan with a month-long retrospective of his music to celebrate the city's designation as UNESCO City of Music, with nine concerts including four Scottish premieres. Works ranged from *Tryst* and *The World's Ransoming* to the first performances in Scotland of the Viola Concerto, Symphony No. 4, the *Stabat Mater* and the Concertino for Horn and Strings (an arrangement of the 2007 Horn Quintet). MacMillan's relationship with the artistic bodies of Scotland remains incredibly strong, and thirty years after the return to his country of birth he has continued to work closely with those orchestras and ensembles that first performed his work.

James MacMillan has come a long way from his early recollections of a Cumnock society 'dominated by machismo, hard-drinking and sporadic violence';[17] he has become an artist of truly international standing, and for a 21st-century composer, that is no small feat. In fact, it is hard to think of another British composer who holds the same position as MacMillan – he has been able to rely on his compositional work (with additional conducting positions) for the majority of his income, never having to resort to teaching

---

[16]   The British Council is an organisation promoting a wider understanding of the United Kingdom, its language and its culture, amongst other things. It regularly promotes British arts and culture across the globe with a particular focus on countries in the Commonwealth. For more information, see https://www.britishcouncil.org/.

[17]   MacMillan, 'Silence of the lambs'.

positions, copying or writing books to supplement his living. He holds an exalted position and for many people he is the model of a successful British composer: internationally prominent, providing for state occasions, embedded in his community, visible in the wider media and writing for the whole gamut of musical life. One suspects that his early career may have benefitted from the support of his wife's work as a lawyer, but the close relationship between husband and wife (both personal and professional) has given MacMillan the stability to reach the heights that his compositions have achieved. MacMillan's success is all the more admirable when his provincial and working-class background is considered: there was no gilded entrance to the London concert scene, nor a celebrated endorsement by a senior figure, from which some of his contemporaries have benefitted. MacMillan has taken the well-trodden path that many composers have taken, but this has resulted in a more successful and lofty destination than others, much of this stemming from his dedication to his art and beliefs.

But it must be admitted that MacMillan has benefitted from being a Scottish composer. Though his relationship with his homeland has been turbulent (and will probably continue to be), it has undoubtedly aided his career in a way that being an English composer would not have done. This is due, in part, to there being far fewer composers in Scotland than in its southern neighbour: opportunities have been more readily available and the pool of applicants shallower. This may seem like a reductive argument, but MacMillan's ascent to 'Scotland's greatest living composer' would have been much more difficult in other countries where competition was fiercer and the embrace of national artistic bodies much harder to achieve. This is not to diminish either his abilities, or Scotland as an artistic nation, but MacMillan's success is inseparably linked with his homeland and a renewed sense of national musical pride.

MacMillan's return to Scotland in 1988 was perhaps the most pivotal moment in his career: if he had remained an émigré it is doubtful he would have had the success and national confirmation that greeted those early works such as *Into the Ferment* and *Tryst*. He undoubtedly benefitted from a change in artistic climate in Scotland, with bodies such as the SCO, the BBC SSO and Scottish Opera finding their feet on a national stage and looking to promote home-grown talent to a wider audience. He was also the beneficiary of much of the groundwork laid down by Peter Maxwell Davies, whose own work with Scotland's orchestras had provided a template for an indigenous successor. Maxwell Davies's support of MacMillan through his *Strathclyde Concertos* projects and his employment of the younger composer on his composition course also added to MacMillan's stature in the late 1980s, all of which would have been much harder to secure if he had resided outside of his homeland.[18]

Being a Scot has not just provided MacMillan with access to world-class orchestras and ensembles, or the promotion that comes from being top of the compositional tree in his birthplace; it has also given him a distinguishing advantage over his contemporaries, who, no matter what their music may sound like, can easily be labelled a 'contemporary composer' with further distinction unnecessary. Being Scottish, and embracing his nationality, culture and history, has given MacMillan a distinctiveness that has seen him promoted over others, and has led to the longevity of his career in the modest spotlight of contemporary music. The adoption of the turns, trills and embellishments of Scottish traditional music into his own may be so commonplace that commentators refer to them as 'MacMillanisms', but they nevertheless represent an easily recognised musical thumbprint to his music: it can often take only one plangent line of melody for the composer to be identified. Not since Tippett, Britten or perhaps MacMillan's early teacher Kenneth Leighton has this been the case.[19] Though the direct influence of his homeland on his music may have waned since 'Scotland's Shame', it is still an ineffable part of his musical DNA, and as important a constituent as his faith has continued to be.

MacMillan has been fortunate to have several distinguishing characteristics to both his music and his beliefs, with early observers recognising his socialism and Catholicism as well as his nationality (perhaps his nationalism too). This mixture of nationality, politics and faith obviously bore early successes with *The Confession of Isobel Gowdie* (which for many still represents MacMillan, body and soul) and *Tuireadh*, though these pieces from 1990–91 represent the zenith of MacMillan's overtly Scottish-influenced works. The tags of 'Scottish, socialist and Catholic' defined MacMillan for most of the 1990s and beyond, and they have made him different, distinguishable and marketable: many composers would have yearned for just one of them to differentiate them from others. If MacMillan's perceived nationalism ceased to be important by the millennium, then his socialism had most definitely waned by the time of his incendiary article in 2008 in *The Spectator*, 'Unthinking dogmatism', which firmly cast aside any latent attachment to present-day left-wing circles amidst

---

18   That is not to say that being Scottish yet not living in Scotland is prohibitive to a successful career. Judith Weir (the current Master of the Queen's Music) has rarely lived in Scotland (and she was born in England, but to Scottish parents) but has benefitted from Scottish endorsement and is one of the country's most respected composers.

19   Wells, 'James MacMillan: Retrospective Modernist', 167.

a tirade of accusations against liberal metropolitan elites. Though he is now firmly of the right or centre right, the commitment to fairness, equality and the highlighting of injustices and persecution that characterised his left-wing pieces (such as *Búsqueda* and *Cantos Sagrados*) still exist, though often now in a purely religiously inspired form.[20]

Amidst everything that has changed in MacMillan's life, the one thing that has remained constant is his unwavering faith: this is what defines him as a composer above anything else, and since the death of John Tavener it is hard to think of another composer who is so identified with his or her religion. Whereas at one point MacMillan's Catholicism was just another part of a colourful mix of influences that resulted in *Isobel Gowdie* and *Veni, Veni, Emmanuel*, it has since become MacMillan's *raison d'être*: virtually everything he does (compositionally or in his wider career) is related to his beliefs. Though he has gone to great lengths not to proselytise his faith, he has nevertheless defended it at all costs and robustly attacked those who have sought to undermine or weaken his beloved church. Certainly his relationship with the church is symbiotic – few in the Catholic hierarchy could have imagined a British composer so openly and continually supportive of the Catholic Church, its history, its current operations and its future. In a period of uncertainty and instability in certain areas of the church (particularly regarding historical misdemeanours) MacMillan has been unswerving in his support, and not since Olivier Messiaen has a composer given so much of his creative life to faith. It is no surprise that MacMillan chose to deal with an aspect of his Catholicism in his Edinburgh Festival speech: it is no surprise that the negative reactions to it caused him so much pain.

Although it would be truly cynical to suggest that MacMillan's wholehearted embracing of the Catholic Church is anything other than an authentic representation of his faith, there is an element of truth to the fact that it has made him a more prominent and successful composer than if it had remained just a constituent part of his musicality. Together with MacMillan's choral renaissance (a product of the further embracing of his faith) much of his recognition today revolves around his Catholicism and is as significant as his nationality that first gained him prominence in the 1980s. Although he remains a composer of significant orchestral, chamber and instrumental works, and there is no suggestion that this will change, his career appears to be taking him more and more to religious institutions and theological departments, to discuss the finer points of religious practice and its dissemination. He is as recognisable today as a commentator on

---

[20]   Thompson, 'MacMillan's Loyalty'.

faith in the arts as an actual practitioner of his art. How this will shape his compositions in his later years remains to be seen, and whether the continuation of The Cumnock Tryst and his love for Scotland will prevent him from embracing fully his theological concerns and the lure of American religious prestige and prominence.

What we can be sure of is that any music MacMillan produces in the coming years (a Fifth Symphony is planned, as are two further Passion settings, a 40-voice motet and a church opera) will be received with the same mix of opinion that has greeted his music since the breakthrough works of the late 1980s. For some, the music will always be too emotional, too direct, too Catholic, but for others it is exactly these things that makes the music so appealing. It is one of MacMillan's greatest strengths and attributes that a new work rarely goes by without some comment, whether positive or negative, and he will always be a divisive but respected composer. He remains a composer of great integrity, compassion, veracity and thoughtfulness and his continued work, whether in dramatic orchestral tableaux or intimate choral moments, will hopefully continue long past his sixtieth birthday to give a corpus of work to rival any of Britain's greatest composers. It seems only fitting that the final words should come from Psalm 96, set so memorably by MacMillan in *A New Song*:

> O sing unto the Lord a new song,
> sing unto the Lord all the whole earth.
> Sing unto the Lord and praise His Name,
> by telling of His salvation from day to day.

Works and Recordings

Works are listed by year, in order of composition (any later revisions are included in the work's main entry). There then follow details of the texts, instrumentation, durations, first performances and recordings. All MacMillan's works are published by Boosey & Hawkes, London. With regards to performance and recording details, the following abbreviations apply:

CO – Chamber Orchestra
PO – Philharmonic Orchestra
SO – Symphony Orchestra
BBC – British Broadcasting Corporation

EARLY UNPUBLISHED WORKS (1978–80)

Poème (1978) – counter-tenor, flute, violin, piano
A Midsummer Night's Dream (1979) – flute, oboe, bassoon,
    percussion, harpsichord
Visitatio Sepulchri (1979) – unknown
Triptych (1979) – flute, clarinet, trombone, timpani, percussion, piano,
    violin, cello
Ostinato (1979) – piano
Für Kommende Zeiten (1979) – soprano and 2 percussion
Tres Passiones Hominis MDCCCCLXXIX (1979) – organ
Canons and Interludes (1980) – flute, oboe, piano
Ainulindalë (1980) – flute, trumpet, piano, double bass

DISCARDED WORKS

Study on Two Planes (1981) – cello and piano
The Piper at the Gates of Dawn (1983) – sulings (Javanese flute), gender
    (Indonesian gamelan metallophone), prepared piano, double bass
Songs of a Just War (1984) – soprano, flute, oboe, clarinet, harp, viola, cello

Litanies of Iron and Stone (1987) – clarinet, soprano saxophone, trombone, tape
Comet New-Born, Arising at Morning (1987) – cabaret singer and seven players
Fons pietatis (1988) – SATB choir
Tourist Variations (1992) – Chamber opera
Fanfare for the Opening of the Scottish Parliament (1999) – Brass Ensemble

PUBLISHED WORKS (1977–2018)

Missa Brevis (1977, rev. 2007)
I. Kyrie; II. Gloria; III. Sanctus; IV. Agnus Dei; V. At the conclusion
Instruments: SATB choir
Duration: c.16'
Premiere: March 1977 (Sanctus only), Ayr Town Hall, Ayr, UK: Cumnock
Academy Senior Chamber Choir, James MacMillan; 22 November 2007
(complete), Greyfriars Kirk, Edinburgh, UK: Cappella Nova, Alan Tavener
Recording: Linn Records, CKD 301, Cappella Nova, Alan Tavener

A child is born in Bethlehem (1978)
Text: Dutch traditional, trans. R. C. Trevelyan
Instruments: ATB choir and oboe
Duration: c.6'
Premiere: 21 January 2012, St John's College, Cambridge, UK: Choir of
St John's College, Cambridge, Andrew Nethsinga

Edinburgh Te Deum (1978)
Instruments: SSATB choir (with bass solo) and organ
Duration: c.8'
Premiere: 20 November 2011, Westminster Cathedral, London, UK:
Westminster Cathedral Choir, Martin Baker
Recording: Hyperion Records, CDA 67970, Westminster Cathedral Choir,
Martin Baker

The Lamb has come for us from the House of David (1979)
Text: St Ephraim (c.306–73)
Instruments: SAATB choir and organ
Duration: c.4'
Premiere: 9 June 1979, St Peter's Church, Edinburgh, UK: Schola Sancti
Alberti, James MacMillan
Recording: Coro, COR 16071, The Sixteen, Harry Christophers

Hymn to the Blessed Sacrament (**1980, rev. 2010**)
Text: St Thomas Aquinas (1225–74), trans. James Quinn
Instruments: SATB choir and organ
Duration: c.3'
Premiere: 4 March 2012, Westminster Cathedral, London, UK: Westminster
Cathedral Choir, Martin Baker

The Blacksmith (**1981**)
Text: Traditional
Instruments: Arrangement of an Irish traditional song for voice
and B♭ clarinet
Duration: c.3'

Symphonic Study (**1981**)
Instruments: Orchestra
Duration: c.11'
Premiere: 11 January 2014, City Halls, Glasgow, UK: BBC Scottish SO, James
MacMillan

Etwas zurückhaltend (**1981**)
Instruments: String quartet
Duration: c.15'
Premiere: 31 March 2010, Canongate Kirk, Edinburgh, UK:
Edinburgh Quartet
Recording: Delphian, DCD 34088, Edinburgh Quartet

The Road to Ardtalla (**1983**)
Instruments: Flute, clarinet, horn, piano, violin, cello
Duration: c.15'
Premiere: 6 November 1987, Manchester University Concert Hall,
Manchester, UK: Manchester University New Music Ensemble,
James MacMillan

Three Dawn Rituals (**1983**)
Instruments: Alto flute, clarinet, bassoon, horn, vibraphone, prepared piano,
violin, cello
Duration: c.9'
Premiere: 2 November 1985, St John's Church, Ladbroke Grove, London, UK:
Nomos Ensemble, Paul Webster
Recording: RCA, 828766428520, Scottish CO, James MacMillan

Wedding Introit (**1983**)
Instrument: Organ
Duration: c.2'
Premiere: 9 July 1983, Chapel of St Albert the Great, Edinburgh, UK:
Michael Bonaventure
Recording: Deux-Elles, DXL 1097, William Whitehead

Beatus Vir (**1983**)
Text: Psalm 112
Instruments: SSATBB choir and organ
Duration: c.8'
Premiere: 2 July 1983, Norwich Cathedral, Norwich, UK: Choir of
Norwich Cathedral

On Love (**1984**)
Text: From *The Prophet* by Khalil Gibran (1883–1931)
Instruments: Treble voice and organ
Duration: c.5'
Premiere: 18 August 1984, Chapel of St Albert the Great, Edinburgh, UK:
Barbara Kelly, James MacMillan
Recording: Hyperion Records, CDA 67867, William de Chazal,
Jonathan Vaughn

Piano Sonata (**1985**)
Instrument: Piano
Duration: c.14'
Premiere: 22 June 1987, BBC Scotland broadcast ('The Musician in
Scotland'): William Wright
Recording: Delphian Records, DCD 34009, Simon Smith; Universal Classics,
00680125106278, John York; Heritage, HTGCD 253, Rolf Hind

St Anne's Mass (**1985, rev. 2011**)
I. Kyrie; II. Sanctus and Benedictus; III. Acclamation; IV. Agnus Dei
Instruments: Unison voices, organ (or piano)
Duration: c.5'

Two Visions of Hoy (**1986**)
Instruments: Solo oboe, flute, clarinet, horn, bassoon, percussion, cello
Duration: c.9'
Premiere: 17 June 1986, Manchester University Concert Hall, Manchester,
UK: Manchester University New Music Ensemble, James MacMillan

The Keening (1986)
Instruments: Orchestra
Duration: c.23'
Premiere: 11 January 2014, City Halls, Glasgow, UK: BBC Scottish SO,
James MacMillan

Festival Fanfares (1986)
Instruments: Brass band
Duration: c.4'
Premiere: 1986, Ayr, UK: Kilmarnock Schools Band

Offertorium (1986)
Instrument: Organ
Duration: c.8'
Premiere: 4 August 1986, St Colman's Parish Church, Co. Down, UK:
James MacMillan

Untold (1987, rev. 1991)
Instruments: Wind quintet
Duration: c.7'
Premiere: 13 September 1988, Ayr, UK: Flaxton Ensemble
Recording: RCA, 828766428520, Scottish CO, James MacMillan

Two Movements for Wind Quintet (1987)
Instruments: Wind quintet
Duration: c.10'
Premiere: 29 June 2007, Royal Scottish Academy of Music and Drama,
Glasgow, UK: RSAMD Faculty Ensemble, James MacMillan

After the Tryst (1988)
Instruments: Violin, piano
Duration: c.3'
Premiere: 19 September 1990, Henry Wood Hall, Glasgow, UK: Members of
the Paragon Ensemble
Recording: RCA, 828766428520, Scottish CO, James MacMillan; Champs
Hill Records, CHRCD039, Diana Galvydyte, Christopher Guild

Búsqueda (**1988**)
Text: Poems from Argentinian Mothers of the Disappeared
(trans. Gilbert Markus); excerpts from the Latin Mass
Instruments: Speaker, 8 actors, 3 sopranos and ensemble
Duration: c.29'
Premiere: 6 December 1988, Queen's Hall, Edinburgh, UK: ECAT Ensemble,
James MacMillan
Recording: Catalyst, 09026626692, Scottish CO, James MacMillan

Into the Ferment (**1988**)
Instruments: Ensemble and orchestra
Duration: c.25'
Premiere: 19 December 1988, Magnum Centre, Irvine, UK: Scottish CO,
Ayr Schools Orchestra, James MacMillan
Recording: Chandos, CHAN 10092, BBC PO, James MacMillan

Variation on Johnny Faa' (**1988**)
Instruments: Soprano, flute, cello, harp
Duration: c.4'

Visions of a November Spring (**1988, rev. 1991**)
Instruments: String quartet
Duration: c.28'
Premiere: 3 May 1989, Glasgow, UK: Bingham String Quartet
Recording: BIS, BIS-CD-1269, Emperor Quartet; Delphian, DCD 34088,
Edinburgh Quartet

Tryst (**1989**)
Instruments: Orchestra
Duration: c.30'
Premiere: 17 June 1989, Kirkwall, Orkney, UK: Scottish CO, Paul Daniel
Recording: Naxos, 8.554167, Ulster Orchestra, Takuo Yuasa; BIS, BIS-
CD-1019, Scottish CO, Joseph Swensen

The Exorcism of Rio Sumpúl (**1989**)
Instruments: Mixed ensemble or chamber orchestra
Duration: c.25'
Premiere: 28 January 1990, Glasgow, UK: Paragon Ensemble, David Davies
Recording: BIS, BIS-CD-1169, BBC Scottish SO, Osmo Vänskä

Cantos Sagrados (1989)
Text: Ariel Dorfman; Ana Maria Mendoza; sacred texts
Instruments: SATB chorus and organ
Duration: c.22'
Premiere: 10 February 1990, Old St Paul's Church, Edinburgh, UK:
Scottish Chamber Choir, Colin Tipple
Recording: Signum Classics, SIGCD507, Elysian Singers, Sam Laughton

... as others see us ... (1990)
Instruments: Mixed ensemble
Duration: c.25'
Premiere: 5 April 1990, National Portrait Gallery, London, UK: Scottish CO,
James MacMillan
Recording: RCA, 828766428520, Scottish CO, James MacMillan

The Confession of Isobel Gowdie (1990)
Instruments: Orchestra
Duration: c.26'
Premiere: 22 August 1990, Royal Albert Hall, London, UK: BBC Scottish
SO, Jerzy Maksymiuk
Recording: LSO Live, LSO0124, London SO, Sir Colin Davis; Chandos,
CHAN 10275, BBC PO, James MacMillan; BIS, BIS-CD-1169, BBC
Scottish SO, Osmo Vänskä

The Berserking (1990)
Instruments: Piano and orchestra
Duration: c.33'
Premiere: 22 September 1990, Musica Nova, Glasgow, UK: Peter Donohoe,
Scottish National Orchestra, Matthias Bamert
Recording: Chandos, CHAN 10092, Martin Roscoe, BBC Philharmonic,
James MacMillan; Red Seal, B000003FZ5, Peter Donohoe, Royal Scottish
National Orchestra, Markus Stenz

Sowetan Spring (1990)
Instruments: Wind band
Duration: c.11'
Premiere: 23 September 1990, Glasgow, UK:
Wind of the Royal Scottish National Orchestra, John Paynter

Catherine's Lullabies (1990)
Text: Sentences from the Creed and Magnificat; from a mother of the
Plaza de Mayo; Isaiah 61:1–2; Ecclesiasticus 4; Litany of the Saints
Instruments: SATB chorus, brass and percussion
Duration: c.20'
Premiere: 10 February 1991, Glasgow, UK: John Currie Singers

Scots Song (1991)
Text: William Soutar ('The Tryst')
Instruments: Soprano and ensemble
Duration: c.6'
Premiere: 10 May 1991, Brighton, UK: Composers Ensemble
Recording: Delphian, DCD34099, Irene Drummond, Iain Burnside

Tuireadh (1991)
Instruments: Clarinet and string quartet
Duration: c.22'
Premiere: 25 June 1991, St Magnus Cathedral, Kirkwall, Orkney, UK:
James Campbell, Allegri String Quartet
Recording: BIS, BIS-CD-1219, Robert Plane, Emperor Quartet

Tuireadh (arr. for clarinet and string orchestra) (1991, arr. 1995)
Instruments: Clarinet and string orchestra
Duration: c.22'
Premiere: 24 November 1995, Filharmonia Baltycka, Gdansk, Poland:
Karol Respondek, Gdansk Philharmonic, James MacMillan

A Cecilian Variation for J.F.K.
(Second movement of Kennedy Variations) (1991)
Instruments: Piano solo
Duration: c.3'30"
Premiere: 22 November 1991, Kennedy Center, Washington DC, USA:
David Owen Norris
Recording: Delphian, DCD34009, Simon Smith

Intercession (1991)
Instruments: 3 oboes
Duration: c.7'
Premiere: 26 November 1991, Art Gallery, Huddersfield, UK:
Chione Oboe Trio

Intercession (arr. for 3 saxophones) (1991)
Instruments: 3 soprano saxophones
Duration: c.7'

Sinfonietta (1991)
Instruments: Orchestra or chamber orchestra
Duration: c.19'
Premiere: 14 May 1992, Queen Elizabeth Hall, London, UK:
London Sinfonietta, Martyn Brabbins
Recording: BIS, BIS-CD-1119 Digital, Scottish CO, James MacMillan

Divo Aloysio Sacrum (1991)
Text: from an inscription on a church wall
Instruments: SATB chorus and optional organ
Duration: c.7'
Premiere: 27 August 1993, St Giles Cathedral, Edinburgh, UK: Royal Scottish
National Orchestra Chorus, Edinburgh Festival Ensemble, Christopher Bell
Recording: Signum Classics, SIGCD507, Elysian Singers, Sam Laughton

Inés de Castro (1991–95, rev. 2014)
Text: Jo Clifford, after the play *Inés de Castro*
Instruments: Soprano, 2 mezzo-sopranos, tenor, bass-baritone, bass, chorus
and orchestra
Duration: c.110'
Premiere: 23 August 1996, Edinburgh Festival, UK: Scottish Opera,
Richard Armstrong

Veni, Veni, Emmanuel (1992)
Instruments: Percussion and orchestra
Duration: c. 26'
Premiere: 10 August 1992, Royal Albert Hall, London, UK: Evelyn Glennie,
Scottish CO, Jukka-Pekka Saraste
Recording: RCA 828766428520, Evelyn Glennie, Scottish CO,
James MacMillan; Challenge Classics, CC72540, Colin Currie,
Netherlands Radio Chamber Philharmonic, James MacMillan

So Deep (1992)
Text: Robert Burns
Instruments: SSAATTBB chorus with optional oboe and viola solos
Duration: c.7'
Recording: Signum Classics, SIGCD507, Elysian Singers, Sam Laughton

Barncleupèdie (with apologies to Erik Satie) (1992)
Instruments: Piano solo
Duration: c.2'
Premiere: 28 February 1993, Queens Hall, Edinburgh, UK:
Catherine Edwards
Recording: Delphian, DCD34009, Simon Smith

Visitatio Sepulchri (1992–93)
Text: Fourteenth-century Easter Day liturgical drama; Te Deum
Instruments: 7 solo singers or 7-part chorus (SSATTB, male speaker) and
chamber orchestra
Duration: c.45'
Premiere: 20 May 1993, Tramway, Glasgow, UK: Scottish CO, Ivor Bolton
Recording: BIS, BIS-SACD-1719, Netherlands Radio Choir, Netherlands
Radio Chamber Philharmonic, James MacMillan; Catalyst, 09026626692,
Scottish CO, Ivor Bolton

... here in hiding ... (1993)
Text: from St Thomas Aquinas ('Adoro te devote'), trans.
Gerard Manley Hopkins
Instruments: Four male voices (or unaccompanied choir)
Duration: c.12'
Premiere: 10 August 1993, Stevenson Hall, Royal Scottish Academy of Music
and Drama, Glasgow, UK: Hilliard Ensemble
Recording: ECM Records, 00028945325927, Hilliard Ensemble

They saw the stone had been rolled away (1993)
Instruments: Fanfare for brass and percussion
Duration: c.6'
Premiere: 27 August 1993, St Giles Cathedral, Edinburgh, UK: Edinburgh
Festival Ensemble
Recording: BIS, BIS-CD-1019, Scottish CO, Joseph Swensen

Epiclesis (1993, rev. 1998)
Instruments: Trumpet and orchestra
Duration: c.25'
Premiere: 28 August 1993, Usher Hall, Edinburgh, UK: John Wallace,
Philharmonia Orchestra, Leonard Slatkin
Recording: BIS, BIS-CD-1069 Digital, John Wallace, Royal Scottish National
Orchestra, Alexander Lazarev

Angel (**1993**)
Instrument: Piano
Duration: c.4'
Premiere: 31 October 1993, Stockbridge Parish Church, Edinburgh, UK:
James MacMillan
Recording: Delphian, DCD34009, Simon Smith

Memoire imperiale (**1993**)
Instruments: Chamber orchestra
Duration: c.5'
Premiere: 13 February 1994, Edinburgh University, Edinburgh, UK:
Scottish CO, Matthias Bamert

Seven Last Words from the Cross (**1993**)
Text: Biblical excerpts
Instruments: SSAATTBB chorus and strings
Duration: c.45'
Premiere: 27 March 1994, BBC TV, UK: Cappella Nova,
BT Scottish Ensemble, Alan Tavener
Recording: Hyperion, CDA 67460, Polyphony, Britten Sinfonia,
Stephen Layton

Kiss on Wood (**1993**)
Instruments: Violin and piano
Duration: c.9'
Premiere: 6 August 1994, Harrogate Festival, UK: Madeleine Mitchell,
John Lenehan
Recording: NMC Recordings, NMCD098, Madeleine Mitchell, Andrew Ball

Kiss on Wood (**cello version**) (**1993**)
Instruments: Cello and piano
Duration: c.9'
Premiere: 15 December 1994, Wigmore Hall, London, UK: Julian Lloyd
Webber, John Lenehan
Recording: Universal Classics, 00680125100825, Raphael Wallfisch,
John York

Ballad (1994)
Text: William Soutar
Instruments: Voice (unspecified) and piano
Duration: c.4'
Premiere: 15 May 1994, Royal Scottish Academy of Music and Drama,
Glasgow, UK: Frances McCafferty, Graeme McNaught
Recording: Delphian, DCD34099, Irene Drummond, Iain Burnside

White Note Paraphrase (1994)
Instrument: Organ
Duration: c.2'
Premiere: 25 June 1994, Kirkcudbright Parish Church, Scotland, UK: Tom
Carrick

Britannia (1994)
Instruments: Orchestra
Duration: c.14'
Premiere: 21 September 1994, Barbican Hall, London, UK: London SO,
Michael Tilson Thomas
Recording: Chandos, CHAN 10092; BBC PO, James MacMillan

Memento (1994)
Instruments: String quartet
Duration: c.4'30"
Premiere: 13 October 1994, Merkin Concert Hall, New York, NY, USA:
Kronos Quartet
Recording: BIS, BIS-CD-1269, Emperor Quartet

Christus Vincit (1994)
Text: from the Worcester Acclamations (tenth century)
Instruments: SSAATTBB chorus with soprano solo
Duration: c.7'
Premiere: 23 November 1994, St Paul's Cathedral, London, UK: joint choirs of
Westminster Abbey, Westminster Cathedral & St Paul's Cathedral, John Scott
Recording: Hyperion, CDA67219, Choir of Westminster Cathedral,
Martin Baker

Adam's Rib (1994–95)
Instruments: Brass quintet
Duration: c.12'
Premiere: 28 March 1995, Usher Hall, Edinburgh, UK:

Members of the Scottish CO
Recording: BIS, BIS-CD-1019, Scottish CO, Joseph Swensen

Màiri (1995)
Text: Evan Maccoll (trans. James MacMillan)
Instruments: 16-part choir (SSSSAAAATTTTBBBB) a cappella
Duration: c.11'
Premiere: 19 May 1995, St John's Smith Square, London, UK: BBC Singers,
Bo Holten
Recording: Chandos, CHAN 9997, BBC Singers, James MacMillan

After the Tryst (**version for soprano saxophone or clarinet**) (1995)
Instruments: Soprano saxophone (or clarinet) and piano
Duration: c.3'
Premiere: 7 July 1995, Royal Pump Room, Leamington Spa, UK: Gerard
McChrystal
Recording: Delphian, DCD34201, Mackenzie Sawers Duo

A Different World (1995)
Instruments: Violin and piano
Duration: c.5'
Premiere: 22 July 1995, Almeida Theatre, London, UK: Madeleine Mitchell,
John Lenehan
Recording: NMC Recordings, NMCD098, Madeleine Mitchell, Andrew Ball

The Children (1995)
Text: William Soutar
Instruments: Mezzo soprano or baritone voice and piano
Duration: c.5'
Premiere: 23 July 1995, BBC Radio 3, UK: Sandra Porter, Graeme McNaught
Recording: Delphian, DCD34099, Irene Drummond, Iain Burnside

Seinte Mari moder milde (1995)
Text: Thirteenth-century anon.
Instruments: SATB chorus and organ
Duration: c.6'
Premiere: 24 December 1995, King's College, Cambridge, UK: King's College
Chapel Choir, Stephen Cleobury
Recording: Hyperion, CDA 67219, Choir of Westminster Cathedral, Andrew
Reid, Martin Baker

The World's Ransoming (1995–96)
Instruments: Orchestra with obbligato cor anglais
Duration: c.21'
Premiere: 11 July 1996, Barbican, London, UK: Christine Pendrill,
London SO, Kent Nagano
Recording: LSO Live, LSO0124, Christine Pendrill, London SO, Sir Colin
Davis; BIS, BIS-CD-989 Digital, Christine Pendrill, BBC Scottish SO,
Osmo Vänskä

A Child's Prayer (1996)
Text: Traditional (remembered by the composer from childhood)
Instruments: SATB choir a cappella, with 2 treble/soprano solos
Duration: c.4'
Premiere: 4 July 1996, Westminster Abbey, London, UK:
Choir of Westminster Abbey, Martin Neary
Recording: Hyperion, CDA67219, Choir of Westminster Cathedral,
Martin Baker

Cello Concerto (1996)
Instruments: Cello and orchestra
Duration: c.41'
Premiere: 3 October 1996, Barbican, London, UK: Mstislav Rostropovich,
London SO, Colin Davis
Recording: BIS, BIS-CD-989 Digital, Raphael Wallfisch, BBC Scottish SO,
Osmo Vänskä

Í (A Meditation on Iona) (1996)
Instruments: Strings and percussion
Duration: c.17'
Premiere: 21 February 1997, City Hall, Glasgow, UK: Scottish CO, Joseph
Swensen
Recording: BIS, BIS-CD-1019, Scottish CO, Joseph Swensen; Challenge
Classics, CC72540, Colin Currie, Netherlands Radio Chamber Philharmonic,
James MacMillan

The Galloway Mass (1996)
Text: English setting of the Catholic Mass
Instruments: Cantor, congregation, choir and organ

Duration: c.15'
Premiere: 25 March 1997, Good Shepherd Cathedral, Ayr, UK:
Congregation of Good Shepherd Cathedral

Ninian (1996)
Instruments: Clarinet and orchestra
Duration: c.35'
Premiere: 4 April 1997, Usher Hall, Edinburgh, UK: John Cushing,
Royal Scottish National Orchestra, Paul Daniel
Recording: BIS, BIS-CD-1069 Digital, John Cushing, Royal Scottish National
Orchestra, Alexander Lazarev

On the Annunciation of the Blessed Virgin (1996)
Text: Jeremy Taylor
Instruments: SATB choir and organ
Duration: c.7'
Premiere: 27 April 1997, Caius Chapel, Cambridge, UK:
Choir of Gonville & Caius College, Andrew Arthur, Geoffrey Webber
Recording: Coro, COR 16071, The Sixteen, Harry Christophers

The Halie Speerit's Dauncers (1996)
Text: James McGonigal
Instruments: Children's choir (unison) and piano (or voice (unspecified)
and piano)
Duration: c.6'
Premiere: 28 April 1997, Corpus Christi Primary School, Glasgow, UK:
Children of Corpus Christi Primary School, James MacMillan

Birthday Present (1997)
Instrument: Piano
Duration: c.2'
Recording: Delphian, DCD34009, Simon Smith

Lumen Christi (1997)
Instrument: Piano
Duration: c.2'30"
Premiere: 11 April 1997, Palazzo Barozzi, Milan, Italy: Carlo Boccadoro
Recording: Delphian, DCD34009, Simon Smith

The Gallant Weaver (1997)
Text: Robert Burns
Instruments: SATB choir a cappella
Duration: c.7'
Premiere: 14 April 1997, Thomas Coats Memorial Church, Paisley, UK:
Paisley Abbey Choir, George McPhee
Recording: Chandos, CHAN 9997, BBC Singers, James MacMillan

Fourteen Little Pictures (1997)
Instruments: Piano trio
Duration: c.25'
Premiere: 21 May 1997, Wigmore Hall, London, UK:
Frank/Pauk/Kirschbaum Piano Trio
Recording: Black Box, BBM1008, Nash Ensemble; Wigmore Hall Live, WH
0026, Gould Piano Trio

Symphony: *'Vigil'* (1997)
Instruments: Orchestra with separate brass quintet
Duration: c.53'
Premiere: 28 September 1997, Barbican, London, UK: London SO,
Mstislav Rostropovich
Recording: BIS, BIS-CD-990 Digital, BBC Scottish SO, Fine Arts Brass
Ensemble, Osmo Vänskä

Raising Sparks (1997)
Text: Michael Symmons Roberts
Instruments: Six songs for mezzo-soprano and ensemble
Duration: c.34'
Premiere: 5 October 1997, Queen Elizabeth Hall, London, UK: Jean Rigby,
Nash Ensemble
Recording: Black Box, BBM 1067, Jean Rigby, Nash Ensemble

A New Song (1997)
Text: from Psalm 96
Instruments: SATB chorus and organ
Duration: c.4'
Premiere: 1 March 1998, St Bride's Episcopal Church, Glasgow, UK:
Choir of St. Bride's Episcopal Church, Peter Christie, Robert Marshall
Recording: Hyperion, CDA67219, Choir of Westminster Cathedral,
Andrew Reid, Martin Baker

Cantos Sagrados (orchestral version) (1997)
Text: Ariel Dorfman; Ana Maria Mendoza; sacred texts
Instruments: Chorus (SATB) and orchestra
Duration: c.22'
Premiere: 21 March 1998, Glasgow Cathedral, Glasgow, UK:
Royal Scottish National Orchestra and chorus, Christopher Bell

Changed (1997)
Text: Wallace Stevens ('The Man with the Blue Guitar')
Instruments: Mixed chorus (SATB), with accompaniment of organ, harp,
string trio or any three like instruments
Duration: c.2'30"
Premiere: 12 December 1998, Walker Hall, Kilbirnie, Ayrshire, UK:
Cunningham Chamber Choir, members of the North Ayrshire Youth
Silver Band, Dorothy Howden
Recording: Hyperion, CDA67219, Choir of Westminster Cathedral,
Andrew Reid, Martin Baker

The Prophecy (version for school choir and ensemble) (1997)
Text: 'The Story of Deirdre' as translated by Kenneth Hurlstone-Jackson
in 'A Celtic Miscellany'
Instruments: School choir (2-part) and ensemble
Duration: c.8'
Premiere: 11 October 1997, Queen Elizabeth Hall, London, UK:
children from Haringey Schools, musicians from The Philharmonia,
James MacMillan, Nicholas Wilks, John Cooney

The Prophecy (version for soprano and ensemble) (1997)
Text: 'The Story of Deirdre' as translated by Kenneth Hurlstone-Jackson
in 'A Celtic Miscellany'
Instruments: Soprano and ensemble
Duration: c.8'
Premiere: 12 March 2001, Teatro alla Scala, Milan, Italy:
Cristina Zavalloni, Sentieri selvaggi

Why is this night different? (String Quartet No. 2) (1998)
Instruments: String quartet
Duration: c.22'
Premiere: 23 April 1998, Wigmore Hall, London, UK: Maggini Quartet
Recording: BIS, BIS-CD-1269, Emperor Quartet

Gaudeamus in loci pace (**1998**)
Instrument: Organ
Duration: c.6'
Premiere: 12 September 1998, Pluscarden Abbey, UK: Joseph Cullen
Recording: Griffin Records, GRF-ED-4054, Daniel Cook

Exsultet (**1998**)
Instruments: Brass quintet and optional percussion
Duration: c.8'
Premiere: 1 December 1998, Royal Scottish Academy of Music and Drama,
Glasgow, UK: players from the RSAMD
Recording: Chandos, CHAN 9997, BBC PO, James MacMillan

Exsultet (**version for symphonic brass**) (**1998, arr. 2000**)
Instruments: Orchestral brass and percussion
Duration: c.8'
Premiere: 30 September 2000, Bridgewater Hall, Manchester, UK:
BBC Philharmonic, James MacMillan

Quickening (**1998**)
Text: Michael Symmons Roberts
Instruments: Counter-tenor, 2 tenor and baritone soloists, children's choir,
SATB choir and orchestra
Duration: c.48'
Premiere: 5 September 1999, Royal Albert Hall, London, UK:
Hilliard Ensemble, BBC SO, BBC Symphony Chorus, Westminster Cathedral
Boys' Choir, Andrew Davis
Recording: Chandos, CHSA 5072, Hilliard Ensemble, City of Birmingham
Symphony Chorus and Youth Chorus, BBC Philharmonic, James MacMillan

Cumnock Fair (**version for piano sextet**) (**1999**)
Instruments: Piano sextet
Duration: c.12'
Premiere: 23 March 1999, Cumnock Academy, Ayrshire, UK: musicians
from the Scottish CO

Cumnock Fair (**version for string orchestra and piano**) (**1999**)
Instruments: String orchestra and piano
Duration: c.12'
Recording: BIS, BIS-CD-1119, Graeme McNaught, Scottish CO,
James MacMillan

Cello Sonata No. 1 (1999)
Instruments: Cello and piano
Duration: c.22'
Premiere: 30 May 1999, Assembly Rooms, Bath, UK: Raphael Wallfisch,
John York
Recording: Universal Classics, 00680125100825, Raphael Wallfisch,
John York

Symphony No. 2 (1999)
Instruments: Chamber orchestra
Duration: c.24'
Premiere: 2 December 1999, Town Hall, Ayr, UK: Scottish CO,
James MacMillan
Recording: BIS, BIS-CD-1119, Scottish CO, James MacMillan

The Company of Heaven (1999, rev. 2016)
Instruments: Solo carnyx and wind band
Duration: c.15'

Magnificat and Nunc Dimittis (1999–2000)
Text: 1662 Book of Common Prayer
Instruments: SATB choir and organ
Duration: c.21'
Premiere (complete): 15 July 2000, Winchester Cathedral, UK:
Choir of Winchester Cathedral, Philip Scriven, David Hill
Recording: Hyperion, CDA67867, Jonathan Vaughan, Wells Cathedral Choir,
Matthew Owens

Magnificat (orchestral version) (1999)
Text: 1662 Book of Common Prayer
Instruments: SATB choir and orchestra
Duration: c.14'
Premiere: 5 January 2000, Wells Cathedral, Wells, UK: Wells Cathedral Choir,
St. John's College Choir Cambridge, BBC Philharmonic, James MacMillan
Recording: Chandos, CHAN 9997, BBC Philharmonic, BBC Singers,
James MacMillan; Challenge Classics, CC72554, Netherlands Radio
Chamber Philharmonic, Netherlands Radio Choir, James MacMillan

Heyoka Te Deum (**1999**)
Text: Latin Te Deum; Lakota native Indian text (trans. English)
Instruments: 3-part treble voices, flute, tubular bells and piano
Duration: c.5'30"
Premiere: 3 May 2001, Great Hall of Cooper Union, New York, NY, USA:
Brooklyn Youth Choir, Dianne Berkon

For Ian (**2000**)
Instrument: Piano
Duration: c.5'
Premiere: 8 February 2000, St. Ninian's Women's Guild, Cumnock, UK:
James MacMillan
Recording: Delphian, DCD34009, Simon Smith

Mass (Original version) (**2000**)
Text: Liturgical
Instruments: SATB chorus and organ
Duration: c.35'
Premiere: 22 June 2000, Westminster Cathedral, London, UK:
Choir of Westminster Cathedral, Andrew Reid, Martin Baker
Recording: Hyperion, CDA 67219, Choir of Westminster Cathedral,
Andrew Reid, Martin Baker

Mass (**New English translation**) (**2000, rev. 2012**)
Text: Liturgical (revised text in English)
Instruments: SATB chorus and organ
Duration: c.25'
Premiere: 2 June 2013, Westminster Cathedral, London, UK:
Peter Stevens, Westminster Cathedral Choir, Martin Baker

Parthenogenesis (**2000**)
Text: Michael Symmons Roberts
Instruments: Soprano, baritone, actress and chamber ensemble
Duration: c.50'
Premiere: 12 September 2000, Corn Exchange, Cambridge, UK:
Britten Sinfonia, James MacMillan

From Galloway (**2000**)
Instrument: Clarinet
Duration: c.2'
Premiere: 1 October 2000, Royal Concert Hall, Glasgow, UK: John Cushing

Northern Skies (seven intermediate pieces) (2000)
Instruments: Cello and piano
Duration: c.14'
Premiere: 9 March 2001, Hutcheson's Hall, Glasgow, UK:
Catherine MacMillan/Fay Jennet/Rachel Brolly/Allison Jones (cello),
Myra Chahin (piano)

Cello Sonata No. 2 (2000)
Instruments: Cello and piano
Duration: c.17'
Premiere: 17 April 2001, Queen's Hall, Edinburgh, UK: Julian Lloyd Webber,
John Lenehan
Recording: SOMM Recordings, SOMMCD0175, Alexander Baillie,
John Thwaites

The Birds of Rhiannon (2001)
Text: Michael Symmons Roberts
Instruments: Orchestra with optional chorus (SATB)
Duration: c.24'
Premiere: 26 July 2001, Royal Albert Hall, London, UK: The Sixteen,
BBC PO, James MacMillan
Recording: Chandos, CHAN 9997, BBC Singers, BBC PO, James MacMillan

Nunc Dimittis (orchestral version) (2001)
Text: 1662 Book of Common Prayer
Instruments: SATB choir and orchestra
Duration: c.8'
Premiere: 16 November 2001, Bridgewater Hall, Manchester, UK:
BBC Philharmonic, BBC Singers, James MacMillan
Recording: Chandos, CHAN 9997, BBC Philharmonic, BBC Singers,
James MacMillan; Challenge Classics, CC72554, Netherlands Radio
Chamber Philharmonic, Netherlands Radio Choir, James MacMillan

Te Deum (2001)
Text: 1662 Book of Common Prayer
Instruments: SATB choir and organ
Duration: c.15'
Premiere: 3 February 2002, Tower of London, London, UK: Colm Carey,
Choir of the Chapel Royal, Her Majesty's Tower of London, Stephen Tilton
Recording: Hyperion, CDA 67460, Polyphony, James Vivian, Stephen Layton

in augustiis ... I (2001)
Instrument: Piano
Duration: c.3'
Premiere: 16 February 2002, Bute Hall, Glasgow, UK: Simon Smith
Recording: Delphian, DCD34009, Simon Smith

in augustiis ... II (version for cello solo) (2001)
Instrument: Cello
Duration: c.8'

in augustiis ... II (version for oboe solo) (2001)
Instrument: Oboe
Duration: c.8'
Recording: Quartz Music, QTZ2081, James Turnbull

in augustiis ... II (version for soprano solo) (2001)
Text: James MacMillan, compiled from various ancient English, Dutch
and Latin sources
Instrument: Soprano solo
Duration: c.8'

Tremunt videntes angeli (2001)
Text: Fifth-century Latin hymn 'Aeterne rex altissime'
Instruments: SATB choir a cappella
Duration: c.9'
Premiere: 9 May 2002, St Mary's Cathedral, Edinburgh, UK: Choir of
St Mary's Cathedral, Edinburgh, Matthew Owens
Recording: Delphian, DCD34017, St. Mary's Cathedral Choir, Edinburgh,
Matthew Owens; Signum Classics, SIGCD507, Elysian Singers, Sam Laughton

Dutch Carol (2001)
Text: Dutch traditional, taken from 'Oxford Book of Carols' (trans.
R. C. Trevelyan)
Instruments: Unison treble voices with piano
Duration: c.2'
Recording: Delphian, DCD34097, Tewkesbury Abbey Schola Cantorum,
Benjamin Nicholas

A Deep but Dazzling Darkness (2001–02)
Instruments: Solo violin, ensemble and tape
Duration: c.22'
Premiere: 27 March 2003, St. Luke's, London, UK: Gordon Nikolitch,
London SO, James MacMillan (private performance)
Recording: Challenge Classics, CC72540, Gordon Nikolitch,
Netherlands Radio Chamber Philharmonic, James MacMillan

O bone Jesu (2002)
Text: Sixteenth-century anon.
Instruments: Chorus a cappella
Duration: c.10'
Premiere: 10 October 2002, Southwark Cathedral, London, UK:
The Sixteen, Harry Christophers
Recording: Coro, COR 16069, The Sixteen, Harry Christophers

To My Successor (2002)
Text: George Herbert
Instruments: SATB chorus a cappella
Duration: c.3'
Premiere: 27 February 2003, Canterbury Cathedral, Canterbury, UK:
Choir of Canterbury Cathedral, David Flood

Symphony No. 3: 'Silence' (2002)
Instruments: Orchestra
Duration: c.36'
Premiere: 17 April 2003, NHK Hall, Tokyo, Japan: NHK SO, Charles Dutoit
Recording: Chandos, CHAN 10275, BBC PO, James MacMillan

25th May 1967 (2002)
Instrument: Piano
Duration: c.3'
Premiere: 6 May 2003, Bateman Auditorium, Gonville and Caius College,
Cambridge, UK: Simon Smith

For Neil (2002)
Instrument: Piano
Duration: c.3'
Premiere: 6 May 2003, Bateman Auditorium, Gonville and Caius College,
Cambridge, UK: Simon Smith

Chosen (**2003**)
Text: Michael Symmons Roberts
Instruments: SAATTB choir and organ
Duration: c.7'
Premiere: 24 December 2003, Paisley Abbey, Glasgow, UK: Oliver Rundell,
Choir of Paisley Abbey, George McPhee
Recording: Signum Classics, SIGCD059, Vasari Singers, Jeremy Backhouse

Le Tombeau de Georges Rouault (**2003**)
Instrument: Organ
Duration: c.15'
Premiere: 18 March 2004, Birmingham Symphony Hall, Birmingham, UK:
Thomas Trotter

Piano Concerto No. 2 (2003)
Instruments: Piano and string orchestra
Duration: c.30'
Premiere: 8 May 2004, Lincoln Center, New York, NY, USA:
New York City Ballet, Cameron Grant, James MacMillan
Recording: Chandos, CHAN 10377, Wayne Marshall, BBC Philharmonic,
James MacMillan

Give me Justice (**Introit for the Fifth Sunday of Lent**) (**2003**)
Text: Psalm 42 (43)
Instruments: SATB choir a cappella
Duration: c.3'
Recording: Linn Records, BKD301, Cappella Nova, Alan Tavener

*A Scotch Bestiary: enigmatic variations on a zoological carnival
at a Caledonian exhibition* (**2003–04**)
Instruments: Organ and orchestra
Duration: c.33'30"
Premiere: 7 October 2004, Disney Hall, Los Angeles, CA, USA:
Wayne Marshall, Los Angeles Philharmonic, Esa-Pekka Salonen
Recording: Chandos, CHAN 10377, Wayne Marshall, BBC Philharmonic,
James MacMillan

For Max (**2004**)
Instruments: Piano quintet
Duration: c.3'

Premiere: 22 June 2004, St Magnus Cathedral, Kirkwall, Orkney, UK:
Nash Ensemble

For Michael (2004)
Instruments: Piano quintet
Duration: c.3'
Premiere: 15 July 2004, Pittville Pump Room, Cheltenham, UK:
Aleksander Madzar, Belcea Quartet

Laudi alla Vergine Maria (2004)
Text: Dante Alighieri
Instruments: SSAATTBB chorus a cappella
Duration: c.9'
Premiere: 6 October 2004, St Janskerk, Gouda, Netherlands: Netherlands
Chamber Choir, Stephen Layton
Recording: GRF-ED-4052, Winchester Cathedral Choir, Andrew Lumsden

HB to MB (2004)
Instrument: Cello
Duration: c.3'30"
Premiere: 7 October 2004, House of Lords, Palace of Westminster,
London, UK: Raphael Wallfisch

Nemo te condemnavit (2005)
Text: Gospel according to St John, 8:10–11
Instruments: SATB chorus a cappella
Duration: c.5'
Premiere: 18 November 2005, Woolsey Hall, Yale University,
New Haven, CT, USA: Yale Glee Club, Jeffrey Douma
Recording: Naxos, 8.570719, Dmitri Ensemble, Graham Ross

From Ayrshire (2005)
Instruments: Violin and orchestra
Duration: c.8'
Premiere: 23 March 2007, Schuster Center, Dayton, OH, USA:
Nicola Benedetti, Dayton PO, Carlos Miguel Prieto
Recording: Universal/DG 476 3159, Nicola Benedetti, Academy of St Martin
in the Fields, James MacMillan; Challenge Classics, CC72638, Linus Roth,
Netherlands Radio Chamber Philharmonic, James MacMillan

The Sacrifice (2005–06)
Text: Michael Symmons Roberts, based on a story from the Mabinogion
Instruments: 6 sopranos, mezzo-soprano, tenor, 2 baritones,
chorus and orchestra
Duration: c.130'
Premiere: 22 September 2007, Wales Millenium Centre, Cardiff, UK:
Welsh National Opera, James MacMillan
Recording: Chandos, CHAN 10572(2), Orchestra and Chorus of
Welsh National Opera, Anthony Negus

The Sacrifice: Three Interludes (2005–06)
Instruments: Orchestra
Duration: c.15'
Premiere: 22 February 2008, Bridgewater Hall, Manchester, UK: BBC PO,
James MacMillan
Recording: Chandos, CHAN 5072, BBC PO, James MacMillan

For Sally (2006)
Instruments: Piano quintet
Duration: c.4'
Premiere: 5 July 2006, Pittville Pump Room, Cheltenham, UK:
Nash Ensemble, Martyn Brabbins

Invocation (2006)
Text: Karol Wojtyla (trans. Jerzy Peterkiewicz)
Instruments: SATB double chorus a cappella
Duration: c.6'
Premiere: 11 July 2006, Tewkesbury Abbey, Tewkesbury, UK:
Oriel Singers, Tim Morris
Recording: Linn Records, CKD439, Cappella Nova, Alan Tavener

Sun-Dogs (2006)
Text: Michael Symmons Roberts ('Sun-Dogs'); Latin from the Roman Missal,
English traditional
Instruments: SATB chorus a cappella (with multiple divisi)
Duration: c.21'
Premiere: 6 August 2006, Auer Hall, Bloomington, IN, USA:
Indiana University Contemporary Vocal Ensemble, Carmen Téllez
Recording: BIS, SACD 1719, Netherlands Radio Choir, James MacMillan

Success (2006)
Text: Bessie Stanley
Instruments: SATB chorus a cappella
Duration: c.2'

Stomp (with Fate and Elvira) (2006)
Instruments: Orchestra
Duration: c.5'30"
Premiere: 3 March 2007, Barbican Centre, London, UK:
London SO, Colin Davis CBE

After Virtue (2006)
Text: Alasdair MacIntyre (from the final paragraph, chapter 18
of the book *After Virtue*)
Instruments: SSAATTBB chorus a capella
Duration: c.5'
Premiere: 18 March 2007, Oslo, Norway: Oslo Soloist Choir, Grete Pedersen

Tenebrae Responsories (2006)
Text: from the Roman Breviary
Instruments: Chorus a cappella (SATB vocal ensemble, with divisi
up to SSAATTBB – 8 singers on stage)
Duration: c.20'
Premiere: 4 April 2007, St Andrews in the Square, Glasgow, UK:
Cappella Nova, Alan Tavener
Recording: Coro, COR 16096, The Sixteen, Harry Christophers

Horn Quintet (2007)
Instruments: Horn and string quartet
Duration: c.15'
Premiere: 9 July 2007, Pittville Pump Room, Cheltenham, UK:
Nash Ensemble

Concertino for Horn and Strings (2007, arr. 2016)
Arrangement of Horn Quintet by the composer
Instruments: Horn and string orchestra
Duration: c.15'
Premiere: 3 March 2017, City Halls, Glasgow, UK:
Alex Franc-Gemmill, Scottish CO, Andrew Manze

... fiat mihi ... (2007)
Text: Stabat Mater; with additional text by the composer
Instruments: Double chorus a cappella
Duration: c.5'
Premiere: 21 March 2008, Wells Cathedral, Wells, UK:
Bath Camerata, Nigel Perrin
Recording: Linn Records, CKD439, Cappella Nova, Alan Tavener

St John Passion (2007)
Text: Revised Standard Version of the Bible; the Vulgate; Stabat Mater;
additional text by the composer
Instruments: Solo baritone, chorus and orchestra
Duration: c.87'
Premiere: 27 April 2008, Barbican Hall, London, UK:
Christopher Maltman, London SO and Chorus, Colin Davis
Recording: LSO Live, LSO 0671, Christopher Maltman, London SO
and Chorus, Colin Davis

String Quartet No. 3 (2007)
Instruments: String quartet
Duration: c.25'30"
Premiere: 21 May 2008, Queen Elizabeth Hall, London, UK:
Takacs String Quartet
Recording: Delphian, DCD 34088, Edinburgh Quartet

Jebel (2007)
Instruments: Brass band
Duration: c.3'30"
Premiere: 1 September 2008, Jordanhill School, Glasgow, UK:
Pupils of Jordanhill School

Chant for John (2007)
Instruments: Piano quartet
Duration: c.2'

Piano Concerto No. 3: *The Mysteries of Light* (2007–08)
Instruments: Piano and orchestra
Duration: c.25'
Premiere: 14 April 2011, Orchestra Hall, Minneapolis, MN, USA:
Jean-Yves Thibaudet, Minnesota Orchestra, Osmo Vänskä

Walfrid, On His Arrival At The Gates of Paradise (2008)
Instrument: Piano
Duration: c.3'

The Song of the Lamb (2008)
Text: Revelation 15:2–4 (Revised Standard Version)
Instruments: SATB chorus and organ
Duration: c.5'
Premiere: 9 March 2008, House of Hope Presbyterian Church,
St Paul, MN, USA: Nancy Lancaster, Motet Choir of the House of Hope
Presbyterian Church, Andrew Altenbach

Padre Pio's Prayer (2008)
Text: Padre Pio (attrib.), interpreted by James MacMillan
Instruments: SATB chorus and piano
Duration: c.11'
Premiere: 3 June 2008, Westminster Cathedral, London, UK:
The Sixteen, Harry Christophers
Recording: Coro, COR 16071, The Sixteen, Harry Christophers

O (**An Antiphon for Advent**) (**2008**)
Text: Liturgical (unknown)
Instruments: 3-part treble choir, trumpet and strings (or organ)
Duration: c.7'30"
Premiere: 23 June 2008, Queen's Hall, Edinburgh, UK:
St Mary's Music School

Lament of Mary, Queen of Scots (2008)
Text: Robert Burns
Instruments: Soprano, tenor, violin, cello and piano
Duration: c.5'
Premiere: 16 January 2009, University of Glasgow, Glasgow, UK:
Lorna Anderson, Jamie MacDougall, Haydn Trio Eisenstadt

Mouth of the Dumb (2008)
Text: James MacMillan, trans. after Latin from the Inchcolm Antiphoner
Instruments: SS soli (or chorus) and harp
Duration: c.4'
Premiere: 4 April 2009, Kings Place, London, UK: Andrew Swait,
Sam Harris, Lucy Wakeford
Recording: NMC Recordings, NMCD150, Andrew Swait, Sam Harris,
Lucy Wakeford

Who Are These Angels? (2009)
Text: Anon. (attrib. St Augustine)
Instruments: Male vocal ensemble and string quartet
Duration: c.6'
Premiere: 28 April 2009, Laurenskerk, Rotterdam, Netherlands:
Doelen Kwartet, Ensemble Amarcord
Recording: Linn Records, CKD 383, Cappella Nova, Alan Tavener

Who Are These Angels? (SATBB version) (2009)
Text: Anon. (attrib. St Augustine)
Instruments: SATBB chorus and string quartet
Duration: c.6'

Jubilate Deo (2009)
Text: Book of Common Prayer
Instruments: SATB choir and organ
Duration: c.3'30"
Premiere: 17 May 2009, Wells Cathedral, Wells, UK: Jonathan Vaughn,
Wells Cathedral Choir, Matthew Owens
Recording: Hyperion, CDA67867, Jonathan Vaughan, Wells Cathedral Choir,
Matthew Owens

Benedictus Deus (2009)
Text: from a fifteenth-century Canterbury pontifical
Instruments: SATB chorus a cappella
Duration: c.4'30"
Premiere: 21 May 2009, Westminster Cathedral, London, UK:
Westminster Cathedral Choir, Martin Baker
Recording: Linn Records, CKD 383, Cappella Nova, Alan Tavener

Summae Trinitati (To the most high Trinity) (2009)
Text: from a fifteenth-century Canterbury pontifical
Instruments: SATB chorus, 4 trumpets, 3 optional trombones,
timpani and organ
Duration: c.4'
Premiere: 21 May 2009, Westminster Cathedral, London, UK:
Westminster Cathedral Choir, Martin Baker

Serenity (2009)
Text: St Thomas Aquinas ('O Salutaris Hostia'); Reinhold Niebuhr (attrib.)
('The Serenity Prayer')
Instruments: SATB choir and organ
Duration: c.5'
Premiere: 21 June 2009, St Aloysius' Church, Rose Street, Glasgow, UK:
Students from St Aloysius' College

Miserere (2009)
Text: Psalm 51:3–21
Instruments: Mixed chorus a cappella
Duration: c.10'
Premiere: 29 August 2009, Carolus-Boromeuskerk, Antwerp, Belgium:
The Sixteen, Harry Christophers
Recording: Coro, COR 16096, The Sixteen, Harry Christophers

And lo, the angel of the Lord came upon them (2009)
Text: Gospel of St. Luke 2:9–14
Instruments: Three mixed-voice choirs a cappella
Duration: c.3'
Premiere: 19 December 2009, St. Paul's Church, Birmingham, UK:
Ex Cathedra, Jeffrey Skidmore
Recording: Linn Records, CKD 383, Cappella Nova, Alan Tavener

The Beneficiaries (2009)
Text: Les Murray
Instruments: Soprano, clarinet and piano
Duration: c.1'
Premiere: 25 February 2010, Purcell Room, Southbank Centre, London, UK:
Jane Manning, Jane's Minstrels

Bring us, O Lord God (2009)
Text: John Donne
Instruments: SATB choir a cappella
Duration: c.5'
Premiere: 1 May 2010, Sheldonian Theatre, Oxford, UK:
Schola Cantorum, James Burton
Recording: Linn Records, CKD 383, Cappella Nova, Alan Tavener

Violin Concerto (2009)
Instruments: Violin and orchestra
Duration: c.25'
Premiere: 12 May 2010, Barbican, London, UK: Vadim Repin, London SO,
Valery Gergiev
Recording: Onyx Classics, 4157, Vadim Repin, BBC Scottish SO,
Donald Runnicles

Tota pulchra es (2009)
Text: Antiphon at the Vespers of the Immaculate Conception
Instruments: Choir and organ
Duration: c.5'
Premiere: 8 July 2010, Basilica of the National Shrine of the Immaculate
Conception, Washington, DC, USA: Choir of the Basilica of the
National Shrine
Recording: Linn Records, CKD 383, Cappella Nova, Alan Tavener

Oboe Concerto (2009–10)
Instruments: Oboe and orchestra
Duration: c.23'
Premiere: 15 October 2010, Birmingham Town Hall, Birmingham, UK:
Nicholas Daniel, Britten Sinfonia, James MacMillan
Recording: Harmonia Mundi, HMU 807573, Nicholas Daniel,
Britten Sinfonia, James MacMillan

Clemency (2009–10)
Text: Anon.; Michael Symmons Roberts; glossolalia
Instruments: 5 singers (STTBrBr) and string orchestra
Duration: c.45'
Premiere: 6 May 2011, Linbury Studio Theatre, Royal Opera House,
London, UK: Britten Sinfonia, Clark Rundell
Recording: BIS, BIS-CD-2129, Boston Lyric Opera, David Angus

Lassie, wad ye loe me? (2010)
Text: Anon.
Instruments: Mixed voices with multiple divisi, a cappella
Duration: c.5'
Premiere: 8 May 2010, St John's Church, Dunoon, UK:
Strathclyde University Chamber Choir, Alan Tavener
Recording: Naxos, 8.573069, Blossom Street Choir, Hillary Campbell

Sonnet (2010)
Text: William Shakespeare
Instruments: Vocal duet a cappella (SS or S, MS)
Duration: c.3'
Premiere: 5 June 2010, The Drummond Hotel, St Fillians, Perthshire, UK:
Catherine and Clare MacMillan
Recording: Albion, ALBCD030, Les Sirènes Female Chamber Choir

Ave Maria (2010)
Text: Latin
Instruments: SATB choir and organ
Duration: c.5'
Premiere: 27 July 2010, St George's Chapel, Windsor, UK: Richard Pinell,
Boys, Girls and Men of All Saints Northampton, Lee Dunleavy

Meditation (2010)
Instrument: Organ
Duration: c.3'
Premiere: 11 August 2010, St Michael and All Saints Church, Edinburgh, UK:
Philip Sawyer

Think of how God loves you (2010)
Text: 1 John 3:1; the baptismal rite
Instruments: SATB chorus a cappella
Duration: c.1'
Premiere: 22 August 2010, St Columba's Church, Maryhill, Glasgow, UK:
The Choir of St Columba's, Maryhill, James MacMillan
Recording: Linn Records, CKD 383, Cappella Nova, Alan Tavener

Mass of Blessed John Henry Newman (**2010**)
Text: New trans. of the Mass
Instruments: Cantor, congregation and organ, with optional SATB chorus, brass and timpani
Duration: c.15'
Premiere: 16 September 2010, Bellahouston Park, Glasgow, UK:
unnamed congregation
Recording: Linn Records, CKD 383, Cappella Nova, Alan Tavener

Tu es Petrus (**Processional**) (**2010**)
Instruments: Organ, brass and percussion
Duration: c.1'
Premiere: 18 September 2010, Westminster Cathedral, London, UK:
London Brass, Peter Stevens, Martin Baker
Recording: Hyperion, CDA 67970, London Brass, Peter Stevens, Martin Baker

Tu es Petrus (**Introit**) (**2010**)
Text: Matthew 16:18
Instruments: SATB chorus, organ, brass and percussion
Duration: c.4'
Premiere: 18 September 2010, Westminster Cathedral, London, UK:
Choir of Westminster Cathedral, London Brass, Peter Stevens, Martin Baker
Recording: Hyperion, CDA 67970, Choir of Westminster Cathedral, London Brass, Peter Stevens, Martin Baker

Seraph (**2010**)
Instruments: Trumpet and string orchestra
Duration: c.15'
Premiere: 17 February 2011, Wigmore Hall, London, UK:
Alison Balsom, Scottish Ensemble
Recording: EMI Classics, 5099967859023, Alison Balsom, Scottish Ensemble

Domine non secundum peccata nostra (**2010**)
Text: Tract for Ash Wednesday
Instruments: SSATTBB chorus with violin
Duration: c.5'
Premiere: 9 March 2011, St John's College, Cambridge, UK:
Margaret Faultless, Choir of St John's College, Cambridge, Andrew Nethsingha
Recording: Linn Records, CKD439, Cappella Nova, Alan Tavener

Since it was the day of Preparation ... (2010–11)
Text: St John's Gospel (Revised Standard Version); extracts from 'O filii et filiæ'
(Jean Tisserand) & 'Salve festa dies' (Venantius Fortunatus) (Liber Usualis);
St Matthew's Gospel (Vulgate)
Instruments: Bass solo, mixed soli or small chorus and ensemble
Duration: c.70'
Premiere: 22 August 2012, Greyfriars Kirk, Edinburgh, UK: William Conway,
Brindley Sherratt, Hebrides Ensemble, Synergy Vocals
Recording: Delphian DCD 34168, Brindley Sherratt, Hebrides Ensemble,
Synergy Vocals

Motet I (**from** *Since it was the day of Preparation ...*)
Instrument: Theorbo

Motet II (**from** *Since it was the day of Preparation ...*)
Instrument: Cello
Premiere: 30 July 2016, The Saloon, Duncombe Park, Helmsley, UK:
Leonard Elschenbroich

Motet III (**from** *Since it was the day of Preparation ...*)
Instrument: B-flat clarinet
Premiere: 24 July 2016, All Saints Church, Helmsley, UK: Andrew Marriner

Motet IV (**from** *Since it was the day of Preparation ...*)
Instrument: Harp
Premiere: 21 July 2016, Castle Howard, York, UK: Catrin Finch

Motet V (**from** *Since it was the day of Preparation ...*)
Instrument: Horn

Missa Dunelmi (2011)
Text: Liturgical
Instruments: SSAATTBB chorus a cappella
Duration: c.16'
Premiere: 27 February 2011, Durham Cathedral, Durham, UK:
Durham Cathedral Choir, James Lancelot
Recording: Linn Records, CKD439, Cappella Nova, James MacMillan

St Patrick's Magnificat (2011)
Text: Latin (unknown)
Instruments: SATB chorus a cappella
Duration: c.7'
Premiere: 31 May 2011, St Patrick's Church, Soho, London, UK:
Choir of St Patrick's Church
Recording: Linn Records, CKD439, Cappella Nova, Alan Tavener

Beatus Andreas (2011)
Text: Versicle at Matins on the Feast of St Andrew
Instruments: SATB chorus and organ
Duration: c.6'
Premiere: 2 June 2011, St Andrew's Cathedral, Glasgow, UK:
Choir of St Aloysius' Church, Dan Divers

Alpha and Omega (2011)
Text: Revelation 21:1–6a
Instruments: SSSAATTBB chorus a cappella
Duration: c.6'30"
Premiere: 4 June 2011, Rockefeller Chapel, University of Chicago,
Chicago, IL, USA: Rockefeller Chapel Choir, Chicago University
Motet Choir, James Kallembach
Recording: Linn Records, CKD439, Cappella Nova, Alan Tavener

Ecce Sacerdos Magnus (2011)
Text: Antiphon for a bishop
Instruments: Unison voices, 2 trumpets and organ
Duration: c.3'
Premiere: 15 August 2011, Aberdeen Cathedral, Aberdeen, UK:
Aberdeen Cathedral Choir

Children are a heritage of the Lord (2011)
Text: Psalm 127 (King James Bible)
Instruments: SSATB chorus a cappella
Duration: c.5'
Premiere: 11 September 2011, Hatfield House, Hertfordshire, UK:
The Sixteen

I Am Your Mother (**2011**)
Text: Words of Our Lady of Guadelupe; Sancta Maria, virginum piissima
Instruments: SATB chorus a cappella
Duration: c.4'
Premiere: 17 September 2011, Blackfriars, Oxford, UK:
Choir of Blackfriars, James MacMillan
Recording: Linn Records, CKD439, Cappella Nova, Alan Tavener

Ave Maris Stella (**2011**)
Text: Vesper hymn to Mary
Instruments: SATB chorus a cappella
Duration: c.3'
Premiere: 3 November 2011, Truro Cathedral, Truro, UK:
Truro Cathedral Choir, Christopher Gray
Recording: Signum Classics, SIGCD536, Gabrieli Consort, Paul MacCreesh

For Sonny (**2011**)
Instruments: String quartet
Duration: c.5'30"
Premiere: 1 March 2012, Peterhouse, Cambridge, UK: Edinburgh Quartet
Recording: Delphian, DCD 34088, Edinburgh Quartet

Fanfare Upon One Note (**2011**)
Instruments: Orchestral brass
Duration: c.2'30"
Premiere: 3 March 2012, Clyde Auditorium, Glasgow, UK:
BBC Scottish SO, National Youth Orchestra of Scotland,
Royal Conservatoire of Scotland, Donald Runnicles

Hodie Puer Nascitur (**2011**)
Text: based on an anonymous fourteenth-century French-Cypriot antiphon
('Hodie mortalis firmiter – Hodie puer nascitur', Biblioteca Nazionale, Turin,
Ms. J. II. 9)
Instruments: Chorus and ensemble
Duration: c.5'
Premiere: 13 April 2012, Concertgebouw, Amsterdam, Netherlands:
Huelgas Ensemble, Royal Concertgebouw Orchestra, Martyn Brabbins
Recording: RCO Live, RCO 14001, Huelgas Ensemble,
Royal Concertgebouw Orchestra, Martyn Brabbins

Gloria (**2011**)
Text: Liturgical (unknown)
Instruments: Tenor soloist, SATB chorus (with divisi), children's choir, organ,
brass and timpani
Duration: c.20'
Premiere: 23 June 2012, Coventry Cathedral, Coventry, UK:
Ian Bostridge, Choral Society of Coventry Cathedral, Saint Michael's Singers,
City of Birmingham SO brass and percussion, James MacMillan

New-made for a king (**2011**)
Text: Michael Symmons Roberts (from 'Her Maker's Maker')
Instruments: SSAA chorus and piano
Duration: c.6'
Premiere: 23 June 2012, Farnham Maltings, Farnham, UK:
Farnham Youth Choir, Andreas Klatt
Recording: Naxos, 8.573427, Wells Cathedral School Choir, Elliot Launn,
Christopher Finch

Credo (**2011**)
Text: Liber Usualis
Instruments: Chorus and orchestra
Duration: c.20'
Premiere: 7 August 2012, Royal Albert Hall, London, UK:
BBC PO, Manchester Chamber Choir, Northern Sinfonia Chorus,
Rushley Singers, Juanjo Mena

Canite Tuba (**2011–12**)
Instruments: Brass band
Duration: c.12'
Premiere: 1 July 2012, Symphony Hall, Birmingham, UK: Black Dyke Band

Woman of the Apocalypse (**2011–12**)
Instruments: Orchestra
Duration: c.27'
Premiere: 4 August 2012, Santa Cruz Civic Auditorium, Santa Cruz, CA,
USA: Cabrillo Festival Orchestra, Marin Alsop

Cum vidisset Jesus (**2012**)
Text: Antiphon on the Feast of the Seven Dolours of the Blessed Virgin Mary
Instruments: Chorus (SATB) a cappella

Duration: c.7'
Premiere: 15 September 2012, University of Notre Dame,
Notre Dame, IN, USA: Notre Dame Festival Chorus, Carmen-Helena Téllez
Recording: Linn Records, CKD439, Cappella Nova, Alan Tavener

One (2012)
Instruments: Chamber orchestra
Duration: c.3'
Premiere: 27 October 2012, Barbican Hall, London, UK:
Britten Sinfonia, James MacMillan
Recording: Harmonia Mundi, HMU807573DI, Britten Sinfonia,
James MacMillan

Cecilia Virgo (2012)
Text: (Latin)
Instruments: Double SATB chorus a cappella
Duration: c.5'
Premiere: 24 November 2012, Royal Holloway, University of London, Egham,
Surrey, UK: Choir of Royal Holloway, University of London, Rupert Gough

Nova! Nova! Ave fit ex Eva (2012)
Text: Fifteenth-century anon.
Instruments: SSA chorus a cappella
Duration: c.5'
Premiere: 21 December 2012, Caird Hall, Dundee, UK:
Royal Scottish National Orchestra Junior Chorus, Christopher Bell
Recording: Naxos, 8.573427, Wells Cathedral School Choir,
Christopher Finch

And he rose (2012)
Instrument: Cello
Duration: c.4'
Premiere: 15 January 2013, Turner Simms Concert Hall, Southampton, UK:
Matthew Barley

The Death of Oscar (2012)
Instruments: Orchestra
Duration: c.10'
Premiere: 11 July 2013, Liederhalle, Beethovensaal, Stuttgart, Germany:
Radio-Sinfonieorchester Stuttgart des SWR, Stéphane Denève

St Luke Passion (**2012–13**)
Text: Bible, Revised Standard Version
Instruments: SATB chorus, children's choir, organ and chamber orchestra
Duration: c.75'
Premiere: 15 March 2014, Concertgebouw, Amsterdam, Netherlands:
Netherlands Radio PO, Netherlands Radio Choir, Vocaal Talent Nederland,
National Jaugdkoor, Markus Stenz
Recording: Challenge Classics, CC72671, Netherlands Radio PO,
Netherlands Radio Choir, National Youth Choir, Peter Dicke, Markus Stenz

If ye love me (**2013**)
Text: John 14:15–17 (King James Bible)
Instruments: SATB chorus a cappella
Duration: c.5'

St Andrews' Suite (**2013**)
Instruments Organ
Duration: c.7'
Premiere: 27 June 2013, University of St Andrews, Scotland, UK:
Tom Wilkinson

Alleluia (**2013**)
Text: Latin (unknown)
Instruments: SSSSAAAATTTBB(B) chorus a cappella
Duration: c.10'
Premiere: 6 July 2013, Silva Concert Hall, Hult Center for the Performing
Arts, Eugene, OR, USA: Berwick Chorus of the Organ Bach Festival,
Matthew Halls
Recording: SWR Classic, CD93.342, South West German Radio
Vocal Ensemble, Marcus Creed

The Offered Christ (**2013**)
Text: 'The Altar Fire' (Armenian Liturgy), trans. Olive Wyon
Instruments: SAATB chorus and organ
Duration: c.5'
Premiere: 20 July 2013, Chichester Cathedral, Chichester, UK:
Chichester Cathedral Choir

Viola Concerto (2013)
Instruments: Viola and orchestra
Duration: c.31'
Premiere: 15 January 2014, Royal Festival Hall, London, UK:
Lawrence Power, London PO, Vladimir Jurowski

Deus noster refugium (2013)
Text: Psalm 46
Instruments: SSAATTBB chorus and organ
Duration: c.5'
Premiere: 29 March 2014, Leeds Town Hall, Leeds, UK:
Leeds Festival Chorus, Simon Wright

A Rumoured Seed (2013)
Text: Michael Symmons Roberts
Instruments: Chorus a cappella
Duration: c.15'
Premiere: 2 April 2014, Perth Concert Hall, Perth, UK: The King's Singers

Piano Trio No. 2 (2013)
Instruments: Piano Trio
Duration: c.13'30"
Premiere: 20 May 2014, Guildhall Banqueting Room, Bath, UK:
Gould Piano Trio
Recording: Champs Hill Records, CHRCD090, Gould Piano Trio

Domus infelix est (The house is unhappy) (2013)
Text: Latin (unknown)
Instruments: SATB chorus and violin
Duration: c.6'
Premiere: 5 October 2014, Cumnock Tryst, Cumnock, UK:
Nicola Benedetti, The Sixteen

I will take you from the nations (2014)
Text: Ezekiel 36:24–26, 28
Instruments: SSAATTBB chorus a cappella
Duration: c.3'
Premiere: 8 June 2014, Merton College, Oxford, UK: Merton College Choir

Emitte lucem tuam (2014)
Text: Psalm 43; Gloria Patri
Instruments: SSAATTBB a cappella
Duration: c.4'
Premiere: 19 September 2014, Westminster Cathedral, London, UK:
Choir of Cardinal Vaughan School

Percussion Concerto No. 2 (2014)
Instruments: Percussion and orchestra
Duration: c.25'
Premiere: 7 November 2014, Tivoli Vredenburg, Utrecht, Netherlands:
Colin Currie, Netherlands Radio Philharmonic, James Gaffigan

Seven Angels (2014)
Text: Revelation 8; 9:1–4, 13–17a; 11:12b, 15–19; 21:1–6a
Instruments: Mixed chorus (with multiple divisi), soloists (from chorus)
and small instrumental ensemble
Duration: c.36'
Premiere: 31 January 2015, Town Hall, Birmingham, UK: Ex Cathedra,
Jeffrey Skidmore

Little Mass (2014)
Text: Liturgical excerpts
Instruments: Children's chorus and orchestra
Duration: c.30'
Premiere: 28 March 2015, Philharmonic Hall, Liverpool, UK:
Royal Liverpool PO, Liverpool Philharmonic Training and Youth Choirs,
Melody Makers, James MacMillan

Playing to the Skyline (2014)
Instruments: Children's string orchestra and ensemble
Duration: c.3'

Ave Verum Corpus (2014)
Text: Latin
Instruments: Treble voices and organ
Duration: c.4'

The Rising Moon (2014)
Text: Robert Burns (from 'Death and Dr Hornbrook')
Instruments: Unison voices and handbells
Duration: c.3'

The Rising Moon (**version for SATB chorus**) (2014)
Text: Robert Burns (from 'Death and Dr Hornbrook')
Instruments: SATB chorus and handbells
Duration: c.3'

Symphony No. 4 (2014–15)
Instruments: Orchestra
Duration: c.37'
Premiere: 3 August 2015, Royal Albert Hall, London, UK:
BBC Scottish SO, Donald Runnicles
Recording: Onyx Classics, ONYX 4157, BBC Scottish SO, Donald Runnicles

The Culham Motets (2015)
Text: Liturgical (unknown)
Instruments: Chorus a cappella
Duration: c.21'

Noli Pater (**2015**)
Text: Anon.
Instruments: SSAATTBB chorus, triplepipe and organ
Duration: c.5'
Premiere: 15 July 2015, St Albans Cathedral, St Albans, UK:
Barnaby Brown, Gonville and Caius College Choir, Cambridge,
Bernhard Haas, Geoffrey Webber
Recording: Delphian, DCD34154, Barnaby Brown, Gonville and Caius
College Choir, Cambridge, James Leitch, Geoffrey Webber

When you see the millions of the mouthless dead (**2015**)
Text: Charles Hamilton Sorley
Instruments: SATB chorus a cappella
Duration: c.3'
Premiere: 3 October 2015, Cumnock Old Church, Cumnock, UK:
Genesis Sixteen

Knockroon Waltz (**2015**)
Instruments: Harp solo
Duration: c.3'
Premiere: 4 October 2015, The Tapestry Room, Dumfries House,
Cumnock, UK: The Cumnock Tryst

Ut omnes unum sint (**2015**)
Text: John 17:20–23 (Vulgate)
Instruments: SSAATTBB chorus a cappella
Duration: c.5'
Premiere: 21 November 2015, St Mary's Metropolitan Cathedral,
Edinburgh, UK: Cappella Caeciliana, James MacMillan

I Awoke Today (**Resurrection Chorus**) (**2015**)
Text: Manchester Streetwise Explore Group, arranged by Penny Woolcock
Instruments: SATB chorus and ensemble
Duration: c.4'
Premiere: 25 March 2016, Campfield Market, Manchester, UK:
Streetwise Opera, The Sixteen, Penny Woolcock

A European Requiem (**2015**)
Text: Requiem Mass
Instruments: Counter-tenor (or alto) and baritone soli, mixed chorus
and orchestra
Duration: c.43'
Premiere: 2 July 2016, Silva Concert Hall, Eugene, OR, USA:
Christopher Ainselle, Morgan Smith, Oregon Bach Festival Orchestra,
Berwick Chorus of Oregon Bach Festival, Matthew Halls

Stabat Mater (**2015**)
Text: Latin, attrib. Jacopone da Todi (c.1230–1306)
Instruments: Chorus and string orchestra
Duration: c.53'
Premiere: 15 October 2016, Barbican, London, UK:
The Sixteen, Britten Sinfonia, Harry Christophers
Recording: Coro, COR16150, The Sixteen, Britten Sinfonia,
Harry Christophers

The Sun Danced (2016)
Text: from the Apparitions of the Angel and of Our Lady and from
the Miracle of the Sun at Fátima
Instruments: Soprano, chorus and orchestra
Duration: c.29'
Premiere: 13 October 2017, The Sanctuary, Fatima: Gulbenkian
Orchetsra and choir, Joana Carneiro

Four Little Tributes (2016)
  1. *For Michael*
  2. *For Max*
  3. *For Sally*
  4. *Chant for John*
Instruments: Piano quintet or quartet
Premiere: 26 July 2016, St Mary's Priory Church, Malton, UK:
Royal Northern Sinfonia

O Give Thanks unto the Lord (2016)
Text: Robert Herrick ('To Music: A Song'); Psalm 105:1–5
Instruments: Chorus and organ (with optional string accompaniment)
Duration: c.5'
Premiere: 30 September 2016, Truro Cathedral, Cornwall, UK:
Choir of Truro Cathedral, City of London Sinfonia, Stephen Layton
Premiere of choral version: 9 October 2016, Liverpool Cathedral,
Liverpool, UK: Choir of Liverpool Cathedral, Choir of
Liverpool Metropolitan Cathedral, Stephen Layton

Hirta (2016)
Instruments: Arrangement of a traditional melody for strings
and recorded piano

Sonata for Violin and Piano *(Before the Tryst)* (2016)
Instruments: Violin and piano
Duration: c.15'
Premiere: 30 March 2017, Weill Recital Hall, New York, NY, USA:
Simone Lamsma, Robert Kulek

Trombone Concerto (2016)
Instruments: Trombone and orchestra
Duration: c.25'
Premiere: 20 April 2017, Concertgebouw, Amsterdam, Netherlands:
Jörgen van Rijen, Royal Concertgebouw Orchestra, Iván Fischer
Recording: RCO Live, 17004, Jörgen van Rijen, Royal Concertgebouw
Orchestra, Iván Fischer

One Equal Music (2016)
Text: John Donne
Instruments: SATB chorus a cappella
Duration: c.5'
Premiere: 21 May 2017, Selwyn College Cambridge choral evensong,
Cambridge, UK: Choir of Selwyn College, Cambridge

Bennett! (2016)
Instruments: Solo contrabass clarinet
Duration: c.5'
Premiere: 2 October 2016, The Tapestry Room, Cumnock, UK: Scott Lydgate

Blow the Trumpet in the New Moon (2016)
Text: Psalm 81:1–4 (Geneva Bible)
Instruments: SSSSAAAATTBB a cappella
Duration: c.5'
Premiere: 29 June 2017, Royal Festival Hall, London, UK:
The Bach Choir, David Hill

A Special Appeal (2017)
Text: (Archbishop) Oscar Romero of El Salvador (trans. Julian Filochowski);
Psalm 31:13, 14
Instruments: SSAATTBB chorus and organ
Duration: c.5'
Premiere: 23 September 2017, Westminster Abbey, London:
Choir of Westminster Abbey, James O'Donnell

Larghetto for orchestra (**orchestration of** *Miserere*) (**2017**)
Instruments: Orchestra
Duration: c.15'
Premiere: 27 October 2017, Heinz Hall, Pittsburgh, PA, USA:
Pittsburgh SO, Manfred Honeck

Sicut Cervus (2017)
Text: Psalm 42:1
Instruments: SATB double choir
Duration: c.5'
Premiere: 12 November 2017, St George's Church, Bristol, UK: Exultate Singers

Saxophone Concerto (2017)
Instruments: Soprano saxophone and string orchestra
Duration: c.15'
Premiere: 11 April 2018, Perth Concert Hall, Perth, UK:
Amy Dickson, Scottish CO, Joseph Swensen

O Virgo prudentissima (2017)
Text: Angelo Ambrogini (1454–94) ('Poliziani')
Instruments: SATB chorus a cappella
Duration: c.10'
Premiere: 22 May 2018, Eton College Chapel, Eton, UK:
The Sixteen, Harry Christophers

Ein Lämplein verlosch (2018)
Instruments: String quartet
Duration: c.5'
Premiere: 17 June 2018, Gewandhaus, Mendelssohn-Saal, Leipzig, Germany:
Gewandhaus-Quartett

Everyone Sang (2017)
Text: Siegfried Sassoon ('Everyone Sang')
Instruments: SSSSAAAATTTTBBBB chorus and organ
Duration: c.6'
Premiere: 2 July 2018, American Guild of Organists' Convention, Kansas City,
MO, USA: Jan Kraybill, Spire Chamber Ensemble, Ben A. Spalding

The Highgate Motet (2017)
Text: Lancelot Andrewes ('Private Preces')
Instruments: SATB choir a cappella
Duration: c.5'

Sing joyfully to the Lord (2017–18)
Text: Psalm 33:1–4 (New International Version)
Instruments: SATB chorus (with divisi) and organ
Duration: c.5'

THE STRATHCLYDE MOTETS (2005–10)

Videns Dominus (When the Lord saw) (2005)
Communion Motet for the Fifth Sunday in Lent
Text: Roman Breviary, John 2:33, 35, 43, 44, 39
Instruments: SATB chorus a cappella
Duration: c.5'30"
Premiere: 13 March 2005, Strathclyde University Chaplaincy Centre,
Glasgow, UK: Strathclyde University Chamber Choir, Alan Tavener
Recording: Coro, COR 16096, The Sixteen, Harry Christophers

Factus est repente (Suddenly, a sound came) (2005)
Communion Motet for Pentecost
Text: Roman Breviary, Acts 2:2, 4
Instruments: SATB chorus a cappella
Duration: c.2'45"
Premiere: 15 May 2005, Strathclyde University Chaplaincy Centre,
Glasgow, UK: Strathclyde University Chamber Choir, Alan Tavener
Recording: Coro, COR 16096, The Sixteen, Harry Christophers

Sedebit Dominus Rex (The Lord will sit on his throne) (2005)
Communion Motet for the feast of Christ the King
Text: Roman Breviary, Psalm 28:10b, 11b
Instruments: SATB chorus a cappella
Duration: c.4'40"
Premiere: 20 November 2005, Strathclyde University Chaplaincy Centre,
Glasgow, UK: Strathclyde University Chamber Choir, Alan Tavener
Recording: Linn Records, CKD 301, Cappella Nova, Alan Tavener

In splendoribus sanctorum
(Amidst the splendours of the heavenly sanct) (2005)
Communion Motet for Nativity Midnight Mass
Text: Roman Breviary, Psalm 109:3
Instruments: SATB chorus and obbligato trumpet or organ
Duration: c.8'10"
Premiere: 24 December 2006, St Columba's Church, Maryhill, Glasgow, UK:
St Columba's Church Choir
Recording: Coro, COR 16096, The Sixteen, Harry Christophers

Mitte manum tuam (Stretch forth your hand) (2006)
Communion Motet for the Second Sunday of Easter
Text: Roman Breviary, John 20:27
Instruments: SATB choir a cappella
Duration: c.3'
Premiere: 23 April 2006, St Columba's Church, Maryhill, Glasgow, UK:
Strathclyde University Chamber Choir, Alan Tavener
Recording: Linn Records, CKD 301, Cappella Nova, Alan Tavener

Dominus dabit benignitatem
(The Lord will bestow his loving kindness) (2006)
Communion Motet for the First Sunday in Advent
Text: Roman Breviary, Psalm 84:13
Instruments: SATB chorus a cappella
Duration: c.5'
Premiere: 3 December 2006, St Columba's Church, Maryhill, Glasgow, UK:
Strathclyde University Chamber Choir, Alan Tavener
Recording: Coro, COR 16096, The Sixteen, Harry Christophers

Data est mihi omnis potestas (It has been given to me) (2007)
Communion Motet for Ascension Day
Text: Roman Breviary, Matthew 28:18, 19
Instruments: SATB chorus a cappella
Duration: c.4'30"
Premiere: 14 May 2007, St Columba's Church, Maryhill, Glasgow, UK:
Strathclyde University Chamber Choir, Alan Tavener
Recording: Coro, COR 16096, The Sixteen, Harry Christophers

O Radiant Dawn (2007)
Advent Antiphon for 21 December
Text: English (unknown)
Instruments: SATB choir a cappella
Duration: c.3'
Premiere: 2 December 2007, St Columba's Church, Maryhill, Glasgow, UK:
St Columba's Church Choir
Recording: Coro, COR 16096, The Sixteen, Harry Christophers;
Linn Records, CKD 383, Cappella Nova, Alan Tavener

The Canticle of Zachariah (2007)
Text: Luke 1:68–79
Instruments: SATB choir a cappella
Duration: c.3'30"
Premiere: 2 December 2007, St Columba's Church, Maryhill, Glasgow, UK:
Strathclyde University Chamber Choir
Recording: Linn Records, CKD 383, Cappella Nova, Alan Tavener

Pascha nostrum immolates est (Our Passover is sacrificed) (2008)
Communion Motet for Easter Day
Text: Liturgical (unknown)
Instruments: SATB chorus a cappella
Duration: c.3'
Premiere: 23 March 2008, St Columba's Church, Maryhill, Glasgow, UK:
Strathclyde University Chamber Choir, Alan Tavener
Recording: Linn Records, CKD 383, Cappella Nova, Alan Tavener

Os mutorum (2008)
Text: Medieval chant from the Inchcolm Antiphoner
Instruments: 2-part women's voices (or 2 solo voices) and medieval harp
Duration: c.4'
Premiere: 22 June 2008, St Columba's Church, Maryhill, Glasgow, UK: Canty
Recording: Linn Records, CKD 378, Canty, Rebecca Taverner,
William Taylor; Linn Records, CKD 383, Cappella Nova, Alan Tavener

Lux Aeterna (Eternal Light) (2008)
Text: Requiem Mass
Instruments: SATB choir a cappella
Duration: c.3'
Premiere: 2 November 2008, St Columba's Church, Maryhill, Glasgow, UK:
Strathclyde University Chamber Choir, Alan Tavener
Recording: Coro, COR 16096, The Sixteen, Harry Christophers;
Linn Records, CKD 383, Cappella Nova, Alan Tavener

Qui meditabitur (2010)
Text: Communion Antiphon for Ash Wednesday
Instruments: SSATTBB chorus a cappella
Duration: c.5'
Premiere: 17 February 2010, St Columba's Church, Maryhill, Glasgow, UK:
Strathclyde University Chamber Choir
Recording: CKD 383, Cappella Nova, Alan Tavener

Benedicimus Deum caeli (**2010**)
Text: Roman Breviary, Tobias 12:6
Instruments: SSAATTB chorus a cappella
Duration: c.3'
Premiere: 30 May 2010, St Columba's Church, Maryhill, Glasgow, UK:
Strathclyde University Chamber Choir, Alan Tavener
Recording: Coro, COR 16096, The Sixteen, Harry Christophers;
Linn Records, CKD 383, Cappella Nova, Alan Tavener

MISCELLANEOUS WORKS (DATES UNKNOWN)

Advent Antiphons
Text: Various, ad lib
Instruments: Cantor, unison voices (congregation), TB chorus and keyboard
Duration: c.18'
Recording: Linn Records, CKD 383, Cappella Nova, Alan Tavener

The Lord's Prayer
Text: Liturgical (unknown)
Instruments: Unison voices with organ accompaniment
Duration: c.2'

O dignissima Christi sponsa
Text: Magnificat Antiphon
Instruments: SATB chorus a cappella
Duration: c.5'

Bibliography

Alvey, Bethany L., 'Spirituality and Scottish Identity in Selected Works of James MacMillan' (PhD, University of Miami, 2016)

Anderson, Martin, 'Southwark Cathedral: A MacMillan Première', *Tempo*, vol. 57, no. 223 (2003), 80–83

Arnold, Jonathan, *Sacred Music in Secular Society* (Farnham: Ashgate, 2014)

Buie, Elizabeth, 'James MacMillan: My Best Teacher', *Times Educational Supplement Scotland* (9 September 2011)

Burrows, Helen. J., 'Choral Music and the Church of England: 1970–1995' (PhD, University of East Anglia, 1999)

Clark, Andrew, 'Devoted to music: Andrew Clark talks to Scottish composer James MacMillan about the inspiration behind his work', *The Financial Times* (19 September 1997)

Clements, Andrew, 'John Casken', *The Musical Times*, vol. 123, no. 1667 (1982), 21–23

——, 'Preview: BBC's Seven Last Words', *The Guardian* (28 March 1994)

Clinch, Dermot, 'James MacMillan: Great Scot or musical Machiavelli?', *The New Statesman* (23 August 1996)

Conway, Paul, 'Cheltenham Festival 2007: James MacMillan and Anthony Payne', *Tempo*, vol. 62, no. 243 (2008), 57–58

——, 'London, Wigmore Hall, Durham Cathedral: James MacMillan', *Tempo*, vol. 65, no. 258 (2011), 51–52

——, 'MacMillan: "A Deep but Dazzling Darkness" et al.', *Tempo*, vol. 67, no. 264 (2013), 103–04

——, 'James MacMillan premieres in Edinburgh, Glasgow and London', *Tempo*, vol. 68, no. 269 (2014), 70–72

Cooke, Phillip. A., Interview with James MacMillan (Eton High Street, 22 May 2018)

——, Interview with James MacMillan (University of Aberdeen, 16 November 2017)

——, Interview with James MacMillan (Candleriggs, Glasgow, 29 March 2017)

——, Interview with James MacMillan (Royal Conservatoire of Scotland, Glasgow, 30 November 2015)

Donohoe, Graeme, 'Sir James MacMillan reveals heartbreak of losing his granddaughter to rare condition', *Daily Record* (26 February 2017)

Downie, Gordon, 'Aesthetic Necrophilia: Reification, New Music, and the Commodification of Affectivity', *Perspectives of New Music*, vol. 42, no. 2 (2004), 264–75

Drakeford, Richard, 'Review of Seven Last Words from the Cross', *The Musical Times*, vol. 136, no. 1832 (1995), 556

'Dunblane Cathedral', https://hymnary.org/tune/dunblane_cathedral (retrieved 27 March 2018)

Dunnett, Roderic, Liner notes to *James MacMillan Miserere*, CORO Records, COR16096 (2011)

——, 'Subtle Celebration', http://www.mvdaily.com/articles/2000/07/macmill7.htm (retrieved 20 June 2018)

Everett, William, 'National Themes in Scottish Art Music, ca. 1880–1990', *International Review of the Aesthetics and Sociology of Music*, vol. 30, no. 2 (1999), 151–71

Frank, Nathan, 'James MacMillan's *St. John Passion*: The Role of Celtic Folk Idioms and The Reproaches' (PhD, University of North Texas, 2014)

Fuller, Michael, 'Liturgy, Scripture and Resonance in the Operas of James MacMillan', *New Blackfriars*, vol. 96, no. 1964 (2015), 381–90

Greaves, Mark, 'Liturgists tried to block my Mass setting for the Pope', *Catholic Herald* (27 October 2010)

Greenfield, Edward, 'James MacMillan', *The Guardian* (25 August 1990)

——, 'An echo of the pure sound of prayer', *The Guardian* (6 August 1992)

Hall, Thomas, '"Crowning Glories": Inés de Castro', *The Musical Times*, vol. 138, no. 1849 (1997), 38–39

Hallam, Mandy, 'Conversation With James Macmillan', *Tempo*, vol. 62, no. 245 (2008), 17–29

Harries, Rhiannon, 'How We Met: James MacMillan & Michael Symmons Roberts', *The Independent* (12 April 2008)

Heffer, Simon, 'James MacMillan and a musical bag of spanners', *The Telegraph* (4 July 2009)

Hewett, Ivan, *Music: Healing the Rift* (London: Continuum, 2003)

'History of Cunninghame Choir', http://www.cunninghame-choir.org.uk/history.html (retrieved 29 May 2017)

'The holy warrior with a baton', *Catholic Herald* (17 December 2015)

Jaffe, Daniel, 'Music Stand: James MacMillan', *BBC Music Magazine* (1 January 2009)

——, 'James MacMillan', http://www.compositiontoday.com/articles/james_macmillan_interview.asp (retrieved 15 March 2018)

'James MacMillan talks about "Tuireadh"', soundcloud.com/hebridesensemble/
    james- macmillan-talks-about- tuireadh (retrieved 5 June 2017)

Johnson, Julian, and Sutton, Catherine, 'Raising Sparks: On the Music of James
    MacMillan', *Tempo*, no. 202 (1997), 1–35

Johnson, Stephen, 'James MacMillan: Veni Veni Emmanuel', *Tempo*, no. 183
    (1992), 34–35

——, 'James MacMillan', *Tempo*, no. 185 (1993), 2–5

——, 'Harnessing Extremes', *Gramophone* (1 May 1995)

——, 'Untitled', *The Independent* (25 September 1997)

——, 'Three in one', *Gramophone* (1 May 1999)

——, Liner notes to *James MacMillan: Into the Ferment*, Chandos Records,
    CHAN 10092 (2003)

——, Liner notes to *MacMillan: Symphony No. 3 'Silence'*, Chandos Records,
    CHAN 10275 (2005)

——, Liner notes to *James MacMillan Sun-Dogs*, BIS CD, BIS-SACD-1719
    (2010)

——, 'MacMillan's *The Confession of Isobel Gowdie*', *Discovering Music*, BBC
    Radio 3 (broadcast 2 June 2014)

Kettle, David, 'Inés de Castro', Programme note to Scottish Opera production
    (2015)

Khalifa, Michel, Liner notes to *St Luke Passion*, Challenge Classics, CC72671
    (2015)

Kilbey, Paul, 'Bachtrack Composers Project: James MacMillan', http://
    bachtrack.com/interview-james-macmillan (retrieved 15 February 2015)

Kingsbury, Stephen, 'The Early Choral Music of James MacMillan: 1983–
    1993' (PhD, University of Illinois at Urbana-Champaign, 2003)

——, 'Aesthetic Meaning in the Congregational Masses of James MacMillan',
    Yale Journal of Music & Religion, vol. 2, no. 1 (2016)

Larner, Gerald, 'New Men for the New Music', *The Guardian* (14 August 1990)

MacDonald, Callum, 'MacMillan, Stevenson and Other Scots', *Tempo*, no. 188
    (1994), 32–35

MacMillan, James, 'MacMillan on University' (unknown YouTube video)
    https://www.youtube.com/watch?v=L8Nm5c-yZvE&t=19s (retrieved 16
    February 2017)

——, 'Music Composition' (PhD, University of Durham, 1987)

——, 'Electro-Acoustic Music', *The Guardian* (6 May 1988)

——, 'Orcadian delights', *The Guardian* (23 June 1988)

——, Programme note to *Into the Ferment* (1988), http://www.boosey.com/
    cr/music/James-MacMillan-Into-the-Ferment/3961 (retrieved 15 May
    2017)

———, Programme note to *Búsqueda* (1988), http://www.boosey.com/cr/music/James-MacMillan-B-squeda/3524 (retrieved 11 May 2017)

———, Programme note to *Tryst* (1989), http://www.boosey.com/cr/music/James-MacMillan-Tryst/5742 (retrieved 18 May 2017)

———, Programme note to *Cantos Sagrados* (1989), http://www.boosey.com/cr/music/James-MacMillan-Cantos-Sagrados/6138 (retrieved 15 May 2017)

———, Programme note to *The Confession of Isobel Gowdie* (1990), http://www.boosey.com/cr/music/James-MacMillan-The-Confession-of-Isobel-Gowdie/3115 (retrieved 29 May 2017)

———, Programme note to *The Berserking* (1990), http://www.boosey.com/cr/music/James-MacMillan-The-Berserking/6452 (retrieved 18 May 2017)

———, Programme note to *Catherine's Lullabies* (1990), http://www.boosey.com/cr/music/James-MacMillan-Catherine-s-Lullabies/5648 (retrieved 1 June 2017)

———, Programme note to *Tuireadh* (1991), http://www.boosey.com/cr/music/James-MacMillan-Tuireadh/1603 (retrieved 1 June 2017)

———, Programme note to *Sinfonietta* (1991), http://www.boosey.com/cr/music/James-MacMillan-Sinfonietta/7163 (retrieved 8 June 2017)

———, Programme note to *Veni, Veni, Emmanuel* (1992), http://www.boosey.com/pages/cr/catalogue/cat_detail.asp?musicid=3051 (retrieved 8 June 2017)

———, Programme note to *Seven Last Words from the Cross* (1993), http://www.boosey.com/cr/music/James-MacMillan-Seven-Last-Words-from-the-Cross/6108 (retrieved 18 October 2017)

———, Programme note to *Visitatio Sepulchri* (1993), http://www.boosey.com/cr/music/James-MacMillan-Visitatio-Sepulchri/5913 (retrieved 26 September 2017)

———, Programme note to *Memento* (1994), http://www.boosey.com/cr/music/James-MacMillan-Memento/3747 (retrieved 7 July 2018)

———, Programme note to *Britannia* (1994), http://www.boosey.com/cr/music/James-MacMillan-Britannia/3918 (retrieved 16 April 2018)

———, Programme note to *Cello Concerto* (1996), http://www.boosey.com/cr/music/James-MacMillan-Cello-Concerto/2478 (retrieved 12 March 2018)

———, Programme note to *The World's Ransoming* (1996), http://www.boosey.com/cr/music/James-MacMillan-The-World-s-Ransoming/281 (retrieved 6 March 2018)

———, Liner notes to *The Berserking*, RCA Victor Red Seal CD, 09026-68328-2 (1996)

———, Programme note to *Lumen Christi* (1997), http://www.boosey.com/cr/music/James-MacMillan-Lumen-Christi/7641 (retrieved 26 March 2018)

——, Programme note to *Symphony: Vigil* (1997), http://www.boosey.com/cr/music/James-MacMillan-Symphony-Vigil/771 (retrieved 26 March 2018)

——, Liner notes to *James MacMillan: Veni, Veni, Emmanuel; Tryst*, Naxos Records, 8.554167 (1998)

——, 'Interview during the Second Annual Vancouver New Music Festival', http://web.archive.org/web/20030418031812/http://www.sfu.ca/twentieth-century-ltd/macmillan1.html (retrieved 14 April 2015)

——, 'Scotland's Shame?: bigotry and sectarianism in modern Scotland', in Devine, Tom, ed., *Scotland's Shame? Bigotry and Sectarianism in Modern Scotland* (Edinburgh: Mainstream, 2000)

——, 'I Had Not Thought About It Like That Before', in Devine, Tom, ed., *Scotland's Shame? Bigotry and Sectarianism in Modern Scotland* (Edinburgh: Mainstream, 2000)

——, 'God, Theology and Music', *New Blackfriars*, vol. 81, no. 948 (2000), 16–26

——, 'Creation and the Composer', in J. Astley, T. Hone, and M. Savage, eds., *Creative Chords: Studies in Music, Theology and Christian Formation* (Leominster: Gracewing, 2000)

——, Programme note to *The Birds of Rhiannon* (2001), http://www.boosey.com/cr/music/James-MacMillan-The-Birds-of-Rhiannon/15179 (retrieved 3 July 2018)

——, 'Parthenogenesis', in Begbie, J., ed., *Sounding the Depths: Theology through the Arts* (London: SCM Press, 2002)

——, Programme note to *A Deep but Dazzling Darkness* (2002), https://www.boosey.com/cr/music/James-MacMillan-A-Deep-but-Dazzling-Darkness/15136 (retrieved 22 July 2018)

——, Programme note to *Symphony No. 3* (2002), http://www.boosey.com/cr/music/James-MacMillan-Symphony-No-3-Silence/15181 (retrieved 22 June 2018)

——, Programme note to *For Max* (2004), http://www.boosey.com/cr/music/James-MacMillan-For-Max/46369 (retrieved 16 May 2017)

——, 'Silence of the lambs', *The Guardian* (28 February 2004)

——, Programme note to *A Scotch Bestiary* (2004), http://www.boosey.com/cr/music/James-MacMillan-A-Scotch-Bestiary/15163 (retrieved 17 April 2018)

——, Programme note to *From Ayrshire* (2005), https://www.boosey.com/cr/music/James-MacMillan-From-Ayrshire/48593 (retrieved 22 July 2018)

——, 'Dangers of Wark's Whinge', *The Scotsman* (6 February 2005)

——, 'How I rattled the deniers', *The Guardian* (7 August 2006)

——, Programme note to *Sun-Dogs* (2006), http://www.boosey.com/cr/music/James-MacMillan-Sun-Dogs/45441 (retrieved 14 June 2018)

——, Programme note to *St John Passion* (2007), http://www.boosey.com/cr/music/James-MacMillan-St-John-Passion/49500 (retrieved 5 July 2018)

——, 'James MacMillan: interview about his *St John Passion*', http://www.boosey.com/cr/news/James-MacMillan-interview-about-his-St-John-Passion/11805 (retrieved 20 June 2018)

——, 'My Mabinogion opus', *The Scotsman* (16 September 2007)

——, 'Unthinking dogmatism', *The Spectator* (30 January 2008)

——, 'Conceived in silence', *The Guardian* (25 April 2008)

——, Liner notes to *James MacMillan: St John Passion*, LSO Live, 0671 (2009)

——, Programme note to *Violin Concerto* (2009), http://www.boosey.com/cr/music/James-MacMillan-Violin-Concerto/52082 (retrieved 10 July 2018)

——, James MacMillan – Violin Concerto, https://www.bbc.co.uk/programmes/p03l64c5 (retrieved 22 July 2018)

——, 'James MacMillan in Scotland', https://jamesmacmillaninscotland.wordpress.com/blog (retrieved 16 June 2018)

——, 'James MacMillan: interview about *St Luke Passion*', http://www.boosey.com/cr/news/James-MacMillan-interview-about-St-Luke-Passion/100345&LangID=1 (retrieved 10 July, 2018)

——, Liner notes to *Clemency*, BIS CD, BIS-2129 (2014)

——, 'About the Festival', https://www.thecumnocktryst.com/about-the-festival (retrieved 11 August 2018)

——, Programme note to *A European Requiem* (2015), http://www.boosey.com/cr/music/James-MacMillan-A-European-Requiem/100418 (retrieved 11 August 2018)

——, 'Interview on BBC Radio 3', *In Tune*, BBC Radio 3 (broadcast 15 March 2016)

——, 'The beat goes on', *Standpoint* (1 May 2017)

McGregor, Richard, 'Laus deo? On composers' expression of their spirituality', *Spirituality and Health International*, vol. 6, no. 4 (2005), 238–45

——, '"Transubstantiated into the musical ...": metaphor and reality in James MacMillan's Veni Veni Emmanuel', in Hair, Graham, ed., *A Companion to Recent Scottish Music : 1950 to the Present* (Glasgow: Musica Scotica Trust, 2007)

——, 'Scots wha hae? James MacMillan and the paradoxes of Scottish cultural identity', *Sixth Biennial International Conference on Music Since 1990*, Keele University, 2–5 July 2009

———, 'James MacMillan: a conversation and commentary', *The Musical Times*, vol. 151, no. 1912 (2010), 69–100

———, 'James MacMillan's "O Bone Jesu."', *Scottish Music Review*, vol. 2, no. 1 (2011), 1–14

———, '"A Metaphor for the Deeper Wintriness": Exploring James MacMillan's Musical Identity', *Tempo*, vol. 65, no. 257 (2011), 22–39

———, 'Exploring Engagement and Detachment in James MacMillan's "Seven Last Words from the Cross"', University of Aberdeen, Music Research Seminar Series (9 February 2016)

Metzer, David, *Quotation and Cultural Meaning in Twentieth-Century Music* (Cambridge: Cambridge University Press, 2008)

———, *Musical Modernism at the Turn of the Twenty-First Century* (Cambridge: Cambridge University Press, 2011)

Miller, Mary, 'Music for a new Scotland', *The Scotsman* (21 March 1992)

Miller, Phil, 'Interview: Composer James MacMillan on his music festival, growing up in Ayrshire … and why he's given up on social media', *The Sunday Herald* (27 September 2015)

Moody, Ivan, Liner notes to *James MacMillan: Magnificat*, Challenge Classics, CC72554 (2013)

Nice, David, Liner notes to *A Scotch Bestiary*, Chandos Records, CHAN10377 (2006)

———, Liner notes to *Quickening*, Chandos Records, CHSA5072 (2009)

———, Liner notes to *MacMillan: The Sacrifice*, Chandos Records, CHAN10572 (2010)

'The night the sea caught fire: Remembering Piper Alpha', http://www.scotsman.com/lifestyle/the-night-the-sea-caught-fire-remembering-piper-alpha-1-1433754 (retrieved 6 June 2017)

Park, Hernho, 'An Analysis of "Seven Last Words from the Cross" (1993) by James MacMillan' (PhD, University of Illinois at Urbana-Champaign, 2015)

Parsons, William. G., 'Metaphor as a Tool for Theologically-Informed Musical Analysis of Sir James MacMillan's "Triduum"' (PhD, University of Sheffield, 2016)

Peattie, Anthony, 'Opera Premiere: Inés de Castro; Edinburgh Festival Theatre', *The Independent* (25 August 1996)

Porter, Andrew, 'So many young candidates for the red-carpet treatment', *The Observer* (16 August 1992)

Potter, Keith, 'Contemporary British composers. I: James MacMillan: A new Celtic dawn?', *The Musical Times*, vol. 131, no. 1763 (1990), 13–18

'Precision', http://ustvolskaya.org/eng/precision.php (retrieved 9 March 2018)

'Proms Featurette, "The Confession of Isobel Gowdie"', www.youtube.com/watch?v=fNPolWpX9no (retrieved 17 February 2017)

Pruslin, Stephen, 'Strathclyde Concertos', http://www.maxopus.com/resources_detail.aspx?key=58 (retrieved 16 May 2017)

Purser, John, *Scotland's Music: A History of the Traditional and Classical Music of Scotland from Earliest Times to the Present Day* (Edinburgh: Mainstream, 1992)

Pyper, Hugh. S, 'Crucifixion in the concert hall: Secular and sacred in James Macmillan's Passion of St John', *Literature and Theology*, vol. 23, no. 3 (2009), 344–55

Ratcliffe, Shirley, 'Cantus in Choro: James MacMillan', *Choir & Organ* (1 May 1999)

——, 'Cantus in Choro: MacMillan 2', *Choir & Organ* (1 July 1999)

Reade, Simon, 'From socialism to salvation', *The Observer* (15 August 1993)

'Robert Burns's "Willie Brew'd a Peck O'Maut"', http://www.robertburns.org/works/281.shtml (retrieved 16 May 2017)

Rohde, Joshua. W., 'James MacMillan's "Seven Last Words from the Cross" and "Stabat Mater": analysis and approach' (PhD, Boston University, 2017)

Rolls, Timothy, 'James MacMillan: An Analysis of Selected Works' (PhD, University of Houston, 2000)

Russill, Patrick, 'Cantos Sagrados', *The Musical Times*, vol. 137, no. 1837 (1996), 35–37

Schellhorn, Matthew, 'Forget the 1960s – it is time the Church once again embraced new music in the liturgy', *Catholic Herald* (19 March 2015)

'Scots Firebrand', *The Economist* (1 November 1997)

Simpson, Anne, 'Faith in a musical vision', *The Herald* (30 August 1993)

Spicer, Paul, Programme note to *Quickening* (1998), http://www.boosey.com/cr/music/James-MacMillan-Quickening/3599 (retrieved 26 March 2018)

——, Programme note to *Mass* (original version) (2000), http://www.boosey.com/cr/music/James-MacMillan-Mass-Original-version/1017 (retrieved 25 April 2018)

——, Liner notes to *MacMillan: Seven Last Words from the Cross*, Hyperion CD, CDA67460 (2005)

——, Programme note to *Miserere* (2009), http://www.boosey.com/cr/music/James-MacMillan-Miserere/54328 (retrieved 25 April 2018)

——, Liner notes to *MacMillan: Choral Music*, Hyperion CD, CDA 67867 (2011)

——, Liner notes to *MacMillan: Tenebrae Responsories & other choral works*, Hyperion CD, CDA67970 (2013)

Stein, Robert, 'London, Royal Albert Hall Proms 2003: MacMillan, Adams, Kancheli', *Tempo*, vol. 58, no. 227 (2004), 51–53

——, 'London, Barbican: MacMillan's "St John Passion"', *Tempo*, vol. 62, no. 246 (2008), 51–53

——, 'London, Barbican: James MacMillan's Violin Concerto', *Tempo*, vol. 65, no. 255 (2011), 58–59

——, 'MacMillan "St Luke Passion", Barbican Centre, London', *Tempo*, vol. 69, no. 274 (2015), 65–66

Tavener, Rebecca, Liner notes to *Tenebrae: New Choral Music by James MacMillan*, Linn CD, CKD 301 (2007)

——, Liner notes to *Who are these angels: New Choral Music by James MacMillan*, Linn CD, CKD 383 (2011)

——, Liner notes to *Alpha & Omega*, Linn CD, CKD 439 (2013)

Telford, James, 'Reconciling Opposing Forces: the Young James Macmillan – a Performance History' *Tempo*, vol. 65, no. 257 (2011), 40–51

Terry, John T. R., 'Shūsaku Endō's Swamp', https://www.firstthings.com/web-exclusives/2016/12/shsaku-ends-swamp (retrieved 2 July, 2018)

Thompson, Damien, 'MacMillan's loyalty', *The Spectator* (4 December 2010)

——, 'Can a great composer revive a tone-deaf Church?', *Catholic Herald* (24 September 2015)

Twiston-Davies, Beth, 'My art is shaped by my faith', *The Times* (9 April 2009)

Wade, Mike, 'My work is haunted by the death of my granddaughter', *The Times* (11 February 2017)

Walker, Lynne, 'James MacMillan: "making sense of chaos"', *Darkness into Light: The Music of James MacMillan*, BBC Proms Publications (2005)

Walton, Ken, 'A contrived silence', *The Scotsman* (27 July 2003)

——, 'Interview: James MacMillan, composer', *The Scotsman* (2 August 2012)

——, 'Preview: James MacMillan conducting the BBC SSO', *The Scotsman* (11 January 2014)

——, 'Row over Catholic Church music takes dramatic turn', *The Scotsman* (8 March 2014)

——, 'MacMillan stages revision of his first major opera', *The Scotsman* (17 January 2015)

Warnaby, John, 'James MacMillan's "Tryst"', *Tempo*, no. 170 (1989), 38–39

Weitzman, Ronald, 'MacMillan's "Inés de Castro" at the Edinburgh Festival', *Tempo*, no. 199 (1997), 29–32

——, 'James MacMillan's Clarinet Concerto, "Ninian"', *Tempo*, no. 201 (1997), 33–34

——, 'MacMillan's Song Cycle, "Raising Sparks"', *Tempo*, no. 203 (1998), 23–24

——, 'Triduum: MacMillan's Easter triptych', *Tempo*, no. 204 (1998), 32–34

——, Liner notes to *The World's Ransoming*, BIS CD, BIS-CD 989 (1999)

——, 'James MacMillan's "Quickening"', *Tempo*, no. 211 (2000), 29–30

Wells, Dominic. P., 'James MacMillan: Retrospective Modernist' (PhD, University of Durham, 2012)

——, 'In the Footsteps of Bach's St Matthew Passion: The Passion Settings of David Lang and James Macmillan', *Tempo*, vol. 67, no. 264 (2013), 40–51

——, 'Sacrificial passions: The influence of Wagner and Scruton in James MacMillan's *The Sacrifice* and *St John Passion*', In Sholl, Robert and van Mass, Sander, eds., *Contemporary Music and Spirituality* (London: Routledge, 2016)

'Whistlebinkies', http://whistlebinkies.co.uk (retrieved 10 May 2017)

Whitbourn, James, Liner notes to *MacMillan: Mass and other sacred music*, Hyperion CD, CDA67219 (2001)

White, Michael, 'MacMillan passes the test of time', *The Independent* (28 August 1993)

Whittall, Arnold, 'Elegies and Affirmations: John Casken at 60', *The Musical Times*, vol. 150, no. 1909 (2009), 39–51

Williams, Hywel, 'At last post-devolutionary Scotland has the subversive music it merits', *The Guardian* (29 December 2004)

Williams, Nicholas, 'Acts of grace', *The Musical Times*, vol. 140, no. 1866 (1999), 44–46

'William Soutar's "The Tryst"', http://www.williamsoutar.com/poems/tryst.html (retrieved 10 May 2017)

Wright, David, 'From the heartbeat', *The Musical Times*, vol. 133, no. 1796 (1992), 532–533

York, John, 'The Makings of a Cycle? James MacMillan's Cello and Piano Sonatas', *Tempo*, no. 221 (2002), 24–28

Index of Works by James MacMillan

General Index